W9-DEA-094

French Society and Culture
Since the Old Regime

Nº 1
ELEUTHERIAN MILLS
1806.
By Chas. Dalmas.

French Society and Culture Since the Old Regime

❦

THE ELEUTHERIAN MILLS COLLOQUIUM, 1964, OF
THE SOCIETY FOR FRENCH HISTORICAL STUDIES
AND THE SOCIETE D'HISTOIRE MODERNE

edited by

EVELYN M. ACOMB
State University College, New Paltz, New York

and

MARVIN L. BROWN, Jr.
North Carolina State University at Raleigh

Franco-American Colloquium

HOLT, RINEHART AND WINSTON, INC.
New York • Chicago • San Francisco • Toronto • London

Foreword

The Society for French Historical Studies was established several years ago by a group of American historians interested in French History, with the idea of having an informal meeting annually to discuss common interests and the hope of starting a journal that would publish such material. Both of these projects materialized gradually, as did a further aim in the happy affiliation established between the *Société d'Histoire moderne* centered in Paris and our younger American group.

At the time of the International Historical Congress in the summer of 1960, enterprising leaders of both societies planned a joint *Colloque* in Paris that American scholars could attend en route to Stockholm. Consequently, early in July 1960 some forty American historians enjoyed three days of papers and discussion, an unusual exhibition at *the Archives Nationales* and a gala dinner with their French friends and hosts.

The success of this meeting led in turn to plans for a similar one in the United States. An organizing committee was formed here under the able chairmanship of Professor Beatrice Hyslop of Hunter College, the prime mover in organizing the Paris meeting and responsible for the American participation on that occasion, as Lucien Genet and J.-B. Duroselle were for the French. To her wide knowledge, persistent hard work and drive, supported by her American committee as well as the French committee, again ably led by Professor Duroselle, we owe the brilliant program for the Franco-American Colloquium held at the Eleutherian Mills Historical Library near Wilmington, Delaware in September 1964. The papers presented on this occasion are recorded in the following pages. They are the *raison d'être* of this book. As they are fully explained in the Introduction, something of the Franco-American significance of the colloquium may be noted here.

When we assembled on September 9 at the Eleutherian Mills Historical Library, it was, for the historians present, an historic occasion. For our modest meeting was a step forward in the long history of Franco-American intellectual, social, and human relations running from colonial days to the present. If the French contribution to the amalgam of American society, to the fulfillment of the American dream, has been quantitatively small, it has been qualitatively high; colorful, varied, intellectual, individualistic. Merely to hint at this rich contribution, we remember the Huguenots who came first, their communities in New York, New Rochelle, and Charleston, their churches, their descendants, Chief Justice John Jay, the poet Freneau, Paul Revere. We remember too the Frenchmen who sought our shores during the Revolutionary era: Saint-Mémin whose portraits of prominent Americans, including Paul Revere and various Indian chieftains, are part of our permanent heritage; Jean Lefebure de Cheverus, the first Catholic Bishop of Boston, one of the founders of the Athenaeum, where some of his books remain; Major Pierre L'Enfant and his famous plan for the city of Washington; and P. S. Du Ponceau, first an interpreter on Baron Steuben's staff, later a prominent citizen of Philadelphia, and for many years president of both the American Philosophical Society and the Historical Society of Pennsylvania. French naturalists come to mind—the botanist André Michaux, and undercover agent for citizen Genet (and Genet himself became an American citizen following his term of office) and the ornithologist J. J. Audubon's incomparable record of the "Birds of America." We recall the Utopian Etienne Cabet and his Icarians moving in mid-nineteenth century from

Champs d'Azile, Texas, to Nauvoo, Illinois, recently abandoned by Brigham Young's followers. Nor can we forget all the travelers and commentators; Crèvecoeur, a cartographer in the French and Indian War, who stayed on to become an "American Farmer," and to interpret us to Europe and ourselves, as did Tocqueville in the nineteenth century and later, André Siegfried, and still later Jacques Maritain.

Outstanding in this record we find Pierre Samuel Du Pont de Nemours, a prominent physiocrat and long-standing friend of Jefferson, who arrived on January 1, 1800 with his whole family to start over again in the New World. This was never easy, but in due course the courageous efforts of his son Eleuthère Irénée Du Pont to establish "manufactures" on the banks of the Brandywine succeeded. Over 150 years later, thanks to the courtesy of his descendants, our colloquium met most appropriately in the new Eleutherian Mills Historical Library, dedicated, through their vision and generosity, to the preservation of American business papers and Franco-American records.

For the Society for French Historical Studies, the colloquium was a landmark. This was our tenth annual meeting, with over 200 in attendance. Indeed, the "mustard seed" sown at our first informal meeting at Cornell with perhaps twenty-five people present, had grown through the successive meetings held in different centers—at Chapel Hill, Cleveland, Michigan State, Harvard—into a flourishing "tree"! This start, it should be noted, was due to the inspiration of Professors Evelyn Acomb of New Paltz and Edward Fox of Cornell. On the happy occasion of our decennial gathering our French friends were with us; this was the first meeting of our two societies in the United States.

Moreover, in order to sustain the colloquium, our society for the first time requested outside aid. Asking modestly, we received abundantly, and were thus enabled to handle our ambitious program with ease and grace. Funds to sustain the meeting came from the American Council of Learned Societies and from the Fund for Scholars, Students and Technicians of the San Francisco Foundation. The cultural services of the French Embassy obtained the round-trip flights for our French speakers through the sympathetic interest of Edouard Morot-Sir, the Cultural Counselor, a supporter of this project, and Jacques Pujol, his associate.

Special thanks go to our host, The Eleutherian Mills Historical Library, whose indefatigable Director, Richmond Williams, gave us his expert knowledge and that of his exceptional staff. To his competence and that of Professor Paul Beik in charge of logistics were due the smooth functioning of our meeting. To the nearby agencies, the Hagley Foundation and the Henry Francis Du Pont Winterthur Museum, we remain grateful for expertly handled tours of their unique collections. In Philadelphia the American Philosophical Society was our host for lunch and the afternoon, the University of Pennsylvania for dinner, thus enabling our French guests to see the Independence Hall nexus. That both of these agencies were inspired by our most cosmopolitan "Founding Father," Benjamin Franklin, beloved of the French, added an appropriate touch! The University of Delaware, a younger agency, indeed, but the one that initiated the Junior Year in France program, so profitably enjoyed by many young Americans, gave us a warm welcome and generous facilities. Finally the beautiful closing dinner in the Longwood Gardens Conservatory, with the gardens open, the fountains playing and illuminated, was the gift of the Longwood Foundation. When that dinner ended and our colloquium moved into history, it had met in distinction and quality the standard of the Franco-American tradition behind us. To all who made this possible the Society for French Historical Studies presents its thanks. This volume is our acknowledgment.

To the signers of the Treaty of Amity and Commerce in 1788, so important in the attainment of our independence and the first recognition of our independence, the term "commerce" probably meant trade. It does not, however, stretch its meaning too far, certainly not etymologically, to apply it to the exchange of ideas between our two societies, an exchange of knowledge in a setting of amity. The hope that this intellectual commerce and amity between the Society for French Historical Studies and the *Société d'Histoire moderne* may continue in the years ahead, remains as the legacy of our 1964 colloquium. Our French friends and we believe it will. *A l'amitié rien n'est impossible.*

Professor Emeritus   *Frances S. Childs*
Brooklyn College

Preface

The twelve essays included in *French Society and Culture Since the Old Regime* present various aspects of France's political, economic, social, and cultural development since the Old Regime and examine the impact of French ideas and events on other states. As described in the Foreword, the papers were originally read by eminent French and American specialists in the history of France at a Franco-American colloquium held in Wilmington, Delaware in September 1964. The subjects discussed are broad in range, yet detailed in treatment: the relation between the French Revolution and French demography, the evolution of peasant society, the effects of social values on French economic growth, some political and religious factors accounting for the revolutions of 1848, the role of political liberals in France from 1840 to 1875, the French image of Russia and the Russian image of France, the influence of the French Revolution on contemporary revolutions, the reasons for the French policy of appeasement in the Rhineland crisis of 1936, and the contributions of Jean Monnet to French and American rearmament in 1939–1940.

These carefully documented papers bring new information and fresh insight to these subjects and reveal the historical approaches favored by scholars in the Atlantic Community today. They should be of interest, however, not only to specialists but also to students of general European history and those concerned with such contemporary problems as the population explosion, the rate of economic growth, the Russian mentality, the various intellectual and social movements within the Catholic Church, and the origins and effects of revolutions and wars.

To provide more unity and continuity, the editors have regrouped the papers into four sections: Economic and Social Developments in France Since the Old Regime; Liberalism, Christianity, and the Revolutions of 1848; the French Image of Russia and Russian Views of France; and France and the Second World War. The relation between the topics of the papers and their relation to French history as a whole are stressed in a general introduction. Each section is preceded by a brief account of the historical background and each essay by a biographical sketch of the author.

In the division of labor the Preface and Introduction were assigned to Evelyn M. Acomb, president of the Society in 1959–1960, and the historical and biographical sketches to Marvin L. Brown, Jr., editor of *French Historical Studies*. We have collaborated, however, in editing the entire book.

The editors wish to express their gratitude to those members of the Society for French Historical Studies and others who translated or assisted in editing the papers of the French participants: Professors Frances S. Childs, Emeritus of Brooklyn College; Shepard B. Clough of Columbia University; John Curtiss of Duke University; Beatrice F. Hyslop of Hunter College; David Landes of Harvard University; Joseph N. Moody of Catholic University; and Nancy L. Roelker of Tufts University. Frances S. Childs, who as president of the society arranged for the colloquium with meticulous care, persistence, and imagination, agreed to write the Foreword and graciously offered her assistance in a number of ways. Beatrice F. Hyslop, chairman of the organizing committee, was always available for advice and aid. Shepard B. Clough, president of the society in 1964–1965, engaged in the negotiations with the publisher that made this book possible.

We regret that in regrouping the papers, which were originally presented in six sessions, we have had to omit the names of the chairmen: Dean Franklin L. Ford of Harvard University; Arthur M. Wilson Jr., of Dartmouth University; Leo Gershoy of New York University; Reverend Guillaume de Bertier de Sauvigny of the Institut Catholique; David H. Pinkney of the University of Missouri; and Gordon Wright of Stanford University.

The papers on archival resources that were presented at the colloquium will be published in various learned journals and therefore are not reproduced here. The participants in this session were: Georges Déthan, Archives du Ministère des Affaires Etrangères; Mme Geneviève Gille, Archives Nationales; Howard C. Rice, Jr., Assistant Librarian for Rare Books and Special Collections, Princeton University; and Marcel Trudel, Laval University.

E. M. A. and M. L. B., Jr.

New Paltz, N.Y. and Raleigh, N.C.
May 1966

Contents

Contents

French Society and Culture
Since the Old Regime

Introduction

The twelve papers and one commentary contained in this
volume were read by distinguished French and American specialists in the history of France at the second Franco-American colloquium sponsored by the Society for French Historical Studies
and the Société d'Histoire moderne, in Wilmington, Delaware
in September 1964.[1] These are the ripe and nourishing fruits of
the close association and intellectual communication of the members of these two societies. The French society, more comprehensive in the scope of its interests, has had a long and productive
history.[2] The American society, founded only a decade ago,[3] has
already won recognition abroad, as will be seen in this comment
upon the 1963 meeting at Harvard University, published in the
influential French newspaper, *Le Monde:*

The Society includes nearly 400 members, of whom more than a
hundred had come to attend the sessions of its annual "convention."
These figures alone excite the imagination. One wonders if there are
not more American professors interested in the history of France . . .
than French? . . . but numbers are not everything. . . . As to quality,
French historians and sociologists are doubtless the first to recognize
the originality and value of the American contribution in recent years
to historical research on France. . . . Will the last word on General
de Gaulle be written by an American? . . . Clio has no fatherland."[4]

Such Franco-American intellectual collaboration has deep roots,
as has been indicated in the Foreword. It will be recalled that

1

Benjamin Franklin's works were published in many editions in
Paris, that in 1772 he was elected one of eight foreign associates
of the Royal Academy of Sciences, and that in 1778 he became a
member of the Masonic Lodge of the Nine Sisters, which received Voltaire at the same time. Franklin, in turn, proposed the
election of many illustrious Frenchmen, such as Buffon, Raynal,
Condorcet, and Lavoisier, to the American Philosophical Society,
and sent copies of the first volume of its *Transactions*, published
in 1771, to France.[5] Since the eighteenth century, Franco-American amity and alliance have been based upon this intellectual
intercourse. They have, of course, also been based upon the French
image of the United States as a land of prosperity, equality, and
freedom,[6] and upon national self-interest, which sought commerce
and military aid in the struggle against a traditional enemy.[7] Although this amity has been weakened at intervals by misinforma-
tion, isolationism, nationalism, and the changing balance of power,[8]
happily the bonds of friendship and mutual appreciation have
proved to be durable, and intellectual cooperation in the historical
field has never been greater than it is now.

The values to be derived from close association among the
members of these two societies are many and obvious: avoidance
of duplication in research, stimulation from new approaches, and
exchange of information about newly accessible archival and
private papers. The foreigner who studies a national history may
have a more objective and critical point of view in regard to subjects that arouse political controversy,[9] as will be seen in the discussion of economic growth in France. The two colloquia have
been notable not only for their scholarship but also for their prevailing amicable spirit.

Since every age rewrites history from its own perspective, the
papers read at the second colloquium reflect the contemporary
issues with which both academicians and the general public are
concerned and have broader implications than the subjects would
indicate. Thus, the paper on the relationship between demography
and the French Revolution describes some of the effects of the
population explosion in France. Those papers discussing the relationship between economic growth and social values and tracing
the economic and social effects of changes in landholding and

methods of cultivation since the French Revolution indicate the need to increase national productivity to provide subsistence for a burgeoning population and to raise standards-of-living. The essays on the revolutions of 1848 are concerned with the influence of scientific progress, liberalism, and socialism on religious thought and institutions, with the role of the established churches and dissident sects in revolutionary periods, and with the means by which revolution can be averted and gradual reform encouraged. The analysis of liberalism from 1840 to 1875 reveals the continuity of certain basic political tendencies in France, the practice of forming a "third force," a coalition of moderate groups to protect the republic against extremists on the Right and the Left, and the need for a strong, constitutional executive. The papers on the Russian image of France and the French image of Russia in the eighteenth and nineteenth centuries throw light on the factors that create a nation's "mirage" of another nation. The essay on the relationship between the French Revolution and the Russian Revolution of 1917 suggests basic problems of causation in history, such as the relative significance of ideas and economic forces as causes of revolution, and the validity of tracing "influences" or "association" through long periods of time. The studies of France's reaction to German remilitarization of the Rhineland in March 1936, and of French efforts to make use of the American arsenal at the beginning of the Second World War are concerned with the problem of choosing between appeasement and resistance in response to military aggression.

These papers not only reflect current preoccupations, but also provide some indication of the approaches most favored by French historians today.[10] The treatment of subjects confirms the decreasing interest in France in purely political, military, or diplomatic history, and the growing stress upon the study of demography, social structure and social values, economic history, the sociology of religion, and the history of ideas, especially public opinion.[11] According to Professor Godechot's comment at the colloquium, French historians leave the philosophy of history to philosophers, who, he said, often do not know much history! American specialists in French history, to judge by their publications, are still interested in political, constitutional, and diplomatic subjects, although they, too, are attracted by the "new" history. In reading the essays presented here, one is struck by the thoroughness with which French historians are searching their archives, the wealth of material still waiting to be utilized, the meticulous care with which these scholars are interpreting their sources, and the use that they are making of statistics, economic theory, and sociology.

At first glance the essays in this volume may seem varied in subject and somewhat unrelated, but one may discern a unifying theme: some causes of revolution and the impact of revolution and war upon French society and on certain nations closely associated with France since the eighteenth century. This theme is apparent in each of the four Parts: Economic and Social Developments in France since the Old Regime; Liberalism, Christianity, and the Revolutions of 1848; The French Image of Russia and Russian Views of France; and France and the Second World War. Other themes, such as the influence of the Industrial Revolution, are, of course, significant in modern French history and are implicit in some of these papers as well.

In Part 1 some economic and social consequences of the great French Revolution and the Napoleonic era are studied, particularly their influence upon demography, agrarian reform, and economic growth. Marcel Reinhard, investigating hitherto neglected parish records and censuses, finds that in the period before the Revolution there was a temporary overpopulation in France. This situation existed despite persistent regional variations, as indicated on Professor Reinhard's demographic maps. The overpopulation resulted from a crisis in social and economic growth, which contributed to the outbreak of the Revolution. Yet contemporary observers did not attribute the prevailing unemployment, poverty, and vagabondage to overpopulation but rather to the need for reform. The demographic behavior of the French, however, showed some realization of the problem. During the French Revolution the marriage rate increased notably, as did the death rate at certain periods; but there was accentuation of the tendency to limit births, a trend that was to continue throughout the nineteenth century. The reasons for these phenomena are analyzed in detail.

Among the permanent reforms of the French Revolution was the abolition of feudalism, seignorialism, serfdom, and primogeni-

ture. What was the extent of peasant property; how was it cultivated; and how did peasant society change from the eighteenth
century to the present? Ernest Labrousse discloses some of the
difficulties involved in making such estimates. From the tax roles
and government surveys he concludes that peasant property grew
from a little more than one-third of the area at the end of the
Old Regime to less than forty percent in 1815, to around forty-five
or fifty percent in 1900, to approximately sixty-six percent today.
Before 1880, the number of small holdings increased at the expense of large properties; after that date, medium-sized holdings
grew. In reply to a question at the colloquium, Professor Labrousse
said that although the law required that the land should be divided
equally among heirs, this practice (which was, according to Reinhard, one reason for the limitation of births) did not result in a
reduction in the size of holdings, because the peasant purchased
additional land. Professor Labrousse's account of the economic
resources of peasant families reveals the hardships they suffered.
Subsistence farming was the rule from 1789 to 1914, and subsistence crises, which had political consequences, were common
until the last decade of the nineteenth century. Yet in this period
the majority of peasants supported the French Revolution and
the Third Republic, from which they benefited. After the First
World War, the farms became commercialized, the peasant population became more homogeneous, and the "peasant-merchant"
turned toward conservatism.

One of the most debated questions in French economic history
is the explanation for the relatively slow growth of the French
economy in the late nineteenth and twentieth centuries. Were
psychological and sociological or economic factors more significant? As one answer to the problem, Shepard B. Clough examines
the importance that the owners of the means of production and
the wage-earning workers attributed to economic growth in their
hierarchy of social values. He finds that under the Fourth Republic those who remained in agriculture because of the values
associated with the acquisition of land during the French Revolution—the bourgeois-minded peasants described by Labrousse—
contributed far less than their proportionate share to the gross
national product and protected an expensive system of production

with tariffs. The leading capitalist group, whose origins were in commerce, banking, and government rather than in industry, had relied on some state economic aid since the Napoleonic era. Their businesses were often family enterprises; their rate of savings for investment was relatively low; and they imitated the social values of the nobility. The working class was uninterested in greater productivity because of its Socialist or Communist economic theories and was convinced by the labor unions that it was exploited. Since the Second World War, however, values have changed, as shown by doubling of the GNP, increase in savings, and decline in labor unrest; moreover, the government has implemented the Monnet Plan and programs for the economic integration of Western Europe. France is in the midst of an industrial revolution.

In the lively discussion that followed this paper, the French historians questioned the low figures given for membership in trade unions and for the working hours of organized French labor. They recalled the period of French economic growth under the Second Empire and again in the 1920s, and asserted that differences in population growth should be taken into account in comparing GNPs. After citing the sources for his statistics, Clough rejoined that there had been economic progress in France, but it was not so rapid as in Great Britain and Germany. He had not intended to compare the French economy with that of the United States. Dean Franklin Ford then diplomatically remarked that American historians in the last two generations have not been inclined to compare the United States with European countries, because they thought it unique, an approach with which the French would sympathize; yet at their distance from Europe the Americans considered such varied European countries as Great Britain, France, and Germany easily comparable!

In Part 2 some causes and effects of the revolutions of 1848 are discussed. William L. Langer investigates these problems through a detailed study of events in Paris, Vienna, Berlin, and London in 1848. He holds that the revolutions were largely urban, although there were significant peasant revolts that brought about agrarian reform. He concludes that although economic and social conditions arising from the early stages of industrialization and the growth of population created agitation and made basic political changes necessary, the revolutionaries were few, divided, and unprepared. The middle classes preferred to attain their ends by political pressure and might well have done so if the rulers on the Continent had made some concessions and acted vigorously. Instead, the latter were weakened by their fear of social revolution and lack of adequate police forces. In London, on the other hand, the government acted with authority and used the police and troops to intimidate the Chartists. According to Professor Langer, the revolutions on the Continent only delayed reforms, increased tension, and led to war.

One of the forces contributing to the outbreak of the revolutions of 1848 was liberalism stemming from the Enlightenment and the French Revolution, as well as from the Industrial Revolution. Louis Girard analyzes the reasons for the support given by liberal monarchists to the Second and Third Republics and explains the paradox that a monarchist assembly alone could create a constitution for a lasting republic in 1875. The Orleanists or liberal monarchists, descended from the liberals of 1789, favored a king who would guarantee the rule of law and civil liberties, but they opposed democracy, which other liberals like Lafayette favored if established gradually. In 1840 these groups were joined by republicans who preferred reform to revolution and were willing to accept a king who did not govern. In 1848, however, because of Louis Philippe's attempt at personal rule, the liberal monarchists supported the republic, although they opposed the election of the president by the people for fear of a dictatorship. With Louis Napoleon's election and coup d'état, their predictions were fulfilled, and they entered into the opposition. Upon his downfall in 1870, and after the election of a monarchist assembly in 1871, liberal monarchists of the Left Center under the leadership of Thiers, who doubted that restoration of a king was possible, joined once more with moderate republicans of the Left to establish a conservative republic. Although the lower house was to be elected by universal suffrage, they intended that its power should be limited by a president elected by a parliament. With the Senate's approval, the president could dissolve the lower house. In practice, however, monarchists of the Right Center thwarted the plans of the Left Center by depriving the president of this right of dissolution as the result of their actions in the crisis of May 16, 1877.

What role did the established churches and other religious groups play in the revolutions of 1848? Jacques Droz shows that at the beginning of the revolutions there was an apparent reconciliation between the Church and revolutionary governments. Christianity was identified by some writers with the ideals of the French Revolution of 1793 and with those of socialism. (Others, however, declared that Christianity, the religion of grace, absolute monarchy, and privilege, was in contradiction with justice.) Indeed, in central Europe religious disunity and theological radicalism preceded political or social revolution. In Germany the *Lichtfreunde* communities stood for democratic ideals and social reform. Some of their members were active in the Frankfort Assembly and had relations with the "German Catholics," who worked for the political unification of Germany through a national church and socialism. In France, after the June Days, when the workers' insurrection was brutally crushed, anticlericalism grew stronger among the working class and peasants, who considered the established churches to be hostile to reform. The Catholic reaction to the Revolution was to support social Catholicism, demand religious liberties, and reorganize the structure and education of the Church, but the short life of the Second Republic did not permit fulfillment of these objectives.

In his paper, Joseph N. Moody is concerned with the role of the liberal Catholics from 1840 to 1875. He wonders why men like Montalembert, who wished the Church to abandon its legitimist affiliations, accept the principles of the French Revolution, and work for a free Church in a free state, remained few in numbers and failed to have a greater influence upon Catholic opinion. Although most Catholics supported the Revolution of 1848, under the Second Empire they reverted to absolutist principles and sought a privileged position for the Church. Monsignor Moody attributes the weakness of the liberal Catholics to a number of factors, including their disinterest in social reform, fear of social revolution, and support of the temporal power of the papacy.

Part 3 is concerned with studies of public opinion, the images that peoples have of other nations, and their attitudes toward revolutions. The evolution of the French image of Russia in the eighteenth century and first half of the nineteenth century is subtly described by Roger Portal through illuminating references to many literary sources. This image, frequently distorted, which revealed more about the French than about Russia, was shaped by the views of writers, government officials, travelers, merchants, and Russian aristocrats resident in Paris. During the reign of Catherine the Great the myth of Russian liberalism was expounded by French philosophers and economists, who extravagantly praised her interest in reform in order to justify their criticism of the French monarchy. After 1815 French opinion of Russia gradually became more critical because of the Russian defeat of Napoleon and the reactionary policies of Nicholas I. Russian military power and Pan-Slavism were feared, yet Russian literature was admired and there continued to be a desire for trade with the Ukraine. Professor Portal finds that the opinion cultivated Frenchmen had of Russia had no effect on the diplomatic relations between France and Russia.

Robert F. Byrnes deals with the other side of the coin, the Russian image of France in approximately the same period, and arrives at the same conclusion, that this image bore little relation to the foreign policy of Russia. In the mid-eighteenth century a few educated nobles and bureaucrats became interested in France through study and travel, and during the reign of Catherine the Great there was enthusiasm for French culture, a feeling that persisted among the nobility until 1848, although the court was German in sympathy. After this date the court, aristocracy, intelligentsia, and Pan-Slavs became more critical of France because of the Revolution of 1848, the Crimean War, and French sympathy for the Poles. After 1870, Russians of all classes, who misunderstood the French political system, were more interested in English and German political thought and were impressed by German industry and power, despite French investments in Russia and the Franco-Russian alliance of 1894.

Crane Brinton is concerned with the problem of the relationship between the eighteenth century Western revolutions (French and American) and twentieth century revolutions, particularly the Bolshevik Revolution of 1917. He also seeks to understand what he terms the ambivalent attitude of American intellectuals, that is, liberals of the non-Communist Left, toward the latter revolutions. The associationists, with whom he sympathizes, trace the origins of the Bolshevik Revolution to Rousseau, Robespierre, and Babeuf; whereas the dissociationists are convinced that the ideals of the Bolsheviks differed from those of the Enlightenment. According to Professor Brinton, they hold this view because of their distrust of the masses, belief in the uniqueness of the historical past, and devotion to the principles of the Declaration of the Rights of Man.

In the interesting discussion following this provocative paper, Professor Robert Palmer, whose work, *The Age of the Democratic Revolution*, was quoted by Brinton, said that there was some general similarity in origins, course, and consequences between all revolutions, but he believed that the Bolshevik Revolution differed from the French Revolution. He warned against reading back into the eighteenth century the concepts of the twentieth century or being prejudiced against all revolutions because of dislike of the Communist Revolution. The nineteenth-century Russian intelligentsia described by Professor Byrnes, he said, did not resemble the French philosophers of the eighteenth century in personal origins, psychology, ideas, or relation to the élite of their society. The Jacobins differed from the Communists in a number of ways, and although the Marxists were close students of the French Revolution, he doubted that the Bolshevik Revolution was really Marxist. He was also skeptical that there was such a thing as a revolutionary tradition. Professor Godechot was not sure whether Brinton's paper should be classified as philosophy, sociology, or a study of opinion. There was need, he said, for a study of French opinion on the French Revolution. Labrousse's paper had shown how tradition had influenced the attitude of the peasantry in the nineteenth century toward the French Revolution. But traditions tended to disappear, and French opinion today toward the Revolution was based more on information that varied according to the type of reading done at each social level. He added that it would be difficult to distinguish between the French views of the eighteenth-century and twentieth-century revolutions. That is, revolutions in both periods would be approved if their consequences were beneficial for mankind, but their Terrors would be condemned by the great majority, who would not question to what extent they were necessary to preserve the reforms of the revolutions. Professor Brinton declared that his paper was a brief discussion of contemporary American opinion of the eighteenth century revolution, the Russian revolution, and anticolonial revolutions. He believed that there was a revolutionary tradition. Whereas almost all Americans disapprove of revolutions, in themselves, he said, American intellectuals are ambivalent toward them.

The effects of France's political, economic, and social problems and of its experiences in the First World War are evident in its hesitant and indecisive foreign policy before the Second World War and in its desperate efforts to rearm. These are the subjects of Part 4. Drawing upon a recently published volume of the *Documents diplomatiques français* for January—March 1936, Jean-Baptiste Duroselle analyzes the attitude of the French government and public opinion before and immediately after Hitler's march into the Rhineland. He finds that the High Military Commission refused the government's request for a plan to meet the emergency, because of political considerations, the generals' defensive outlook, their belief in the inferiority of French effectives, and lack of confidence in British and Italian support. The general public, which was surprised by the occupation of the Rhineland, was opposed to strong action because of its memory of losses in the last war, divided attitude toward Italy and Russia, and fear that Great Britain would not help France.

At the colloquium, however, John C. Cairns was less enthusiastic about these diplomatic documents, and in his commentary on Duroselle's paper and on John McVickar Haight, Jr.'s paper on Jean Monnet, he stressed the lack of records for much of this period, blaming the politicians, French foreign office, and the British as much as the French generals.

After Hitler's seizure of Austria and occupation of the Sudetenland in 1938, the Daladier government engaged in a feverish effort to rearm. Monnet was sent on two missions to the United States to obtain aid, and in 1939–1940, after overcoming many obstacles, he persuaded Daladier to accept plans that resulted in orders for thousands of American combat planes, expansion of the American aircraft industry, establishment of a joint Anglo-American Purchasing Commission in the United States, and creation of an Anglo-French Economic Coordinating Commission in London, chaired by Monnet. Professor Haight, who describes these achievements, has had access to the Monnet Papers. After the war Monnet organized a plan to increase production in French industry and agriculture; the European Coal and Steel Community; and the Common Market. The Monnet plan and these institutions contributed to the resurgence of France described by Clough. Cairns agrees that the major credit should go to Monnet for increasing American capacity to build aircraft engines, but he suggests that Arthur Purvis and Daladier himself also contributed.

In the freshness of their approach and in the significance of their subjects these essays prove that opportunities for research in the history of France are by no means exhausted. They suggest new avenues to explore and new relationships to examine. They confirm once more the profound influence of the French Revolution and Napoleonic period upon the political, economic, social, and cultural life of France and the Western world and the continuity of France's historical development. It was the descendants of the liberal monarchists of 1789 and moderate republicans who joined to support the Second Republic in 1848 and created a conservative republic in 1875. Liberal Catholics and members of radical sects, who accepted the principles of 1789, prepared the way for the revolutions of 1848. The liberal ideas and cultural achievements of France during the Enlightenment won the admiration of the Russian nobility until the Revolution of 1848, and radical French revolutionaries of 1793–1796 may have inspired the Bolshevik Revolution of 1917. The Revolution of 1789 helped to retard the natural increase in population in France for a century, and through its reforms in landholding created a society of peasant proprietors whose methods of cultivation and pride in property slowed the economic growth of the country. The tradition of state economic aid, the bourgeoisie's desire to imitate the social values of the nobility, and the alienation of the working class, which became more acute after the Revolution of 1848 and the Paris Commune, also explain the lack of dynamic economic development. The effects of this economic retardation, as well as such factors as political and social divisions, a weak executive, obsolete military policies, manpower shortages, pacifism, and distrust of its allies may be adduced to account for the failure of France to resist the German challenge in 1936 and for its crushing defeat in 1940.

Nevertheless, as Professor Wolf noted at the colloquium, France's performance in the cultural field under the Third Republic was in dramatic contrast to its economic record. Moreover, since the Second World War there has been a notable economic and social revival in France, the result in part of the Monnet policies inaugurated under the Fourth Republic, and continued under the stable and firm government of President Charles de Gaulle and his imaginative technicians. In the realm of the intellect, France, as evidenced by this colloquium, continues to represent meticulous and original scholarship and brilliance in interpretation.

Evelyn M. Acomb

Notes

1. The first Franco-American Colloquium, sponsored by these two societies, was held in Paris, July 1–3, 1960. Both French and American historians participated. The papers, which were published in a special number of the *Bulletin de la Société d'Histoire moderne*, 12e série, 59e année, were concerned with the question whether the French Revolution was an Atlantic and Western revolution, with the French image of America from 1734 to 1870, with Franco-American diplomatic and commercial relations under the Second Empire, with the status of contemporary historical studies of France, and with sources for the study of France in some American archives and libraries.

2. The Société d'Histoire moderne, founded July 6, 1901, holds monthly meetings, to which foreign scholars are welcomed, at the Sorbonne during the academic year. Summaries of the papers presented there are published in a *Bulletin*, which is issued three times a year as a supplement to the *Revue d'Histoire moderne et contemporaine*, which succeeded the *Études d'Histoire moderne et contemporaine* (1947–1952) in January 1954. (*Annuaire de la Société d'Histoire moderne*. Paris: 1958, p. 1.)

3. The Society for French Historical Studies, founded April 1–2, 1955, holds annual meetings, generally in the spring, at a university in the North, South, or Middle West. Since 1958 it has published a scholarly journal, *French Historical Studies*, which, beginning in 1960, appears twice a year.

4. "Alain Clément in *Le Monde* April 10, 1963." *French Historical Studies*, vol. 3 (Spring 1963), pp. 139–140.

5. Durand Echeverria, *Mirage in the West*. Princeton: Princeton University Press, 1957, pp. 27–29.

6. Echeverria, pp. 31–38, 67–78.

7. Samuel F. Bemis, *The Diplomacy of the American Revolution*. Bloomington: University of Indiana Press, 1957, pp. 16–28.

8. René Rémond, *Les États-Unis devant l'Opinion française, 1815–1852*. Paris: 1962, vol. 2, pp. 449–867.

9. David H. Pinkney, "The Dilemma of the American Historian of Modern France," *French Historical Studies*, vol. 1 (1958), pp. 21–23.

10. Since the Program Committee for the Colloquium asked the French historians what subjects they would like to propose, before it invited American historians to participate in the sessions, this is a valid conclusion.

11. Jacques Godechot, "Chronique," *French Historical Studies*, vol. 1, (1960), p. 366; vol. 2 (1962), p. 516; vol. 3 (1963), pp. 284–285. See also Pierre Renouvin, "Research in Modern and Contemporary History: Present Trends in France," *The Journal of Modern History*, vol. 38 (March 1966), no. 1, pp. 1–12, published after these lines were written.

part 1

ECONOMIC AND SOCIAL

DEVELOPMENTS IN FRANCE

SINCE THE OLD REGIME

Many historians of France regard the French Revolution as an essentially French phenomenon, while others put forward a newer view, stressing the broader Western, or Atlantic, nature of the revolutionary era.* In either case, however, social and economic factors are increasingly cited to explain and interpret the changes. Moreover, the long-range political effects of the French Revolution are paralleled by interacting social and economic changes of similar importance. Among the most significant results of the Revolution were the heightened importance of the bourgeois capitalist-entrepreneur and the gradual passing of some portions of the lands of the nobility to the peasants, accompanied by a great tendency (which lasted until late in the nineteenth century) to subdivide landed holdings into small parcels. While the government of the restored Bourbons (1814–1830) altered political institutions more than economic conditions, discontent on the part of middle-class groups, supplemented by unrest of the urban working-class elements, explains much of the background of the Revolution of 1830. With the establishment of the July Monarchy (1830–1848) came the entrenchment of the bourgeoisie and the introduction of many of the features of British economic life. France never became so highly industrialized as Great Britain, Germany, or the United States, and the tertiary trades of France remained relatively more important than in more highly concentrated industrial centers of the Western world, but the real impact of the industrial revolution was brought to bear on France in that era. The French Revolution had destroyed the older corporate organization of craftsmen, but labor unions of contemporary sorts emerged during the nineteenth century, becoming legal, however, only near the end of the Second Empire (1852–1870). With the further growth of industry during that regime, and throughout the period of the Third Republic (1875–1940), the struggle between socio-economic groups intensified. In spite of a considerable economic growth throughout the nineteenth and twentieth centuries,

* The introductions to each of the four Parts and biographical sketches preceding each paper were prepared by Marvin L. Brown, Jr.

many observers have noted the static nature of business leadership and of the membership of the various components in social and economic classes, and, at least until the eve of the Second World War and the policies of Jean Monnet, there was considerable justification for these views.

With industry drawing peasants to the cities as recruits for the new labor class, a great urban migration occurred. A true picture of this or other social and economic change is impossible without statistical studies of population, and recent demographic and other similar studies have increasingly made the historian a social scientist. Data concerning the composition of labor unions, the size and ownership of landholdings, the movement of various groups to urban areas, and the many uses of capital in the financial and industrial aspects of French life are increasingly used by the "new" historian. Developments following the First World War, with the complexities of urban life giving special urgency to the issues of capital and labor, have multiplied the problems of the student of social and economic history. Yet many practices and attitudes of much earlier periods still exist in the economy and social organization of France, to complicate the problems of its economic and social historians.

⤳ MARCEL REINHARD

In recent years Marcel Reinhard, a professor at the Sorbonne, has worked primarily in demography, a field in which he has been a trailblazer, particularly in relating his research to the French Revolution and subsequent history. His doctorate at Paris was awarded on the completion of his study, *Le Département de la Sarthe sous le régime directorial,* which stressed administrative and financial problems in an area in which the clash of royalist intrigues and Jacobin propaganda was especially sharp. He is the founder of the *Société de Démographie historique,* the director of the *Institut d'Histoire de la Révolution française* at the Sorbonne, and a codirector of the *Annales historiques de la Révolution française.* Among his publications are a biography of Henri IV (1943), *Avec Bonaparte en Italie* (1946), and an important two-volume biography of Lazare Carnot (1950–1952), the "organizer of the victory," whose methods offered a real opportunity for statistical investigation. Professor Reinhard attacked a universal problem in his *Histoire de la population mondiale de 1700 à 1948* (1949; a second edition appeared with the collaboration of Professor Armengaud). His highly specialized studies of population problems at the time of the French Revolution can thus be placed in the broadest possible frame of reference. His present research is concerned with the city of Paris during the Revolution. In his works Professor Reinhard stresses the "originality" of the French Revolution and the features that distinguish it from the American Revolution. One of his approaches and his theme in the paper that follows is that the key to the events of 1789 and thereafter is the measurable conditions of the masses.

Demography, the Economy, and the French Revolution

The historiography of the French Revolution has long ceased to be limited to the political arena; instead, it has been directed into economic and social fields.* It is surprising, then, that demographic factors, which are so closely related to these economic and social issues, have received so little consideration.

Actually, the revolutionaries, and especially those who held power, did make a continuous effort to gather and understand statistical data on the nation's population. Official inquiries were more numerous than ever, as the revolutionary régimes sought to establish exact numbers: of citizens, active and passive; of the defenders of the country; of taxpayers; of the indigent; of the aged; of children. Revolutionary France wanted to organize on the basis of numbers; hence, in this respect, the statistical era begins in France in 1789.[1]

Why, then, have historians not studied the fundamental problem of historical demography: To what extent existing demographic trends may have provoked or influenced the Revolution, and reciprocally, to what extent the Revolution modified demographic evolution in France? If one admits that the birth rate and the marriage rate are closely related to the convictions of a people and the death rate to their difficulties, certainly profound demographic repercussions are to be expected from the French Revolution.

Today we are acutely sensitive to the role of demography in the development of national and international problems, and the neglect of these factors seems strange. The most obvious explanation is the wide scattering of statistical documents for the Revolutionary period. Indeed, it has become customary not to search farther back than the Consulate period in statistical studies. While a first study of these factors was published immediately after the

---

* Translated by Frances S. Childs, Professor Emeritus, Brooklyn College.

First World War, when the French demographic situation was causing concern, they have been neglected by historians as well as by demographers.[2] Only since the Second World War have sustained efforts been made to catalogue and utilize the sources.[3]

The primary difficulty of obtaining adequate sources was further complicated by the changes in methods, measures, and boundaries made in the revolutionary years. Even the Old Regime's effort to understand natural population growth was interrupted when the Revolution dropped the former lists of marriages, baptisms, and deaths in favor of censuses. National territory expanded and surface measurements were transformed at the same time as were the administrative divisions. Subsequently, the revolutionary calendar caused another statistical break.

It is not, however, impossible to overcome these obstacles. Indeed, the present state of research in the field lends itself to a preliminary balance sheet.

French Demography Around 1788

The interpretation of parish records on a national scale makes clear certain general themes. The history of English demography has shown the advantages and weaknesses of this technique. In France, these records begin in 1770. They have been used by political statisticians, administrators, and ministers.[4] These records indicate growth by the usual increase in baptisms or births. Deficits in these records indicate the frequency of crises, but these are slight and not to be compared with the peak "mortalities" of the preceding 150 years. The situation remained unstable, however, as demonstrated by the economic crisis that followed the Franco-British treaty of commerce of 1786 and that was aggravated by a concomitant agricultural crisis and a very severe winter in 1788–1789. (Figure 1)

In the spring of 1789, at the time of the elections for the Estates General, the conjuncture of circumstances was ominous and bore heavily on the electoral climate, provoking agitation in the towns and rural areas—a prelude to the Great Fear of the summer of 1789. Does this not imply a crisis in the social structure, similar to that in the economy demonstrated by Ernest Labrousse, or more precisely, a problem of "overpopulation"?

Such was not the opinion of contemporaries. Neither the *cahiers de doléances* [lists of grievances] well inventoried by Miss Beatrice F. Hyslop [*A Guide to the General Cahiers of 1789 with the texts of unedited cahiers* (1936)] nor the debates in the assemblies stress this factor. The concept had, however, been defined: For example, the Committee on Mendicancy, speaking from the state's viewpoint of public assistance and security, held that population can be "excessive" if "ample employment opportunities" are not accompanied by "abundant agricultural production."

In considering the employment situation, it is clear that unemployment was endemic, and led to mendicancy, vagabondage, poverty, and insecurity. That employment was inadequate was, to tell the truth, hardly admitted; instead, laziness and debauchery were blamed. The problem was placed on a moral, not an economic plane. Production was held to be abundant, and average yearly yield was held above basic need; therefore, speculators were blamed for the shortages. Overpopulation was not seen by contemporaries as one of the causes of the Revolution. There was no question of stemming population growth, for such growth bore witness to the health of the nation and made for a strong state.

Actually, however, there was an acute imbalance. The "masses" had trouble finding an employer or the means of production or lands. But to many contemporaries, and especially to the revolutionaries, this was caused by the faulty organization of the economy, by the methods of production and distribution, by the social structure, and by the distribution of financial assessments and feudal rights. Their reform program was expressed in social and economic rather than demographic terms. To the historian, such an imbalance may be called temporary overpopulation, due to a crisis in economic and social growth. Few historians, however, conditioned by the reports of contemporaries and by their knowledge of subsequent economic spurts due to industrialization, have drawn this conclusion. Yet the fact most worthy of attention is that the French demographic behavior indicated some awareness of overpopulation.

Before dealing with this important factor, it is well to remember that neighboring states were also aware of a demographic surge, and were also troubled by imbalances; but their total population was less than that of France. In France the population was measured by the classical technique of relating the coefficient [the coefficient was a number used as a multiplier to get the total population figure. Despommelles used 25.75 as a coefficient] to the mean annual number of births. The resulting figure, about twenty-six million, was probably somewhat too low an estimate in relation to the revolutionary censuses, but it indicates a level. In the same period, the English population numbered around nine million, that of the United States four million. This differential is of fundamental importance both as regards the power of her forces at the time France faced the coalitions, and also for the collective mentality of the French, convinced of the irresistible power of the armed masses—of the *levée en masse*.

The final demographic characteristic of pre-Revolutionary France is the diversity of regional trends, almost as extreme as in England.[5] This diversity appeared in area densities, in natural population growth, and in displacements due to migration. A careful study would explain it in terms of the natural setting, economic organization, customs, and religious points of view, and might throw some light on the regional diversity of revolutionary phenomena. In any case, the population level of the seaports was reduced by the commercial crisis, and for several of these ports was only slowly re-established.

In the present state of our knowledge, prudence dictates that we limit our discussion to three major zones—north and northwest, east and southeast, and an intermediary zone. The continuity of these zones throughout the periods commands attention. (Figures 2, 3, and 4)

The presence of marked peripheral population densities was conducive to centrifugal movements that can be called "federalism," and the peripheral distribution of the regional capitals— Lille, Strasbourg, Lyon, Marseilles, Toulouse, Bordeaux, Rennes, and Caen—reinforced this tendency.

The revolutionary role of the cities is also clarified by demographic studies; it was due not to the urban mass (around fourteen percent of the total) but to the crisis resulting from the cumulative effects of unemployment and food shortages. The cities contained

both the "enlightened" and the poverty-stricken (the latter virtually rioters). The unemployed crowded into the cities, especially
Paris. Their hungry bands explain the myth about brigands that
played a decisive role in the Great Fear of the summer of 1789.
The electoral system for the Estates General indicated a distrust of
the cities, for the representation of the cities was proportionally
lower than that of the country areas. This was especially true for
the large cities and most particularly for Paris. Conversely, the
tight network of little towns was the most influential. In these,
the Revolutionary clubs were born.

Demography and the Developing Revolution

The progress of the Revolution associated demographic factors
with other revolutionary forces in a pattern of reciprocal interaction. Moreover, certain permanent factors clearly continued to
exert their long-range influence—human factors such as creeds,
habits, customs; economic factors such as production techniques
(primarily in agriculture), the system of internal and external exchanges; and natural factors, such as the climate.

For statistical information three censuses, each better than the
last, are available: the group for 1790–1791, figuring the inquiry
of the Committee on Mendicancy; that for 1793–1794, or the
census of the Year II, already known to scholars; and the group for
1796 or the Year IV, until recently disregarded. The census of
1801, so-called, carries on these earlier ones, in methods and
results, to the point of not meriting its status as the first French
census, except insofar as its results are well-known for all of France
while there are gaps in the others.

The French population total fluctuated around twenty-seven
million with variations that cannot be used, as they fall within the
margin of relative uncertainty. Relating the figures to the France
of the Old Regime and to that of the nineteenth century suggests
a slight advance in population in spite of the Revolution, contrary
to the convictions of contemporaries and above all of the counter-
Revolutionaries.

The distribution of population density (Figures 5, 6), of the
birth rate, and of the death rate (Figures 7, 8, 9), all confirm the

three-zone classification noted at the end of the Old Regime. Thus, in the overall picture, the census techniques validate the earlier estimates based on birth records. On the other hand, the administrative divisions, three times as many as in the Old Regime, introduce nuances. Finally, the censuses, especially where basic documents are available (that is, local documents that have been summed up in the national tables), lead to a more penetrating understanding of the nature of the population, to its divisions by sex, age, family, even professional activities—divisions not found thereafter, at least until the mid-nineteenth century.

Natural population growth appears in the census of the Year II, which contains the returns for 1792, and which can be completed by the abstracts for the first three months of the Year VII. Beyond these two returns on a national scale, one must be content with regional reports, departmental or local (the latter based on the civil registers). Already intensive microdemographic studies provide a few scattered samples, and analyses of these samples outline interesting trends.

The most striking trend is the marked increase in the marriage rate. Comparing the annual mean with that of the two decades preceding and following 1789, the increase is often from twenty to twenty-five percent, sometimes fifty and even sixty percent or more, both in the rural areas and the towns (for example, in the canton of Chaumes, at Nancy, Strasbourg, Montpellier, at Paris. See Figures 10, 11, and 12). Marriages took place younger and at all times of the year. To sum up, the major effect of the Revolution was the increase in the number of marriages.[6]

This may be explained by the disappearance of certain traditional restrictions, such as the system of guild controls; guilds demanded a certain number of apprenticeship years, with the apprentices remaining bachelors. Specific legal conditions, such as parental consent, were also removed. This occurred at a time when celibacy was considered unpatriotic. Finally, the periods of the year when marriages were forbidden without dispensations (Advent and Lent) disappeared, so that the marriage calendar ceased to be seasonal. The revolutionary élan and the great hope accompanying it should also be noted as operative here. These factors, however, do not explain the size of the increase.

A more exact explanation can be found in the military levies, from the first call for volunteers in 1791 up to 1797–1798 and beyond, when conscription was established by the Jourdan-Lebrel law. This was noted by contemporaries who were reluctant to continue the exemption from military service that married men enjoyed.[7]

This powerful surge in the marriage rate is evident even in such adverse circumstances as during food shortages, and in the most harassed regions such as the frontier towns, for example, Strasbourg (Figure 11). The effects of such a phenomenon could have had a powerful demographic reverberation in a parallel increase in the birth rate, but there was none. In fact, if we relate the birth rate to the marriage rate (Figure 7), we find a drop from one-tenth to one-third.[8] As births are not limited to new households, and as there were in the France of the Old Regime ordinarily five times more births than marriages per year, this surge in the marriage rate could not be clearly reflected in the birth rate until some five years later. But no parallel surge then appears. How do we explain this?

Microdemographic studies furnish stricter analyses: In Crulai, the average was 425 births for 100 marriages between 1781 and 1789, and only 366 between 1790 and 1799. The fecundity rate dropped one-third between the first half of the eighteenth century and the opening of the nineteenth.[9] In the *Three Villages* [of J. Ganiage] the mean number of births per 100 marriages dropped from 670 to 530, the fecundity rate from 475 to 337.[10]

These examples indicate the limitation of births, already noted in pre-Revolutionary France, and due to become more widespread. Among the factors favoring this decline, the weakening of religious practice may be noted as well as the new inheritance laws requiring an equal division of property among all the heirs. Divorce has also been mentioned as encouraging unions that could be broken up, but it was not sufficiently common to have important statistical effects (Figure 10). A serious study of the birth rate and the fecundity rate would be most opportune, as a demographic trend characteristic of France in the nineteenth century is in question here. The political and social aspect of the Revolution itself would certainly have favored this revolution in the demographic field. On this issue the consequences are long-range as well as short-term.

The third demographic variable, the death rate, is no less noteworthy. An excess of deaths appears at several intervals. The geographic distribution of these excesses shifts in 1792.[11] They are frequently larger in 1793, in 1794, and even more so in 1795–1796, the years of the uprisings of the *ventres creux* [empty stomachs], as the insurgents in the Paris riots of April 1, and May 20, 1795, called themselves in opposing the successful *nouveaux-riches*, speculators called *ceintures dorées* [golden belts]. At the moment, two explanations are obvious, war and famine, the old scourges resurrected by the Revolution (Figures 11, 12, 13).

Preliminary studies of these classic factors are rare, so fascinated have historians been by the Napoleonic Wars. In 1799 François d'Ivernois spoke of a million and a half deaths, but from then on calculations dealt with losses of the consular and imperial eras.

Before counting the dead, it is necessary to number the mobilized. Contrary to tendencious propaganda claims, there were never a million men under arms; 750,000 can be counted in the Year II; the census of the Year IV notes 720,000; that of 1801, 641,000. But these totals, swollen by the new levies, had in reality been reduced by deaths and desertions.

The census of 1796 mentions 178,000 deaths for 75 departments, so the total for all 83 departments must have exceeded 200,000. Moreover, from 1796 to the end of 1800, there were at least 100,000 deaths. Thus the total from 1796 to 1800 is around 300,000. It is interesting to remember that calculations based on the mortality tables led Bourgeois-Pichat to estimate some 330,000 deaths.[12] These were military deaths only, but many civilians were also, directly or indirectly, victims of war, and they are difficult to count.

The food crises, defined simultaneously in terms of demand by the population, by the nature of the harvests, and by prices, weighed heavily on the Revolution and precipitated popular disturbances from 1789 to 1795. Some of these were successful, some evoked bloody repression. These crises form a tight link between demography and the Revolution, but famine on a national scale did little to raise the death rate. The most obdurate areas, reminiscent of the Old Regime, were extremely localized: in regions, bordering on production zones and commercial axes, in some of the big cities. This localization produced outbreaks of violence comparable to the stages of the Great Fear, but the human losses were serious only in these areas.[13] Striking the elderly, and women and children, they reduced the imbalance between the sexes and age levels caused by the military losses (Figure 13).

Conclusion

The picture at the end of 1799 shows France economically active, weakened in her male population, less prolific, but with more numerous households. All this is evidenced in the census of 1801. Geographic distribution indicates that the three zones evident before 1789 and in 1793 still exist. On the other hand, through deaths and migration, the urban population has definitely declined in the large cities. The major demographic effect of the Revolution is certainly the accentuation of the tendency to limit births. This is an extraordinary factor, as an increase in fecundity is evident in Belgium and England at the same time.[14] Poverty and unemployment were somewhat relieved by the war industries and the draft; nevertheless, not all of the unemployed were reabsorbed. The demographic imbalance remained.[15]

Notes

1. M. Reinhard and A. Armengaud. *Histoire générale de la population mondiale*, chap. 18, with bibliography.

2. P. Merriot, *Le recensement de l'an II*, 1918.

3. *Bulletin de la Commission d'histoire économique et sociale de la Révolution française depuis 1959*. *Diplômes, d'études supérieurs*, submitted by Professors Godechot, Chaunu Laurent, Livet, Castellan, and put at my disposition by these scholars. *Contributions à l'histoire démographique de la Révolution française*, 1st series 1962, 2nd series in press.

4. E. Esmonin, *Les relevés de baptêmes, mariages et sépultures 1770–1789*. In *Etudes et chroniques de démographie historique 1964*, in press.

5. D. E. C. Eversley, *Population in England in the XVIII Century*. New York: International Congress on Population, 1961.

6. Proportions based on the national returns mentioned and on studies dealing with the regions of Versailles, Fontainebleau, Melun, Caen, and Bourges, and the cities of Strasbourg, Toulouse, and Montpellier.

7. Notably, Delbrel himself.

8. Same sources as Note 6.

9. E. Gautier and L. Henry, La population de Crulai, p. 119.

10. J. Ganiage, Trois villages de l'Ile de France, p. 86. In a communication delivered after the Wilmington Colloquium M. Leroy-Ladurie stated that the same conditions prevailed in Languedoc. He also stressed the development of the limitation of births as one of the consequences of the French Revolution.

11. In 1792 the relations between births and deaths are the reverse of what they were before the Revolution in Brittany and the southwest.

12. Bourgeois-Pichat, Evolution de la population française depuis le XVIII siècle. Population, 1951.

13. Same sources as for Note 6, plus statistics for Colmar and Paris.

14. P. Deprez, Récherches récentes sur l'évolution démographique belge au XVIII siècle; J. T. Krause, English Population, Movements between 1766 and 1850. New York: International Congress on Population, 1961. It is true that the marriage rate went up in the Scandinavian countries in 1791 and 1792.

15. See also the paper by Professor Reinhard describing the demography of France from 1789 to 1815, which he presented at the Twelfth International Congress of the Historical Sciences in Vienna in 1965: "Bilan démographique de l'Europe: 1789–1815." Comité International des Sciences Historiques, Rapports. I, Grands Thèmes. Vienna, 1965.

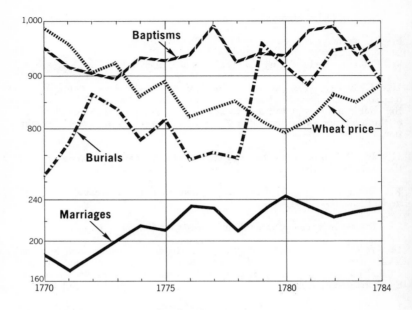

Figure 1. Demographic Evolution in France at the End of the Old Regime (1770–1784). From E. Esmonin, *Les relevés de baptêmes, mariages, et sépultures, 1770–1789*. This graph is based on parish records of baptisms, deaths, and marriages. There were mortality crises during this period, but less severe than in the preceding 150 years. Mortality increased in 1778, resulting in birth deficits in 1779 and 1783. To compare with population growth in Paris, see Figure 12.

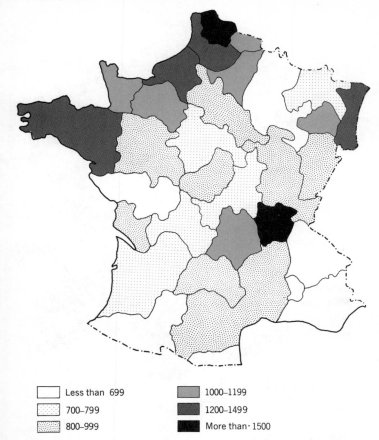

FIGURE 2. Distribution of the French Population at the End of the Old Regime (1778–1787). Density per square league (16.7 square kilometers). From Despommelles, *Tableau de la population de la France, 1789.* In the northern and northwestern zone there is heavy density, especially in Flanders, Picardy, and Brittany. In the eastern and southeastern zone there is also heavy density (except in the mountains) in Alsace, the Center and Burgundy, Cévennes, Languedoc, and Provence. There is approximate correlation with religious practice and some attachment to the Old Regime, but little correlation with the regional economy. In the intermediary zone, northest-southwest, in Champagne, Beauce, Sologne, Poitou, and the southwest, there is little density and uneven poverty.

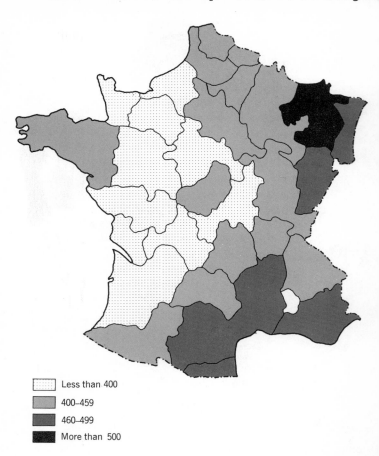

FIGURE 3.   Distributions of Fecundity at the End of the Old Regime
(1778–1787). Baptisms per 100 marriages (measured by the square
league). From Despommelles, *Tableau de la population de la France,*
1789.

In the northern and northwestern zone births were numerous,
especially in Brittany, Flanders, and Picardy. Normandy was divided
in this respect. In the eastern and southeastern zone fecundity was
strong throughout. It was weak in the intermediary zone.

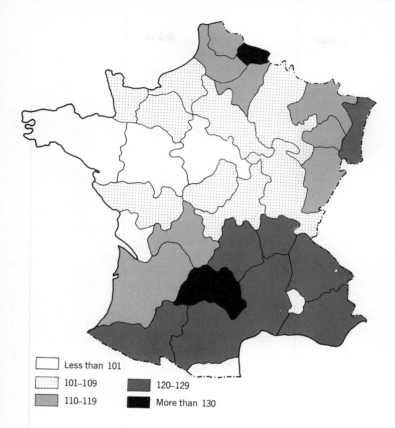

FIGURE 4.   Distribution of Births and Deaths at the End of the Old Regime. Baptisms per 100 burials (by the square league). (From Despommelles)

In the northern and northwestern zone mortality was strong in Brittany, average in Normandy, and weak in Flanders and Picardy. There was poverty in Brittany. In the eastern and southeastern zone mortality was low in all areas. In the intermediary zone mortality was moderate.

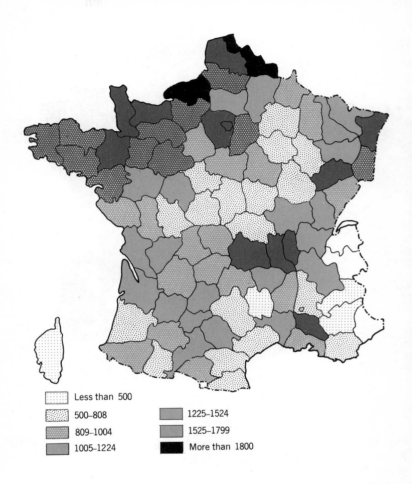

Less than 500
500–808
809–1004
1005–1224
1225–1524
1525–1799
More than 1800

FIGURE 5. Distribution of the French population (1793). Density (by square league). Note the continuation of the three zones of the Old Regime. The districts are departments of France.

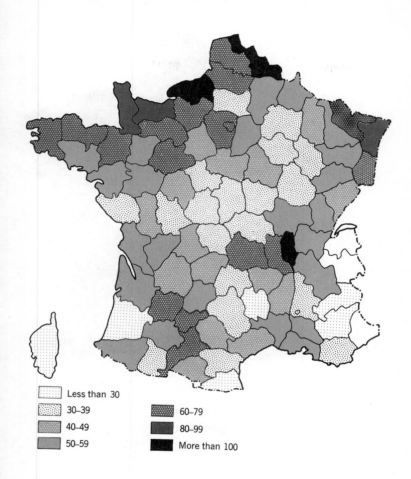

FIGURE 6.   Distribution of the French population (1801). Density (per square kilometer). Compare with Figures 2 and 5.

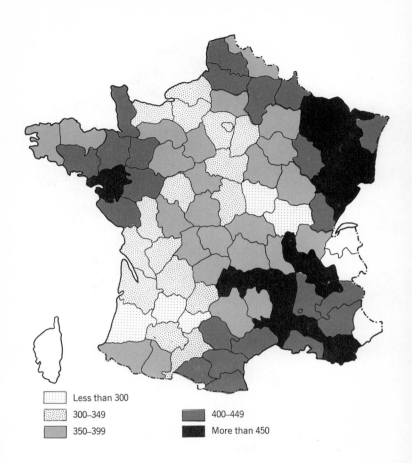

FIGURE 7. Distribution of Fecundity (1792). Births per 100 marriages, by departments. Compare with Figure 3. The zones continue, but there are greater nuances. There is a drop in the relationship between the birth rate and the marriage rate from one-tenth to one-third.

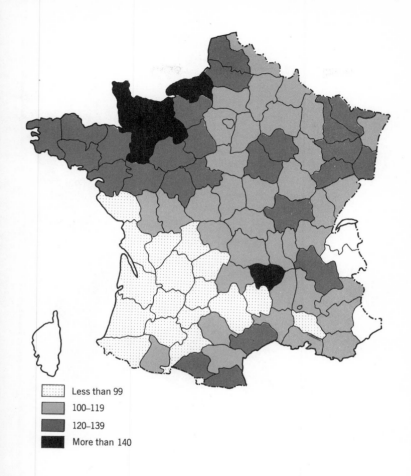

FIGURE 8. Births and Deaths (1792). Number of births per 100 deaths, by departments. Compare with Figure 4. The excess of deaths is more frequent, especially in the southwest. The excess of births is maintained in the southeast and northwest, even in Brittany.

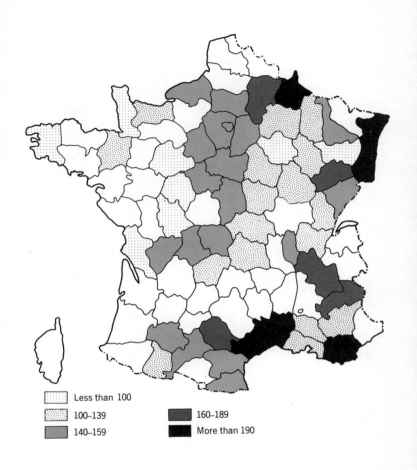

FIGURE 9. Births and Deaths, Year VII (1798), fourth quarter. Births per 100 deaths, by departments. Compare with Figure 8.

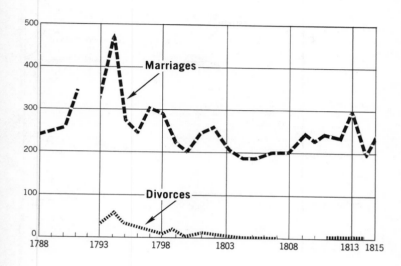

FIGURE 10.   Marriages and Divorces at Nancy (1788–1815). Note
the marriage peak reached in 1794. The break in the line indicates a
lack of figures for this period. (From M. Clémendot)

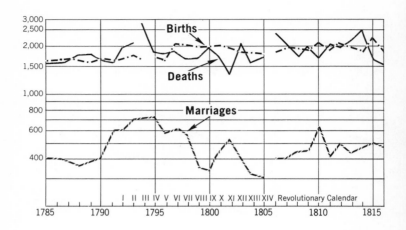

FIGURE 11. Normal Population Growth, Strasbourg (1785–1815). Note the increase in the number of marriages from 1791 to 1797 and the excess of deaths over births from 1791 to 1796, in this frontier town. (From Y. Le Moigne, "Population et Subsistence à Strasbourg au XVIIIᵉ Siècle," in Commission d'Histoire economique et sociale de la Révolution française. *Mémoires et Documents*, XIV, *Contributions à l'Histoire démographique de la Révolution française.* Paris, 1962.)

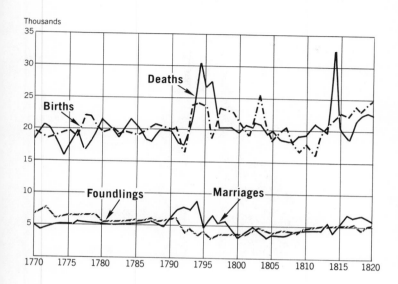

FIGURE 12. Normal Population Growth in Paris (1770–1820). Note the rise in marriages and the decline in the numbers of foundlings from 1790 to 1795. In 1772 there were 7676 foundlings in Paris, or forty percent of the total number of baptisms. (From Roger Mols, *Introduction a la démographie historique des villes d'Europe du XIVᵉ au XVIIIᵉ siècle*. Louvain, 1955, vol. 2, pp. 303–305.)

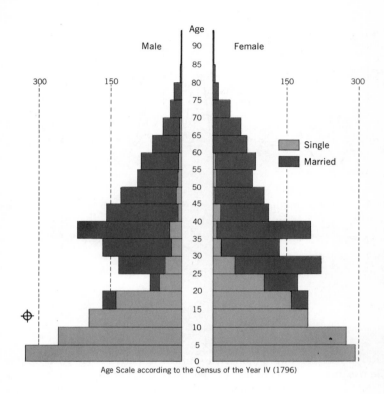

FIGURE 13. Distribution of Population in the Canton of Versailles (outside the walls) According to Age and Sex (1796).

↗ *ERNEST LABROUSSE*

Camille-Ernest Labrousse, who has taught at the Ecole des Hautes Etudes since 1935 and at the Sorbonne since the Second World War, has made a major contribution to historical science by his use of special techniques in the application of statistical analysis to the interpretation of the French Revolution. His two-volume *Esquisse du mouvement des prix et des revenus en France au XVIIIᵉ siècle* (1933) demonstrated unprecedented use of statistical evidence in the study of the decline in the standard-of-living of the lower classes during the eighteenth century, and went far toward altering the long-standing impression, initiated by Tocqueville, that the French Revolution was produced by prosperity, hope, and expectation, rather than by misery. He has made the French Revolution appear once more as a product of "hunger." Georges Lefebvre, himself, reversed his conclusions in line with these findings.

In 1944 Professor Labrousse published the first part of a projected six-part study on *La crise de l'économie française à la fin de l'ancien régime,* which dealt with the crisis in agriculture. Subsequent volumes (unfortunately not completed) were planned to develop the thesis that the adverse economic conditions that caused the Revolution radiated from a general agricultural crisis. This finding constitutes something of a departure from his conclusions of 1933.

Professor Labrousse has also published a study of the labor movement and social ideas in France from 1815 to the end of the nineteenth century. Indeed, the organizing purposes and activities of the working classes, agricultural as well as industrial, have been thoroughly treated in his work. Through his stress on wide collection of data, investigation of the business cycle, and the relationship between economic theory and institutions, social structure, and cultural factors, Labrousse has created new styles in research. His

43

work has attracted a large number of scholars. He has also contributed with Roland Mousnier a broad survey in the volume on the eighteenth century, *Histoire générale des civilisations* (1953), edited by Maurice Crouzet. The following discussion reflects his interest in the development of French agrarian society from the eighteenth century to the present.

The Evolution of Peasant Society in France from the Eighteenth Century to the Present

Within the confines of this communication, already bursting under the pressure of the subject matter, one can at best offer brief insights into a very limited number of problems.* What I am going to present is essentially a study in development—a triple analysis in which I shall touch successively on the nature of peasant property, on the peasant economy, and on the social composition of the peasantry from the end of the eighteenth century to the present.

I must admit to some embarrassment on all these points, but perhaps especially on the first theme, that is, on the distribution of landed property in France, and particularly on the share held by the peasantry at the end of the Old Régime. How can one not feel embarrassed to offer so little on so old a subject! To be able, even today, to do no more than present uncertain and provisional orders of magnitude. Indeed, in this case, our accuracy will vary inversely with our precision.

I shall therefore proceed at once to round numbers. And these give us the following well-known proportions for the distribution of French land on the eve of the Revolution: clergy, less than ten percent; nobility, one-quarter; bourgeoisie, one-quarter; peasants, undoubtedly a good third; the rest in the form of commons.

---

* Translated by Professor David S. Landes, Harvard University.

Remember, moreover, that these ostensibly national percentages vary widely from one region to another, from one *pays* to another, from one locality to another.[1]

At least that gives us a first general approximation. In terms of the social categories listed, peasant property comes first, however small the average holding. Furthermore, its quality, its suitability for cultivation, does not appear to have been inferior to that of the other categories. The peasants, for example, had little woodland, a type of holding that yielded a relatively low income. Undoubtedly they also had a smaller share of heath and moor. But they had an abundance of vegetable garden, of vineyard, and a more or less proportional share of meadow. Above all, they had cultivable land, which accounted at that time, for the country as a whole, for more than half the agricultural surface. In sum, peasant property was worth slightly more than its proportional share of the land area.

But all that is an old story. For the eighteenth century, the great new problem lay elsewhere, and unfortunately we have no answer as yet. Was peasant property increasing? The records of the Old Regime—those of land registry (*enregistrement*) and those of the recording of transfers (*insinuation*)—seem to tell us, in the few local instances that we have, that there was more going into than going out of the peasant patrimony. Clearings promoted this tendency by making available mediocre land for leasing (*afféagement*) against payment of a *champart*. It is not impossible—indeed it fits in with the general economic evolution of the eighteenth century—that the property of the peasant cultivating for market grew, in part at the expense of the very small holder,[2] while the total sum of peasant land increased.[3]

All these are only hypotheses. On the other hand, it is certain that these lands increased during the French Revolution. The peasants profited from the sale of national lands (*biens nationaux*); and from the sale of communal lands, in execution of that parody of the [much-demanded] Agrarian Law—the decree of June 10, 1793. It was, to be sure, an "Agrarian Law" of insignificant consequences, but it did result in leaving a few parcels in the hands of the peasants. Not, as everyone knows, that they were the ones who profited most from these various operations. Nor did the different categories of peasants gain equally. Nor, most important, did the share of the peasantry as a whole increase substantially. For we must not forget the relatively small proportion of the land in the hands of the Church before this redistribution. And noble property—or that of other kinds of émigrés—seems to have suffered only moderately in the last analysis. One cannot say how much the nobility lost. But according to the electoral lists [which take into account payment of the land tax],[4] they continued to hold a considerable share of the soil under the Restoration and the July Monarchy—a share that declined comparatively slowly over the course of the nineteenth century.[5] On the hypothesis that ten percent of French agricultural land changed hands as a result of the revolutionary laws and that the peasantry succeeded in shifting to itself from the privileged classes a fraction of this ten percent, its total share nevertheless was undoubtedly less than forty percent at the time of the return of the Bourbons.

This share increases little by little in the course of the nineteenth century. And we are in a position to appreciate this trend thanks to that incomparable source, the *cadastre*. Unfortunately, unlike the tax rolls of the eighteenth century, the manorial rolls (*terriers*), and sundry other sources used for the study of the distribution of land under the Old Regime, the Napoleonic cadastre did not mention the occupation of the proprietor. We shall therefore have to guess at the identity of our peasants. For this purpose, we shall make use of three criteria: the area of the holding, its value, and the character of cultivation, that is, whether it is direct and manual. It would be too much to say that our presumptions implicit in these criteria are the equivalent of a formal juridical proof. For our friends, the jurists, will settle for nothing less than serious, precise, and concordant presumptions. Ours will generally be serious but they can never be precise. And while they are concordant for the whole of the nineteenth century, they cease to be thereafter.

The special mediocrity of the criterion of size is well-known. It has significance in à statistical study of land distribution only in a homogeneous geographical and agricultural context. Thus it makes no sense to compare desert land and irrigated land, vineyard and forest. What we need is data on the cultivated surface, and not the simple area. Moreover, even cultivated land can vary widely in quality. Think in that regard of the innumerable land categories of some of our old cadastres. In other words, one should really count value and not surface.

Unfortunately, historians up to the present time have usually considered land holdings in terms of size, and we are obliged to do the same if we want to make comparisons. To be sure, one may argue that although the distribution of properties by size is not very significant in cross-section, it may be much more informative over a period of time—for example, if from one period to another, the pattern remains more or less stable. This is another case of the well-known story of old scales that, though not balanced, nevertheless give accurate weight. But can we not say more? Even though distribution by size is not acceptable in certain cases and is sometimes hazardous for small samples, are not these errors eliminated when we consider large areas? Do they not cancel out at the national level? We shall see that the national distribution of property works out about the same whether one measures by size of holding or by cadastral value.

Thus in the course of this overview we shall speak of "surfaces" without too bad a conscience.

Let us now establish the criteria of a "peasant" holding on the national level. We shall use two: small area and direct working of the land. The notion of smallness will obviously vary considerably according to the crop, capital requirements, and geographic location, among other variables. The series of great official inquiries at our disposal—and on which we depend—will not permit us to make these distinctions. All we can use is aggregate areas. It is not a question of aggregate areas in the absolute; we are concerned here only with the evolution of the global areas and with global comparisons. Moreover, smallness will be construed broadly, with an elastic upper limit of fifteen or sometimes twenty hectares [one hectare = 2.471 acres]. To be sure, the peasantry was also elastic, for it was not limited to the lowest sizes of holding, but rather was mixed at all levels with other social groups. But we make the assumption that the peasantry predominated below fifteen hectares, although there were also some larger peasant holdings.

In the nineteenth century and even during the first third of the twentieth, the global figure of the area imputed to peasant holdings seems to correspond more or less with the global area under direct exploitation. To be sure, this concordance of our criteria would not be enough to convince a meticulous jurist. For one thing, direct working of the land does not always imply that the owner shares personally in the work. And yet manual labor is—at least by general agreement—one of the clearest signs of peasant status. The fact is, one can work the land directly without manual participation: through an agent or steward; or even with the proprietor himself living on the farm but limiting his activity to the direction of others. Yet this is not a serious difficulty. Direct nonmanual working is to be found on only a few hundredths of the cultivated area.

The more serious difficulty lies elsewhere. The two categories—area imputed to peasant proprietorship and area under direct working—are composed of different elements. "Bourgeois" holdings of less than twenty hectares will naturally be leased to peasant farmers. By the same token, a certain number of genuine peasant holdings will be let out on leasehold or on sharecrop arrangements. Most inconvenient from our present point of view is the fact that the latter has occurred frequently enough to alter seriously the significance of the most recent inquiries into direct working of land. Rental by peasants become more and more common as rural emigration picks up and as the older peasants adopt the practice of semiretirement. The figures on the area under direct exploitation tend therefore increasingly to underestimate the area owned by the peasantry.

The concordance between the two categories during the nineteenth century, and even that to be found in the *Statistique agricole* of 1929, nevertheless retains a certain significance. It is as though the total area in small holdings and that under direct land exploitation—though often comprising different pieces of land—tended by some pattern of compensation toward rough equivalence, which in turn possesses some positive value. Thus the provisional sketch of movements that we are attempting here is not without foundation.

Balzac is not alone in denouncing the irresistible nibbling of the "termite" peasantry, which is accused of reducing the domain of France to crumbs. Also blamed are the *Code civil* (a creation of the French Revolution) and the ruinous pattern of inheritance [giving each child the right to an equal share] (also considered a little hastily as the work of the Revolution). The target of such analysis is the Revolution itself. And this brings us to the famous question of "morselization."

No one has done more to answer it than a high departmental tax official of more than three-quarters of a century ago. I am referring to Gimel and his investigation of the cadastres.[6] Gimel had been a director of direct taxes in four departments in the four corners of France, in the Isère, the Gers, the Yonne, and the Nord. In these departments he studied the chronological period from the beginning of the Napoleonic cadastre to a terminal period between 1857 and 1873. Within this context, Gimel noted unbuilt properties, as listed on the cadastre of each commune. He grouped these parcels by size, by character, and by ownership at the beginning and end of the period considered. He then divided them into nine and sometimes more categories.

What were his findings? At the top of the scale there was the expected diminution of the larger properties. This was very slow, however, in the aggregate. At the bottom of the scale was the proliferation, but not the morselization, of small properties (defined as those of less than six hectares). To be sure the average area of the smallest holdings, those for example of less than half a hectare, tended in some places to diminish slightly. At this level, of course, various factors played a role: notably the swarm of tiny building lots, multiplying even more rapidly than agricultural parcels. For tax purposes, the law separated building and land, and the statistics therefore include these lots with the parcels of unbuilt agricultural land. Thus the decrease in average area of properties smaller than one hectare does not necessarily imply a fall in the average agricultural property of that category. Besides, the figures show that holdings of less than six hectares increased their number while maintaining their average size.

From six to ten hectares, the pattern is less clear, less stable, though fundamentally analogous to that of the preceding category. Beginning with the ten- to twenty-hectare classification, there was a slight fall in the number of owners and in area. It is thus the smallest holdings that were multiplying at the expense of the others, even of the "middling" variety. But the figures vary considerably from one department to another. This first and fundamental inquiry—the limits of which are, however, obvious—has since received strong confirmation, in particular by the results of two national inquiries of the *Administration des Contributions Directes*. The first, in 1884, classified unbuilt properties by area. It was national in scope, comprising the entire agricultural surface, with the exception of the city of Paris and 364 communes in Corsica, the Savoie, and the Haute-Savoie, not yet registered in the cadastre.[7] The other inquiry, in 1894, classified property, not by area, but by value.[8] Tax collectors and controllers examined tax rolls of unbuilt property for the whole of France and classified the parcels by cadastral value. These two great inquiries yield for the two final decades of the nineteenth century a pattern of distribution fairly close to that found by Gimel. They testify, moreover, to the substantial advance of presumably peasant property in both area and value from the beginning to the end of the century.

The inquiry of 1884 imputes to holdings of less than twenty hectares forty-eight percent of the total agricultural surface. If one confines the category to holdings of less than fifteen hectares, the percentage drops to forty-two. What does the inquiry of 1894 show for value of holdings? A similar division, based on the average cadastral income per hectare, yields more or less the same proportions. The category equivalent to holdings of less than twenty hectares seems to be worth 51.4 percent of the total value; that of less than fifteen hectares, 43.9 percent.

The proportion of land directly exploited by or on behalf of the owner comes very close to these figures: nearly 52.8 percent, according to the agricultural inquiry of 1892. We are talking here once again of area, and the proportion may seem a little high. But the inquiry excluded from the calculation heath and land that had passed out of cultivation—to say nothing of woodland, which large landowners often worked for themselves. The inquiry thus focused on cultivable land, meadow, and vineyard, categories in which peasant ownership was strongest. To the extent that peasant ownership and direct land exploitation go together, this high proportion is reasonable.

In short, the triple criterion of area, value, and mode of exploitation does not yield contradictory results. But one should not forget the uncertain "peasant" character of each of these, and the very diverse realities that lie behind them.

What do the global figures tell us? If peasant property comprised a little more than one-third of total land holdings at the end of the eighteenth century, and something less than forty percent around 1815, it reached or passed perhaps the forty-five percent mark by the end of the nineteenth century. Perhaps it was almost one-half by that time.

The overall trend was clearly a slow but substantial advance of peasant property. To be sure, the land remained unequally distributed. Large noble and bourgeois property holdings remained. And there persisted, from the top to the bottom of the scale, great disparities among the different peasant groups. But in the general peasant advance, the advantage lay with the small landholders.

From 1880/1890 to the present, however, a new tendency developed. Now the greatest gains were made by medium holders. There was a concentration of peasant property, as evidenced by contrasts in the tax returns on unbuilt land before and after the decade. There was, to begin with, a slow fall in the number of taxable peasant holdings, which had increased steadily since the Restoration, and perhaps since much earlier. The number of such holdings went from between 14 and 14.5 million in 1883/1884 to between 13 and 13.5 million in 1911/1913. The trend was downward and accelerated between the First and Second World Wars, in spite of the new taxable holdings recovered with Alsace-Lorraine. By 1962, the figure had fallen to something under 9.5 million.[9]

This trend toward concentration most severely affected the smallest holdings, to the advantage of middling parcels of ten to twenty hectares. We shall look at these more closely later when we study modes of exploitation.

What, now, of our criterion of direct exploitation of land as an indicator of the national dimensions of peasant property? The agricultural inquiry of 1929 throws light on this, especially by comparison with that of 1892. Between these two dates, the proportion of land under direct exploitation rose from 52.8 to 60 percent.[10] But the two figures are not strictly comparable. The latter tends to exaggerate slightly the area presumed to be peasant in character. There is a small bias resulting from the inclusion of the statistics of Alsace-Lorraine; and an even stronger one owing to the incorporation of those on woods and forests in private hands. (We have already noted that the large wooded property lends itself to direct exploitation by an owner who is in no way of peasant character.) On the other hand, there is reason to believe—on grounds already stated[11]—that in 1929 a larger proportion of peasant land than in 1892 was to be found in the leasehold and sharecrop categories.

The census of agricultural holdings of 1946 comes closer to the pattern of 1892. On the other hand, it tends to underestimate the share of direct exploitation by excluding units of less than one hectare. Also it tends more than ever to exclude land authentically peasant, a growing proportion of which was being leased to other cultivators. The percentage yielded by the inquiry of 1946— 53.9 percent—thus seems to fall far short of reality; shorter still fall the figures given by the inquiry of 1955, which are lower than those of 1946.[12]

The old criterion of direct land exploitation has thus lost its traditional significance in the contemporary period. Should one, then, simply go back to the 60-percent figure of 1929 as a base? Should one raise this percentage for 1965 in order to take into account the manifest advance of peasant property that has taken place in the interval? It is not impossible that as of now this property is approaching twice its old one-third proportion. And this overall development divides into two parts: the first, to about 1880/1890, when the smallest holdings continued to proliferate; and the second, when the chief gains have been in the category of medium holdings.

The heterogeneous category of peasant property has thus changed in aggregate size, composition, and character. The holding [*exploitation paysanne*] has changed from a subsistence-oriented unit, furnishing all or part of family needs, to a small commercial enterprise, with all the social consequences that such a transformation implies.

We have just used the term *exploitation paysanne*. We must understand its meaning, as well as that of *exploitation agricole*. And then we shall turn to the *exploitation agricole paysanne* [peasant farm unit]. The definitions given these terms by the central administration on the occasion of the great statistical inquiries of the nineteenth century were not always the same. And their meaning has perhaps varied even more in practice. But the fundamental concept has not varied, from the inquiry of 1862 to the general agricultural census of 1955. A farm unit consists of a parcel or group of parcels, owned or leased, and exploited for the production of livestock or crops. The great majority of these units are naturally managed by a person whose principal occupation is that of *agriculteur* [farmer]. The statistics of the nineteenth century denote him as "proprietor-farmer," or "tenant, sharecropper, day laborer."

But can one speak of a farm unit without some notion of minimal size? One can, in principle, for all units engaged in specialized cultivation. But policy has varied for units of less than one hectare, which are not counted in this category. A more or less firm principle was established in 1882, along the lines one would expect. From that time, so long as a landholder was primarily a farmer, all lands cultivated by him were treated as farm units [*exploitations agricoles*]. Thus a parcel of less than one hectare belonging to a day laborer-proprietor would be treated as farm land; or even that of a day laborer-tenant. Such a definition corresponds to the historical circumstances of peasant life, in which a whole world of farmers of multiple occupations are engaged at the same time in the cultivation of plots of some tens of ares [100 ares = 1 hectare] or of a few hectares. Accumulation of part-time employments is the rule: One is at once proprietor-cultivator, tenant-cultivator, and farm laborer—each on part time. As for the "peasant" unit of exploitation, the same criteria apply to it as to "peasant" property above. It consists, in effect, of a peasant property filled out with rented land. And it is this kind of holding that we shall focus on here, leaving aside sharecroppers and tenants working the land of others and exploiting large "bourgeois" properties of over 40 hectares. What we are interested in is the mass of small and middling peasants.

For it is in this group that we touch the heart of French peasant reality. And this leads us to the characteristics of the kind of farm unit that brings the peasant family security and independence. The point is to give concrete meaning to the areas discussed above. There are actually two problems here, which have been confused on occasion. One problem is the nature of the *subsistence unit* that covers the needs of a "normal" family. That is, is this a strict subsistence unit, one that furnishes the grain required by the family's consumption of bread; or is it a full subsistence unit, one that assures the life of the family by providing it with a minimum standard of living? The second problem is the nature of the *full-employment unit*. One can easily conceive of a family that, though living on a full-subsistence unit, is nevertheless underemployed. The production of the unit, in other words, does not absorb the entire labor power of the family. Physiocrats would call the increment yielded by full utilization of the working capacity of these peasants net product; Marx would call it surplus value.

Let us confine ourselves for the moment to the subsistence farm, yielding enough to satisfy the needs of a so-called normal family. Let us begin by considering the requirements of a peasant family of five people, three of whom are young children—a family of the kind that appears so frequently in the economic and social literature of the revolutionary and imperial periods. A typical peasant family. And let us consider their bread ration and the land required to furnish it. In this way we shall be able to infer the dimensions of the subsistence farm unit—whether strict- or full-subsistence—in the meanings defined above. In other words, what is the minimal space required by a family?

Our calculations are based on the consumption of farm families, in particular on that of families of day laborers, which has been estimated more or less well for the beginning of our period, and even for the first half of the nineteenth century. Our only sources are the estimates of private individuals or of the prefectoral administration.[13] All the sources agree on the huge consumption of bread. Year in, year out, this one item accounts for about half the total expenses. The proportion of bread decreased only slowly, in spite of the increasing share of the potato in the common diet.

Our information becomes more detailed with the great national inquiries of the Second Republic and the Second Empire. The inquiry by the Committee on Labor of the Constituent Assembly, in execution of the decree of May 25, 1848, extended to all of France.[14] It left in Paris and in the provinces a considerable residue of archives in which one may find a number of estimated budgets for agricultural households. The share of expenses accounted for by bread varies from thirty to sixty-one percent. Most often, it is over forty percent. Moreover, these figures are biased downward, for they are based on households of four people, whose expenditure for bread is proportionately a little less than for the family of five persons considered above.

The agricultural inquiry of 1852,[15] also national in scope, was carried out by the cantonal statistical committees established by decree of January 1, 1852. This study, like the estimates of the late eighteenth century, is based on the five-person family. Once again, to be sure, we are confined to estimates. The results finally obtained rest on data often disquietingly poor in quality but considerable in volume. The errors, as we know, will tend to cancel out. And once again, the figures coincide more or less with those of the preceding periods. Bread absorbs on the average something more than forty percent of the budget. Once again, the figures vary considerably from one department to another. But they also agree more or less from one inquiry to another. There is no doubt that on the whole bread remains the basis of the peasant diet, and especially of the poorer groups of the peasantry.

We have tried to check these estimates by an elementary control calculation. The presumed consumption of the poor peasantry has been integrated into the general consumption—also presumed—of the peasantry as a whole, and that integrated into the general consumption—still presumed—of total population. The figures seem to agree with those for the total production, taking into account the amounts required for seeding and for other uses than human consumption and making allowance for imports and exports. The basis of our calculations for the end of the eighteenth century has been obtained by extrapolating from a vast body of statistical data as close in time as possible to the revolutionary and imperial periods—specifically, from the figures on production and consumption of the different cereal grains during the years 1815–1821.

What expenditure was required for bread? At what weight per loaf? At what weight or volume of grain? The quantities will obviously differ according to the nature of the grain, the rate of waste in milling, the techniques of domestic or commercial baking, with the former particularly important in this connection. It does not seem unreasonable to speak of an average consumption toward the end of the eighteenth century of about 1250 kilograms per year, or something less than 3.5 kilograms per day (seven *livres poids de marc*), for a family of five persons.[16] This figure diminished only very slowly in the nineteenth century, in spite of the massive incremental nourishment provided by the potato. One comes within ten percent of it—whether in bread or in other forms of flour—at the outbreak of the First World War. The diet of the French peasant, substantially improved over our whole period, nevertheless essentially maintained its old reliance on bread as the staff of life.

But now we come to the important question what is minimum living space. Theoretically, how much land does a peasant family need to furnish its bread ration? Note that I say "theoretically." Even on that level, the question is of the greatest importance. Later we shall compare these results with the reality.
    Four main factors are relevant:

1.   The nature of the cereal grain. Are we talking about the major grains: wheat, rye, or a mixture of the two [*méteil*]? Rye requires more space than wheat; while for the mixture, everything depends in principle on the proportions used. Are we talking about certain secondary, or simply regional, grains? Corn (maize), for example? For this, less space is needed.
2.   The bread yield of the grain in question. Once again, the yield varies with the grain, and with milling and baking practice, which vary from period to period.
3.   The cultivator's land must produce not only grain and, eventually, bread, but also the seed needed for the production of the next year's grain. In rye production, nineteen percent of total output was required for this purpose from 1815 to 1830. This proportion varies with the specific reproduction rate of each cereal.
4.   In addition to the land required for seed, one must also consider the land left in fallow. The practice of fallow diminished but did not disappear throughout the period studied.

Finally, let us not forget that under the Old Regime supplementary land was also required in order to produce the tithe and the seignorial fees, levied on the gross harvest (seed included), and amounting altogether to about ten percent of the harvest.

We shall limit our inquiry into the minimal land requirements of the peasantry to the period during which bread remained a crucial problem. (As we shall see later on, it ceased to be such during the last third of the nineteenth century.) Our estimates of this minimum, corresponding to the family bread ration, have been calculated with regard to the various factors enumerated above and their variation. The results are necessarily approximations. The area estimates are of the following order of magnitude, for a holding planted partly in wheat, partly in rye:

PERIOD	FAMILY OF FIVE	FAMILY OF FOUR
End of Old Regime	3.33 hectares	2.82 hectares
1815–1821	2.74	2.32
1840–1852	1.87	1.58
1882–1892	1.37	1.16

The important difference between requirements at the end of the Old Regime and for the period 1815–1821 is due largely to the removal of the tithe and seignorial fees, which constituted heavy direct taxes bearing primarily on grain production.[17] By contrast, the continuing diminution of the minimal land area required to feed a family throughout the remainder of the nineteenth century seems to have been the result of obvious technological advances. Need one add that another aspect of these advances is that productivity increased not only per unit of land, but also per unit of labor? As a consequence, the old family of five or four persons, which constituted the human nucleus of the small farm unit, tended to break up. The flow of emigration from the countryside —not taken into account in the table of area estimates, which treats family size as constant—becomes increasingly important; so much so, that by the end of the century, the minimum areas might be reduced to 1.03 hectares. The sharp fall in minimum land requirements is thus even greater than the table shows.

In other words, our estimate of the *trend* is insufficiently optimistic. On the other hand, our *absolute* area figures are probably too low. Even in the simple production of a family's bread, additional expenses, sometimes substantial, are incurred. These have not been taken into account in the table. Leaving aside minor outlays, what of taxes? What of the rent or the share of the crop due the landlord on those parcels that are combined with the actual holding of the peasant in his unit of cultivation? Remember, moreover, that bread represents only forty to fifty percent of the expenses of the family. The rest must also come from the land. To be sure, one needs little space for vegetables, potatoes, and the rest. Even for wine. But the cultivator, in order to insure full subsistence for his family, must pay for other things than food.

To sum up, there are three major cases to be distinguished in this vast world of the small farm unit: 1) the cultivator works his own land only; 2) he works both his own land and parcels that he holds by rental or by sharecrop; 3) he works only the land of others. The last case is rare. As for the two others, both require considerable increases in our estimate of the minimum subsistence area—the second more than the first.

Thus, our analysis has enabled us to calculate bottom limits—considerably underestimated—below which a whole class of cultivators find themselves in the position, not of sellers, but of buyers of grain. Our task now is to substitute for this theoretical minimum a real minimum.

We have been treating the farm exploitation of the eighteenth and nineteenth centuries as though it were exclusively devoted to the production of grain. But in fact multiple crops were the rule. Judging by the average crop distributions of the nineteenth century, the area estimates above should be increased by half to take this into account. And this agrees with some of our earlier observations. The real minimum area necessary to the full subsistence of a family of five persons in the final years of the Old Regime was thus not 3.33 hectares, but about 5. And this corresponds more or less to the figures suggested by a number of other authors. At the end of the nineteenth century, this figure falls, for the same family, not to 1.37 hectares, but to a little more than 2.

These are very small holdings, which doubtless do not provide more than a minimal living by eighteenth-century standards, a minimum that increased considerably over the following century. We shall nevertheless make use of these low estimates and try to see what proportion of cultivators in our period owned or had the use of land adequate to provide this minimal living, theoretical or real.

A long series of agricultural inquiries, more or less comparable, provide us with some elements of an answer from the Second Empire on. The data are usable either in their crude form, or after some manipulation. They enable us to perceive a number of turning points.

The first of these comes in 1850–1860. The problem of grain, bread, survival, continues to obsess the mass of the peasantry. This is still an era of subsistence crises. Between 1851 and 1854/1856, the price of grain doubled. And from 1865 to 1867/1868 it rose by more than sixty percent, and we have Thiers speaking before the Corps Législatif of the economic storm with its price waves "as high as the waves of the sea." In such a world, the theoretical conception of land devoted strictly to the production of bread is not completely divorced from reality. Now, as we have seen, 1.5 to 2 hectares—an irreducible minimum, almost certainly underestimated—were needed at the time to produce the bread of a family. Half of the farm holdings, however, were smaller than this limit: about 3 million of a total of 5.5 million.[18] To be sure, we are not speaking necessarily of a peasant populace at the extreme point of deprivation. Rather, this is more or less the world visited by Frédéric Le Play and his disciples. It was a world that scraped by more or less, and sometimes even succeeded in setting something aside—a world of proprietor-day laborers, proprietor-tenants, proprietor-sharecroppers, habitual or occasional migrants, ready to leave the farm in the care of the family during the dead season, and combining when necessary all of these roles! The holding could cover only part of the family's needs. In particular, grain had to be bought in the market; and the cost was covered by the various activities enumerated.

The full-subsistence holding is another story. The effective minimum, devoted to more than one crop, ran from two to three hectares. The vast majority of cultivators were below that level.

Farms able to sell cereals in the market—often in the smallest quantities—would rarely be less than five hectares. Only in the category of five to ten hectares does one get the beginning of a sense of security. But it was a security not immune to a bad harvest year. That kind of security was had only by those who could sell grain regularly, who were themselves of very unequal means. One crosses this frontier—an economic, but certainly not a social, frontier— with the category of ten to twenty hectares. But these units of more than ten hectares comprise a scant fifteen percent of the total. (Even if one calculates the proportion omitting the very smallest parcels—those of less than one hectare—one obtains a figure of only twenty-five percent.)

Thus, many holdings did not produce enough, or barely sufficed, to maintain a family. At the other end of the scale there were a relatively small number of holdings secure from the commercial consequences of subsistence crises (that is, from the catastrophic drop in the marketable surplus of grain, net of the amount required for seed and domestic consumption). The same situation, only worse, characterized the first half of the nineteenth century and the end of the Old Regime, with a pattern of cultivation that changes only slowly and a minimum area requirement that increases as we go back in time.

Circumstances substantially changed by 1882–1892. There were no longer subsistence crises, no dramas of bread. Nevertheless, subsistence agriculture persisted. But it stagnated rather than advanced. Even so, in spite of the loss of Alsace-Lorraine in 1871, the number of farm units continued to go up. The main gains were in the moderate-sized categories of five to ten hectares. Units from ten to twenty hectares also gained markedly. (We have already noted the increase in the number of middling properties.) What we are observing is a general movement from subsistence cultivation of food to the cultivation of market crops.

The great turning point came at the beginning of the twentieth century. There was a "revolution" in the years following the First World War. The number of units receded markedly. After a steady rise over what may be a period of centuries, they fell from a maximum of 5.7 million in 1892 to 4 million in 1929. This fall is consistent with that in the number of property units already noted above. For the first time there was a clear tendency to concentration, at the expense of the small holdings. The farmer abandoned the old subsistence unit. For that matter, his "subsistence" of 1929 was very different from that of old. The greatest drop was in holdings of less than one hectare, which fell from 2.2 million in 1892 to one million in 1929. By comparison those from one to five hectares fell from 1.8 to 1.1 million. Even those of five to ten hectares, which had multiplied most rapidly in the earlier period, fell, though to a much smaller degree. The big gain was in holdings from ten to twenty hectares and, to some extent, from twenty to thirty, both categories that were reinforced by the purchase of peasant parcels.

The years following the last war have seen even more drastic changes. The *Recensement général de l'agriculture* of 1955 counted no more than 2.3 units of exploitation—only forty percent of the 1892 figure. Pieces of less than one hectare have just about disappeared. Those of less than two hectares (a majority in 1892), no longer represent in total number more than fifteen percent. But between 1892 and 1955, the holdings of five to twenty hectares have risen from a little more than one-fifth to half the total number. Commercial peasant agriculture has replaced the old subsistence agriculture, which was forced to obtain part of its bread by purchases in the market. The French peasant has today become a peasant-merchant, a *petit bourgeois* and entrepreneur.

What of the peasant's values and attitudes? Are these too not becoming those of the middle classes? Certainly this new type of peasant has become the majority, a majority that has gained in numbers and homogeneity.

In the old days the weight of numbers lay elsewhere—with the domestic servants, day laborers, part-and full-time workers, and the innumerable small landholders who sometimes hired themselves out. These, with the exception of the domestic servants, joined with or followed the rural craftsmen in the subsistence riots then so common, especially in the cities and towns. It was they who constituted the rural market for grain. Their very existence, even without a clear class conscience, introduced an element of division into the peasantry.

These little peasants have left. Rural emigration, like most mass emigrations, is a flight of the poor. This was largely an exodus of day workers; so much so that today wage labor seems to be little more than a regional peculiarity of the occupied farm population. The rural craftsman has also disappeared. The small rural tradesmen, who have replaced the others, are like the commercialized peasantry, entrepreneurs with similar attitudes and values. With these departures, with the disappearance of the frontier between buyers and sellers of grain, this society of entrepreneurs has become stronger and more united. The category comprises the whole range from small cultivator to the tenant farmer. Antagonisms between cultivators and noncultivating landowners have softened, despite remaining disputes about the character of the leasehold. The old hostility to the small aristocrat (*hobereau*) tends to lose its force. The peasant is less concerned with ownership than with full management of the land. Besides, he already owns the greater part of the land. His business associations comprise all categories of cultivators. There is no separate organization of tenants (*"preneurs" de terre*) as against owners. There is nothing any more to remind us of the old sharecroppers' and tenants' unions. Farm unionism is a unionism of the middle classes. The class-consciousness of the peasantry is a consciousness of middle-class status.

What of the ideology of this majority of peasant-merchants, and beyond them, of rural society as a whole?

The land reform of the Revolution and the tradition it established, always found in the countryside, in spite of Royalist movements (*les chouanneries*), numerous and ardent defenders. This pro-Revolutionary stance persisted into the nineteenth century, as did the tradition of the *chouannerie* for that matter. The fact of a certain Bonapartist sympathy should not mislead us. As André Siegfried correctly observed, the Bonapartist tendencies of the countryside were (I would modify the verb by the word "often") a variant of the democratic conviction. After the fall of the Second Empire, a majority of the inhabitants of the countryside rallied quickly to the Republic, the custodian of the tomorrows of the Commune, the Republic of peasant proprietors. The great political problem of those days was still, almost, one of a "French

Revolution." The choice seemed to be between a consecration of the Republic and the risk of a monarchical restoration under the patronage of dignitaries (*notables*)—traditional or bourgeois aristocrats (*hobereaux*)—whose sentiments were only too well known.

But the nature of the political problem was changing. Instead of a choice between a Republic of proprietors and the Old Regime, it came to be one between a republic of proprietors and a more or less "social" republic. The prospect was not one to frighten everybody, at least theoretically; and the parties of the extreme left maintained in the rural departments a solid following. The old republican tradition contributed to this, as did many other factors.

But have times not changed? Can old traditions not fade? And for that matter can not the peasant populations of the fiercest districts themselves fade and disappear? The subsistence riots of the propertyless and the smallholders of yesteryear have been replaced by the riots of entrepreneurs. The "red" uprisings of old, of the kind seen in Languedoc in 1907 or in Champagne in 1911, have given way to a very different type. The peasant agitation has changed camps.

And so I shall conclude by asking a question. Looking back at the historical process as we have, is not the French peasantry of today tending slowly though not necessarily ineluctably, to shift from the "Revolution" to conservatism?

Notes

1. See G. Lefebvre, *Études sur la Révolution française. Répartition de la propriété et de l'exploitation foncières à la fin de l'ancien régime.* Paris: 1954, p. 201 ff.; and *Les Paysans du Nord pendant la Révolution française*, 1924.

2. A. Soboul, *Les campagnes montpelliéraines à la fin de l'ancien régime. Propriété et cultures d'après les compoix*, 1958, p. 53.

3. P. Bois, *Paysans de l'Ouest*, 1960, p. 368 ff. See also Baehrel, *Une croissance: la Basse Provence rurale. . . .* 1961, p. 406 ff.

4. See G. Dupeux, *Aspects de l'histoire sociale et politique du Loir-et-Cher (1848–1914).* Paris: 1962; A.-J. Tudesq, *Les grands notables en France (1840–1849).* Paris: 1964.

5. Dupeux. See P. Vigier, *Essai sur la répartition de la propriété foncière dans la région alpine.* Paris: 1963.

6.   Gimel, "Etude sur la division de la propriété foncière dans le département de l'Isère." In *Bulletin de la Société de Statistique de l'Isère*, 3rd series, vol. 4 (1875); *De la division de la propriété foncière, Extrait de l'Annuaire des agriculteurs de France pour 1875; Sur la division de la propriété dans le département du Nord.* Lille: 1877.

7.   *Bulletin de statistique et de législation comparée* (1884).

8.   *Renseignements statistiques relatifs aux contributions directes* (1897).

9.   *Renseignements statistiques relatifs aux contributions directes*, years 1956 ff.

10.   *Statistique agricole de la France. Résultats généraux de l'enquête de 1929.* Paris: 1936.

11.   See *Statistique agricole*, p. 6.

12.   The crude figure is almost fifty-three percent; a minimum refined figure would be sixty-two percent.

13.   See Ernest Labrousse, *Esquisse du mouvement des prix . . . au XVIIIe siècle*, p. 584 ff.

14.   See Y. Bernardin, "Recherches sur les salaires au milieu du XIXe siècle, d'après l'enquête du Comité du Travail de l'Assemblée Constituante" (typewritten manuscript; Faculté des Lettres, Paris, 1952).

15.   *Statistique agricole décennale de 1852.* Paris: 1858–1860.

16.   *Esquisse*, pp. 584–590.

17.   It would seem—though this is not the place to consider the question—that what was then recuperated in kind by peasant holdings and exploitations was later completely lost in value to the new tax on land.

18.   On these figures as well as those which follow, see Statistique Générale de la France, *Résultats généraux de l'enquête agricole décennale de 1862.* Strasbourg: 1868–1870; Ministère de l'Agriculture, *Statistique agricole, Enquête décennale de 1882.* Paris: 1886; *Enquête décennale de 1892.* Paris: 1897; *Statistique agricole . . . Résultats généraux de l'enquête de 1929.* Paris: 1936; Institut National de la Statistique et des Etudes Economiques, and Ministère de l'Agriculture, *Recensement général de l'agriculture de 1955, Caractéristiques générales des exploitations.* Paris: 1958. These various figures have been compared and manipulated so as to make them comparable and to make sure that the differences in principle between the various inquiries did not compromise their comparability in any fundamental way. The census of 1946 on agricultural exploitations, which excludes those of less than one hectare, has not been used.

↗ SHEPARD B. CLOUGH

Born in Bloomington, Indiana, in 1901, Shepard B. Clough obtained his A.B. degree at Colgate in 1923 and, after studies at the Sorbonne and Heidelberg, received his Ph.D. in 1930 at Columbia University, where he has long taught. Besides his identification with Columbia, where many outstanding younger members of the profession have written their dissertations under his guidance, he has been a professor at the *Institut d'Études Politiques* in Paris (1952) and the Institute of European Studies in Turin (1957).

Although he has worked in many fields of history and the social sciences, throughout all his work he has concentrated on economic development, educational change, and political theory in relation to the whole course of Western civilization. His historical outlook is revealed in his article, "Change in History," in *The Social Sciences in Historical Study* (1954, pages 106–127), published by the Social Science Research Council, of which he has been a member. Some of his earlier works, including *Making Fascists* (with Herbert Schneider in 1929) and *History of the Flemish Movement in Belgium* (1930), influenced by his association with the late Carlton J. H. Hayes, were concerned with nationalism. Later works revealed a greater interest in economic history: *France, A Study in National Economics* (1939); *An Economic History of Europe* (1939; written in collaboration with Charles W. Cole, the book that has gone into many editions); *The Economic Development of Western Civilization;* and *An Economic History of Italy, 1861–1963* (1963). For many years Professor Clough was an editor of the *Journal of Economic History.* His *Histoire économique des États-Unis* (1954) presented to the French his interpretations of American phenomena. His more recent special studies and textbooks have been concerned with the broadest treatment of civilization. In the following analysis Clough brings his different interests to bear on French economic and social change since the Revolution.

French Social Structure, Social Values, and Economic Growth

Although economic growth, defined as an increase in goods and services per capita of the population, or of the labor force, has been one of the most distinctive characteristics of the history of the Western world in the last two centuries, and although scholars have devoted much attention to the economic factors involved in growth, relatively little consideration has been given to the place that a given society has allocated to growth in its hierarchy of social values. Nor have satisfactory analyses been made of the interconnections between the emphasis placed on growth by those various interest groups that give structure to a society and those other ideas and attitudes that influence the behavior of members of these groups. Because of these lacunae and because of the force that a burning desire for economic growth can have—as has been demonstrated in Western Europe in the post-Second World War period—a new look at the relationships among social structure, social values, and economic growth seems worthwhile. Such an investigation regarding France may help to explain why economic growth in that country was less rapid than in some of the other states of the West during the period of the Third Republic.[1] This lack of growth had a direct bearing on many aspects of French public life and on France's power position in the world; hence it is an important phase of French general history.

To investigate this condition, we need to identify those interest groups (and particularly their top leadership) that were so strategically placed as to influence strongly economic behavior. For this purpose we may begin with the traditional concept of two major classes,[2] the owners of the means of production and the wage-earning workers, although we realize that such a classification puts too many disparate social elements in the same baskets. A hurried glance at the distribution of wealth in France shows: 1) that some two percent of the population has for some time owned about a third of the wealth; and 2) that a large majority of the population has very meager resources and is composed for the most part of workers.[3] Accordingly, on the one hand, a very small minority was in a strategic position to influence growth; the former group could use their savings from current production for investment, furnish entrepreneurial drive, influence state economic policy, and adopt values regarding the use of resources that would serve as a pattern for many in the lower strata. The economic elite, however, did not have the entrepreneurial dynamism characteristic of English and German businessmen and did not put maximum effort into economic achievement. For their part, the great majority was never able to exploit the strength that its numbers and the system of "one man, one vote" provided. The workers, mostly poorly educated, and divided in a hundred ways,[4] adopted rather desultory attitudes toward economic growth and toward the gains to be had from great exertion on their part. Indeed, in the course of time many subscribed to some Socialist doctrine, especially Marxist, and to the surplus theory of value. Obviously, a worker who believed that he was being exploited by a system every working day could hardly be expected to produce with much enthusiasm, and certainly not to increase his production.

Although this two-class concept of society may be useful as a first step in trying to understand the structure of French society, a need exists for further refinements in order to ascertain how attitudes have been formed and actions taken relative to economic growth.[5] One of the first steps in this refining process is to consider the occupational distribution of the active population in order to get more homogeneous groups than sheer wealth stratification can furnish. The breakdown of the active population of France in 1954 by major economic sectors showed that 27.5 percent were engaged in agriculture; in the United Kingdom where income per capita was 15 percent higher than in France, only 6.2 percent of the population was thus engaged. The same study showed that a smaller percentage was in industry in France than in the United Kingdom (42 percent compared with 53.5 percent), and that a smaller percentage was in the tertiary trades (30.5 percent compared to 40.2 percent). Such a distribution is of significance, for, French agriculture contributes only 11.1 percent of the gross national product, whereas industry contributes 47.1 percent. Opportunities for growth have accordingly been much greater in industry than in agriculture, the rate of increase in industry having been nine times that in agriculture in the period 1950–1960.[6] Furthermore, the development of the tertiary trades, especially communications and transportation, indicates the degree of division of labor in an economy—a *sine qua non* of economic growth —and here, too, France was laggard.

Clearly, the fact that a large segment of the active population of France has continued in agriculture, a field in which production is low per capita, has been a retardative factor. So many Frenchmen have remained in farming, even though it has not been one of the more economically rewarding occupations, largely because of their attitudes and values. The well-to-do acquired land during the French Revolution and after, when estates came onto the market, and they retained their holdings very largely for the social prestige that the ownership of land has continued to bring. Smaller landowners, who at the same time got land title free from any manorial encumbrances, to a considerable extent even today display the peasant's idealized love for his land, a love well illustrated by members of the Fouans family, who quarreled so bitterly for small fields in Emile Zola's *La Terre* (1886).

The tenacity with which French farmers have stuck to their trade is most remarkable. The actual number of holdings over ten hectares has remained amazingly steady, and the consolidation of scattered holdings (so universally advocated by experts), has been limited.[7] French landowners have been loathe to migrate to cities and seem to have pride in their status. Lastly, French agriculturalists have traditionally sought to protect a relatively high cost method of husbandry by tariffs and embargoes rather than to reduce costs by greater efficiency of operations.[8]

Important as the agricultural factor has been, the attitudes and behavior of those who went into industry and commerce have affected French economic growth even more. The business élite in France constitutes a relatively small group. As stated, wealth has long been concentrated in the hands of a few, and the wealthy have dominated the business scene.[9] Of the 2000 "personalities" in *Le Dictionnaire biographique français contemporain* in 1955,[10] investigated by Alain Girard in his *La Réussite sociale en France —Ses caractères, ses lois, ses effets*,[11] sixty-eight percent came from five percent of the active population, and between ten and twelve percent came from the top echelons of business, although the top managerial elements in *sociétés anonymes* and in *sociétés de responsabilité limitée* constituted only 1.25 percent of the active population. Here is a group small enough to permit close study and so influential that its attitudes and values have a direct bearing on economic activity.

The bulk of this economic group had its origins in commerce, banking, and government rather than in industry, and frequently its members owed their start to some action by the state. In the Napoleonic period, for example, they were showered with favors, because the Little Emperor wanted their support. Their productive enterprises were protected by the Continental System; they were given an interest in the Bank of France, which became a controlling interest;[12] they were granted titles of nobility with large honoraria and offices with extravagant stipends;[13] and they were ceded rights for the exploitation of subsoil wealth in perpetuity.[14] During the Restoration, loans made by the state to pay off the indemnity to the Allies turned out to be profitable for bankers, and their branch of economic activity flourished to such an extent that several of the great fortunes were firmly established or enlarged. Two such fortunes were those of Jacques Laffitte, who was associated with Frédéric Pérrégaux, of Guillaume Mallet, formerly a protégé of Necker, who helped found with government support the important insurance companies (Assurances Générales and the Phénix), and of Hans Conrad Hottinguer, a Regent of the Bank of France. Further, during the July Monarchy franchises for the building of railways added to the economic empire of the Rothschilds; and the building of railways, as well as the furnishing of war matériel, gave an impetus to certain industrial enterprises, such as that of Joseph Eugène Schneider at Le Creusot.

In general, I am inclined to agree with the view of E. Beau De Loménie, expressed in *Les Responsabilités bourgeoises*,[15] that both the time at which and the manner in which the top capitalist group came into being had much to do with the values by which it lived and the methods it adopted to attain these values. To a considerable extent, members of this group made the *train de vie* of the noble class its way of life. French family budgets indicate that this group wanted to have a town house and a place in the country, spent much more than members of similar groups in other Western European countries on food and drink, and as a proportion of its expenditure made high outlays on recreation and reading.[16] Members of this top economic group favored a classical education for their children, and until recently had, along with other relatively wealthy people, a quasi-monopoly of education above the primary level.[17] They wanted to live in Paris, or to visit the city frequently, and took on urban rather than rural values—an interest in the arts, in small families, and in national politics.[18] In fact, of the *personnages* cited in *Le Petit Larousse* in 1960, born after 1450, thirty-one percent were born in Paris (and many more resided there), although Paris accounted for only seven percent of the French population.[19]

Furthermore, members of this top category in French economic life had a tradition of going to the state for assistance in their enterprises. They seemed to have less entrepreneurial fervor and less self-reliance than businessmen in neighboring states. If they could not easily raise capital for their undertakings, they went to the state to get it. If they could not compete with the production of other nationals, they sought state action through tariffs, subsidies, and embargoes so that they might make France "safe" for inefficient production. For example, they got through the railway concessions of 1842, which provided that the state would acquire rights of way and build roadbeds at its expense; later, in 1859, they got the agreements whereby earnings on their investments in railways were guaranteed by the state. Under the Third Republic they obtained large subsidies for the merchant marine and for the airplane industry. And they had a protective tariff system, except for the ten years following the Anglo-French commercial agreement of 1860, which had one of the highest rates in Western Europe.[20]

This dependence on the state for support of economic activity and the high place that values of a noneconomic character had among businessmen had important consequences for French economic growth.

1. The rate of savings for investments was relatively low in France. Economists at the Commissariat au Plan estimated that in 1938 it was sixteen percent of national income and they proposed to raise it to between twenty-three and twenty-five percent. Yet in the decade from 1950 to 1960 it was only 19.1 percent of national income compared with West Germany's 24.1 percent.[21]

2. Because of the low rate of savings and investment, France's industry operated with antiquated equipment; the average age of machines in the machine tool industry in 1938 was nineteen years, compared with half that number in the case of the United States and Germany.[22]

3. France had relatively small-scale plants, in most cases well below the optimum size, with only 506 establishments in 1958 employing more than 1000 workers.[23]

4. The investment per capita of the labor forces was low, a factor that contributed to a relatively low output per worker.[24]

5. The French were slow to adopt the corporate form of business organization, which had such advantages as amassing capital from several sources for investment, of diminishing the risk of a business falling into incompetent hands, and of assuring a continuation of operations in the case of the demise of owners. In fact, the act of incorporation required such specific governmental authorization until 1867 and such divulging of business information that French businessmen were reluctant to seek corporate charters.

6. Dependence on the state meant that the directorial leaders in French society devoted large amounts of their time and energy to politics rather than to business affairs. Moreover, many of the chief issues in French politics, such as forms of government, the rôle of the Church, the control of education, and reforms of the army, had little to do with economic growth and diverted attention from it.[25]

7. Family tradition has been so strong in France (67.5 percent of the "personalities" studied by Alain Girard followed the same career as their fathers and seventy-nine percent in the case of *chefs d'entreprises*)[26] that businesses were often family affairs operated for limited family ends, a fact that contributed to the

disposition of the wealthy not to swallow smaller establishments and, in truth, to protect small businesses.[27] Cartels to preserve the less competitive were almost nonexistent prior to the depression of the 1930s because they were unnecessary; the peak trade association, now known as the Conseil National du Patronat Français, was not created until 1919 and then at the urging of the state; and one of the strongest elements of this association has been the Confédération Générale des Petites et Moyennes Entreprises.[28]

Not only did the top French business community lack the drive for economic expansion found in the more aggressive economies, but it also had an exceptionally good record of perpetuating itself.[29] The relative absence of a strong spirit of competition undoubtedly contributed to the longevity of some families on the business scene, but other forces were at work to prolong the life of business families and with them their values and practices. Sons have followed their fathers in their callings, especially in business, as we have seen.[30] The top economic group has had a strong position in the higher levels of education (sixty-six percent of the graduates of *les grandes écoles* between the years 1947 and 1953 came from its ranks). Partly because of this advantage in education and partly because of "connections" this group was able to get many of the best positions in France for its scions (before 1946 it had eighty-four percent of the Inspecteurs des Finances, the bulk of the higher posts in the foreign service, and the highest positions in the civil service.[31] To be sure, a certain social mobility has existed in France, but persons who have moved far up the social scale have usually been absorbed by the élite. The top families are forever looking for bright and successful young men to whom to marry their daughters;[32] they bring some of the most brilliant graduates of the *grandes écoles*, especially of the Ecole Polytechnique and engineering schools, into managerial posts in their businesses; they take those who do well in medical examinations or legal examinations into their offices; and they instill in these young men their own social and business values. In general, they set standards of values and conduct that most middle-class people—smaller businessmen, professors, technicians, members of the liberal professions, middle-grade civil servants, and politicians—follow. In fact, they have a dominant position in French society.[33]

Yet, in spite of the strategic role that the top economic group plays in matters pertaining to economic growth, the part played by labor is by no means insignificant. Workers are to be differentiated by occupation, place in the hierarchy of employees, length of employment, expectations regarding the future, residence, family status, religion, political orientation, and the like. Consequently, for a consideration of workers' attitudes, values, and behavior having a bearing on economic growth, we shall concentrate primarily on workers in industry, and secondarily on those in transportation and communications, for these were areas crucial to expansion.

At the outset let us be clear about the numbers with which we are concerned. The census of 1954 found that the French labor force consisted of some nineteen million persons, of whom 64.8 percent or some 12.2 million were wage earners (the remainder were employers, self-employed workers, and unpaid family workers).[34] Of the wage earners, 4.5 million were in industry (3.2 million in manufacturing, 880,000 in construction, 270,000 in mining and quarrying, and the remainder in gas, electricity, and water), and 4.4 million in the tertiary trades, of whom 1.2 million were in transportation and communications. Thus the group with which we are dealing numbers about six million persons.

Some evidence regarding the economic views of this group can be deduced from the voting behavior of its members[35] and some evidence from trade union affiliations and activity. In the elections of June 1951 the Communist and Socialist parties got 2.5 million worker votes, which was 62.6 percent of the total worker vote.[36] So far as trade unionism is concerned, note should be taken of the facts that trade unionists are divided into three main groups— the Communist-oriented Confédération Générale du Travail, the Socialist-oriented CGT-Force Ouvrière, and the Catholic-oriented Confédération Française des Travailleurs Chrétiens—that membership claims are usually exaggerated, and that membership has fluctuated widely and wildly.[37] After the Second World War the unions claimed over seven million members, but in 1953 the CGT had only a million, the CGTFO had 275,000, and CFTC

300,000.[38] This meant that even after the inclusion of members of agricultural unions and some minor bodies only about twenty percent of the organizable workers of the ocuntry were actually enrolled in unions.[39] Clearly, the militancy of labor was tempered by events.

Volatile as membership in trade unions may have been, the doctrines preached by labor-union leaders have, by contrast, been remarkably stable. For over a century now these men have maintained that there is a conflict of interests between workers and the owners of the means of production.[40] This idea is explicit in classical economic theory (or, as it is called in France, liberal economic theory), and is implicit in the admonition of leaders of the CFTC in their pleas to both capital and labor to treat each other according to Christian principles. It has, indeed, been raised to the level of a dogma by both Socialists and Communists, who believe that the labor theory of value and the surplus value theory have been "scientifically" proved, that they are an integral part of capitalism, and that they will continue to exist so long as the dictatorship of the proletariat is not realized. Thus the economic theory with which Socialist, Communist, and Anarchist trade unionists have been indoctrinated asserts that the less a worker produces while on the job, the less he will be exploited.

Evidence of this attitude on the part of trade-union leaders and their followers is abundant. In the first place, French trade unions have always opposed wage rates based on piece work, and in fact have been successful in preventing the system of piece-work compensation from becoming widespread in France. Secondly, they have called strikes when the cessation of work would do great damage to the national economy, as in 1920 in the midst of recovery from the First World War when twenty-three million days of work were lost, and in 1948 in the period of recovery from the Second World War and the beginning of American aid, when even maintenance men were taken off their jobs in coal mines, six million tons of coal production were lost out of a total annual production of forty-seven million tons, and the index of industrial production fell from 116 in June 1948 to 100 in October, the month of the strike.[41] Thirdly, the productivity of French labor has been low, even when allowances are made for antiquated machinery, low investment per worker, and the lack of optimum-size plants.[42] Finally, French trade unions have stressed demands that reduce work-time rather than those that would increase labor's purchasing power, allow the worker to buy more of what he has produced, and thereby expand the domestic market and encourage investors to save more for investment. The forty-hour week and paid vacations are characteristic of what unions have sought and won, with the result that the French worker works fewer days per year than workers in any other of the major industrial countries and below the average for Western Europe.[43]

Although it is difficult to establish how deep-rooted these views of labor are, or how widespread their effect is, it is clear that French labor leadership as well as capitalist leadership has not placed economic growth at the masthead of values. Now the question remains whether or not a change in attitudes has taken place since the Second World War and whether or not economic growth in France, which amounts to just about a doubling of the gross national product since 1938,[44] is to be attributed to changes in values, as many economists have argued.[45] Some changes in attitude have indeed taken place, and have led to greater than usual rates of saving and investment, to improvements in technology, to greater managerial skill, to reduced labor disturbance, and, basically, to the support of a government dedicated to maintaining domestic stability. At least France has achieved its economic growth without any drastic changes in its resource base, although it has had working for it a high level of international trade.

The changes that have taken place in attitudes toward economic growth have been effected chiefly by relatively young economists and technicians. One of the most prominent was Jean Monnet, a successful businessman who had made so fine a reputation for his managerial abilities that his services were sought prior to the Second World War by foreign states. The "Monnet Plan" was a call-to-arms of French economic forces with the nationalist argument that without growth France would wither away; and it was an appeal to produce more in order to raise the standard of living of even the most humble worker. These ideas he sold both to the government (which cooperated in implementing his plan) and to businessmen and labor through planning committees for a great variety of industries. He was instrumental in dispelling the traditional French fear of competing with foreign producers through the establishment of the European Coal and Steel Community and was one of the leading exponents of European economic integration.

But Jean Monnet was not alone in the partial rejuvenation of French entrepreneurial spirit. Professional business managers and technicians, whose very *raison d'être* is to increase production, became more aware of their societal role—if one may judge from the activity and contentions of their trade association, the Confédération Générale des Cadres, founded in 1944. Economic experts, such as Professor Jean Marcel Jeanneney, were brought into high governmental posts; and others from whom results were expected were placed in positions of importance in nationalized industries. Young economists, like Jean Fourastié at the Commissariat au Plan, raised the banner of productivity (produce more to have more) to a position of theoretical respectability among economists and organized effectively such agencies for disseminating their views as the French Centre de Productivité (connected with the Commissariat), the French Association pour l'Accroissement de la Productivité, and the European Productivity Agency within the Organization for Economic Cooperation and Development.[46] Even French labor seems to have become more reformist—more willing than it had been to seek improvements for workers within the existing economic framework of the country, and less concerned with the sudden and violent overthrow of the capitalist system. Its members have offered no serious opposition to the technical assistance program of the United States whereby French workers were brought to America to learn production techniques; and they have been less prone to strike than formerly, especially for political causes.[47] Economic growth has become one of the major political issues in France.

New winds seem indeed to be active in France's social structure, stirring those social values that pertain to economic growth. These winds may not be of hurricane force, and it is possible that they will blow themselves out. While they last, they will have a profound effect on the French economy. At long last France appears to be having its "industrial revolution."

Notes

1. French national income figures for the early years of this period are not entirely satisfactory, but new ones are being prepared by Professor Jan Marczewski of the Faculté de Droit of Paris. Colin Clark in his *Conditions of Economic Progress* (London: Macmillan and Co., 2nd ed., 1951, pp. 63, 80, and 101) believes that between 1870–1876 and 1938 French national income failed to double, but that Germany's increased five times and Great Britain's more than tripled. French national income per person in work in 1938 was thirty-five percent less than the German and forty-eight percent less than the British.

2. At the end of the eighteenth century the two-class concept of society, based on economic functions, took the place of the three-class system based on legal status and legal privilege. Adam Smith accepted this new notion, although he did speak of three groups: the proprietors of land, employers, and workers, in his *Wealth of Nations* (1776, book I, chapters XVIII to XXXI). David Ricardo followed much the same procedure in his *Principles of Political Economy and Taxation* (1817). Karl Marx made the two-class concept a hallowed one, and explained all historical development in terms of the struggle between the two. He insisted in *The 18 Brumaire of Louis Bonaparte* (1852) that "insofar as millions of families live under economic conditions of existence that divide their mode of life, their interests, and their culture from those of other classes and put them in hostile contrast to the latter, they form a class." In *Das Kapital* (1867, book III, sections 6 and 14) he contends that a true class does not exist unless it has an organization for political action, that the struggle between classes is a political struggle, and that the struggle between antagonistic classes is the source of social change. Interesting as these views may be, Marx's rigidity of position and propensity to prophesy diminished the usefulness of his concept of classes for analytical purposes. See Rolf Dahrendorf, *Class and Class Conflict in Industrial Society* (Stanford: Stanford University Press, 1959, pp. 16 and 17. A useful survey of various views on stratification is the book of readings prepared by Reinhard Bendix and Seymour Lipset, *Class, Status, and Power* (New York: The Free Press of Glencoe, 1953).

3. In 1920 in Paris 79.1, percent of the deceased had inheritances so small that no declaration had to be made; 4.1 percent of the declarations were for fortunes of from 500 to 2000 francs (well-to-do workers), 8.4 percent were for 2000 to 20,000 francs (the petite bourgeoisie), 7.5 percent were for 20,000 to 500,000 francs (the middle class), and 0.3 percent were for sums over 500,000 francs. See Adeline Daumard, *La Bourgeoisie parisienne de 1815 à 1848* (Paris: École Pratique des Hautes Études, 1963, pp. 63–64). In 1902, 27 percent of those who died when they were over 20 years of age did not leave enough to require an inheritance tax declaration. Of those required to file a return, 59 percent had estates less than 2000 francs; 26.0 percent had estates of between 2001 and 10,000 francs; 10.0 percent, estates of between 10,001 and 50,000 francs; 1.8 percent between 50,001 and 100,000 francs; 2 percent between 100,001 and 1 million francs, and .011 over

1 million francs. See A. de Foville, "La Richesse de France," Revue Economique internationale, April 1906.

In 1933, about one-half of those who died during the year had estates large enough to require an inheritance tax return. In Paris, 94.1 percent of the declarations accounted for 7.65 percent of the wealth, 4.7 percent in the middle brackets accounted for 20.2 percent of the amounts inherited, and 1.18 percent accounted for 72.31 percent of the inheritances. See Paul Beik, "Evidence Concerning the Distribution of Wealth in France," Political Science Quarterly, vol. 56 (September 1941), p. 373.

4.   Richard F. Hamilton in an unpublished doctoral dissertation at Columbia University, The Social Bases of French Working Class Politics (1963) has made an interesting study of these very points. His data show that 82 percent of workers have only a primary education. Deep cleavages exist between the skilled and unskilled. The greatest disparity is found in towns of 5000 to 20,000 where contacts among workers are very close. Workers appear to be less religious than the middle class, for only 13 percent versus 26 percent of the middle class consult a clergyman regularly. The younger skilled workers are less revolutionary than the unskilled, as they hope for early rewards. Only 55 percent of skilled workers read a national daily newspaper regularly.

5.

	Party Votes, June 1951	
	PERCENTAGE OF TOTAL NATIONAL VOTES	PERCENTAGE OF WORKER VOTES
PC	25.7	47.8
SFIO	14.3	14.8
RGR	9.9	4.4
MRP	12.3	11.5
RPF	21.6	15.9
Moderates	12.3	5.6
Others	3.9	

See Maurice Duverger, Parties politiques et classes sociales, Cahiers de la Fondation Nationale des Sciences Politiques. Paris: Colin, 1955, no. 74, p. 33. The distribution of workers' votes was obtained from an investigation made by the Institut Français d'Opinion Publique and published in Sondages, March 1952, no. 3.

5a.   The Centre d'Etudes Sociologiques distinguishes twenty-three categories of economic groups. See Duverger, p. 19.

6.   For occupational distribution of the active population see United Nations, Statistical Yearbook, 1957. New York: United Nations, 1963, p. 61. For gross national product by economic sector consult United Nations. The Growth of World Industry. New York: United Nations, 1963, p. 270. The increase in French gross national product by sector was 6.8 percent for agriculture, 52.7 for industry, and 40.5 for the tertiary trades for the period 1950–1960. See Angus Maddison, Economic Growth in the West. New York:

The Twentieth Century Fund, 1964, p. 63. Maddison derived his data from OECD *General Statistics* for September, 1962.

7.

	Landholding in France (1908)
SIZE OF HOLDINGS	NUMBER OF HOLDINGS
(in hectares)	
Very small: less than 1	2,087,851
Small: 1 to 10	2,523,713
Medium: 10 to 40	745,862
Large: 40 to 100	118,497
Very large: over 100	29,541
Total	5,505,464

See E. O. Golob, *The Méline Tariff: French Agriculture and Nationalist Economic Policy.* New York: Columbia University Press, 1944, pp. 20–26, 62–66. See also *Rapport général sur le premier plan de modernisation et d'équipement. Deuxième session du Conseil du Plan.* Paris: Commissariat Général au Plan, 1946, p. 58.

8. On migrations see Louis Chevalier, *La Formation de la population parisienne au XIX siècle.* Paris: Presses Universitaires de France, 1950. See also Chevalier's *Classes laborieuses, et classes dangereuses.* Paris: Plon, 1958, p. 270, Alfred Sauvy, *Richesse et population.* Paris: Payot, 1944, p. 177, and Natalie Rogoff, "Social Stratification in France and the United States," *American Journal of Sociology,* vol. 58 (January 1953), p. 355.

9. See Francis Delaisi, *La Banque de France aux mains des 200 familles.* Paris: Comité de Vigilance des Intellectuels Antifascistes, 1936, and Henri Coston, *Le Retour des "200 familles."* Paris: La Librairie Française, 1960. Both of these are "muckraking" books, but they are not without a great deal of information. See also Henry W. Ehrmann, *Organized Business in France.* Princeton: Princeton University Press, 1957, chap. I.

10. Paris: Agence Internationale de Documentation Contemporaine, 2nd ed., 1954–1955.

11. Paris: Presses Universitaires de France, 1961 (notebook 38 of *Travaux et Documents* of the Institut National d'Etudes Démographiques, pp. 61, 334–335). See also a comparable study by Nicole Delefortrie-Soubeyroux, *Les Dirigeants de l'industrie française* (Paris: Colin, 1961). Another interesting survey of industrial leaders is "Evolution de la population active en France depuis cent ans d'après les denombrements quinquennaux," *Etudes et conjonctures. Economie française,* May–June, 1953. An idea of the various forms of business organization used in France and their respective importance can be obtained from the following table from an article "Les Bénéfices industriels et commerciaux déclarés en 1953," in *Revue statisque et études financières,* no. 75, March, 1955, p. 20.

Types of business according to taxes paid	Number of businesses	Percent of total	Gross business done (billions of francs)	Percent of total gross (billions of francs)
Nationalized industries	58	—	1,653.9	7.0
Sociétés anonymes et en commandites par actions	22,323	1.3	8,691.7	36.8
Sociétés à responsabilité limitée	136,491	7.9	6,188.7	26.1
Other sociétés	7,840	0.5	460.3	1.9
Individual ownerships and partnerships	277,185	16.2	4,615.2	19.5
Businesses taxed according to bénéfices forfaitaires	1,271,966	74.1	2,041.1	8.7

12. Delaisi, La Banque de France.

13. E. Beau De Loménie, Les Responsabilités des dynasties bourgeoises. Paris: Edition De Noël, 1948, vol. 1, p. 50. By a decree of March 1, 1808 barons were to receive endowments equal to 5000 francs annual income from the state, counts 30,000 francs, and dukes 200,000 francs.

14. Subsoil wealth belonged to the French state, but the granting of its exploitation to private interests in perpetuity was something new (Law of April 21, 1810).

15. Beau de Loménie, vol. 1, chap. 1. See also Adeline Daumard, La Bourgeoisie parisienne de 1815 à 1848. Paris: SEPEN, 1963, pp. 172 ff., and Charles Morazé, La France bourgeoise, XVIII–XX. Paris: Armand Colin, 1947, pp. 84 ff.

16. Family budgets for France are not very satisfactory, but they are being improved all the time. See J. Frederic Dewhurst, John O. Coppock, P. Lamartine Yates, and Associates, Europe's Needs and Resources. New York: Twentieth Century Fund, 1961, pp. 153 ff. and 954.

17. In 1930–1931 there were 161,492 students in private secondary schools, 77,137 in secondary classes of boys' lycées and public colleges, and 29,934 in schools for girls; this constituted about 6.4 percent of the population in the age groups that might have been in secondary schools. See Annuaire statistique. Paris: Imprimerie Nationale, 1947, pp. *36 and *38. Alain Girard, La Réussite sociale en France: Ses caractères, ses lois, ses effets, pp. 192 ff., reports

that 66 percent of the students in the *Grandes Ecoles* came from the top 5 percent of the population and 8 percent from the top 18 percent. Education has been a quasimonopoly of the wealthy for a long time. See François de Dainville, "Effectifs des collèges de scolarité aux XVIII siècles dans le Nord-Est de la France," *Population*, July–September, 1955, Year X, no. 3, p. 475. Between 1731 and 1757 about 80 percent of students in *collèges* were from cities and at Châlons-sur-Marne about the same percentage was from the Third Estate (p. 479).

18.   Girard, pp. 327 ff.

19.   Girard, p. 261. See also Alfred Odin of the University of Sofia, *Genèse des grands hommes: gens de lettres français modernes.* Paris: 1895.
   The concentration of business at Paris is well-known. The Parisian region of the Seine—Seine et Oise, Seine et Marne, and Eure et Loir—has 25 percent of French industrial production and 33 percent of its commerce, but has 18 percent of the French population. See *Rapport annuel sur l'exécution du plan de modernisation.* Paris: Commissariat au Plan, 1955, p. 432. An attempt was made in 1955 (decree of January 5) to require businessmen to get governmental authorization for the extension of existing plant or the building of new plant in the Parisian region. This effort had very little effect. See Jean Marcel Jeanneney, *Forces et faiblesse de l'économie française, 1945–1956.* Paris: Armand Colin, 1956, p. 254.

20.   See Simon Kuznets, "Economic Growth and Income Inequality," *The American Economic Review*, vol. 45 (1955), p. 25; Shepard B. Clough, *France 1789–1939: A Study in National Economics.* New York: Scribner, 1939; Kimon A. Doukas, *The French Railroads and the State.* New York: Columbia University Press, 1945, pp. 22 ff., 33 ff., and 43 ff.; and Warren C. Baum, *The French Economy and the State.* Princeton: Princeton University Press, 1958.

21.   *Rapport général sur le premier plan de modernisation et d'équipment,* p. 88, and Angus Maddison, *Economic Growth in the West,* p. 76.

22.   *Rapport général sur le premier plan,* p. 148. France was also backward in agricultural equipment. In 1938 it had one tractor for every 200 farmers, whereas the United Kingdom had one for every 22 farmers.

23.   Jeanneney, p. 258; John Sheahan *Promotion and Control of Industry in Postwar France.* Cambridge, Mass.: Harvard University Press, 1963, pp. 239 ff.; and Maddison, p. 80.

24.   Maddison, p. 40 and Dewhurst *et al.,* pp. 452–453, 467. In 1938 the production of coal per coal worker in France was 831 kilograms compared with 1190 kilograms in the United Kingdom. In the same year France had 7500 horsepower per member of the active population and the United Kingdom had 20,000 horsepower. (Ingvar Svennilson, *Growth and Stagnation in the European Economy.* Geneva: United Nations, 1954, p. 252).

25.   Beau De Loménie, vol. 1, pp. 10–12.

26. Girard, p. 334.

27. Before the Second World War France had legislation that limited the extension of chain stores. See Sheahan, *Promotion and Control of Industry in Post War France*, pp. 140–141.
David Landes has stressed the family aspect of French business. See his "French Entrepreneurship and Industrial Growth in the Nineteenth Century," *Journal of Economic History*, 1949, pp. 45–61.

28. See Ehrmann, pp. 29 ff.

29. Coston, pp. 166–168 and *passim*. Also Beau De Loménie.

30. Girard, p. 189. A sample of the alumni of these schools, who had been graduated in the years 1947–1953 inclusive, showed the following distribution of their fathers by occupation: workers, 2.3 percent; farmers 6 percent; retail merchants and artisanal workers, 11.2 percent; employees, 4.5 percent; middle and subordinate civil servants, 10.6 percent; middle and superior *cadres*, 22.8 percent; liberal professions, 7.4 percent; high civil servants, 16.5 percent; heads of businesses, 18.7 percent.

31. Girard, pp. 189 and 309. Even in the Ecole Nationale d'Administration in the years 1952–1958, 61.8 percent of the students were from the middle and superior cadres upward. See also Henri Laugier, Mlle. Weinberg, and Mlle. Charretier, "Le Recrutement du personnel du ministère des Affaires Étrangères avant la Guerre de 1939," in Girard, pp. 297 ff. and 310 ff. See also Pierre Lalumière, *L'Inspection des finances*. Paris: Presses Universitaires de France, 1959, chap. 2; Daumard, pp. 272 ff.; and Guy Palmade, *Capitalisme et capitalistes français au XIX siècle*. Paris: Colin, 1961.

32. See Coston, *passim*; Jean Meynaud, *Les Groupes de pression en France*. Paris: Colin, 1958; and Georges E. Lavau, Henry W. Ehrmann (Ed.), *Interest Groups on Four Continents*. Pittsburgh: University of Pittsburgh Press, 1958, pp. 60–95.

33. Institut National de la Statistique et des Etudes Economiques. *Etudes statistiques*. Quarterly supplement of the *Bulletin mensuel de Statistique*, Paris: July–September 1956 and July–September 1957.

34. One might add that 8.2 million of the 12.2 million wage earners were males.

35. In addition to the references given in note 4, consult Mattei Dogan, "Le vote ouvrier en Europe occidentale," *Revue française de sociologie*, vol. 1 (January–March, 1960): J. Stoetzel, "Voting Behaviour in France," *The British Journal of Sociology*, June 1955; Russell Planck, "Public Opinion in France after the Liberation, 1944–1949," in Mirra Komarovsky (Ed.), *Common Frontiers of the Social Sciences*. New York: The Free Press of Glencoe, 1957, pp. 184–241; and various works by François Goguel.

36. *Sondages*, March 1952.

37. Georges Lefranc, *Histoire du syndicalisme ouvrier en France*. Paris: Cours de l'Institut d'Etudes Politiques, 1954–1955 maintains that 60 percent of the members of the CFTC in Alsace were Protestants. See also Gerald Thormann, *Christian Trade Unionism in France! A History of the French Confederation of Christian Workers*. Unpublished dissertation at Columbia University, 1951; Henry W. Ehrmann, *French Labor, from Popular Front to Liberation*. New York: Oxford University Press, 1947, chap. 7.

The Confédération Générale du Travail was not constituted until 1895 and up to 1914 did not have a membership of more than 400,000; and in the same period other unions, of which the Catholic were the most important, could not count more than 200,000. The First World War was a turning point in trade union history when membership in the CGT soared to a claimed 2 million in 1918 and the strength of Catholic unions was increased with the founding of the CFTC. This *essor* of trade unions turned out to be somewhat of a flash in the pan, for subsequently splits between those supporting communism and those adhering to Socialist doctrines greatly weakened the movement. In 1920 at the Congress of Tours, the CGT split along political lines into the CGT Unifié, which was Communist, and the CGT, which was Socialist. These two groups merged in 1936, but split again in 1947, with the CGT this time being Communist and the CGT Force Ouvrière being Socialist.

Membership fluctuated from a claimed 600,000 for the CGT in 1934, 300,000 for the CGTU, and 100,000 for the CFTC to 5 million in 1937 for the CGT and 500,000 for the CFTC. After the failure of a strike in 1938 membership in the CGT fell to 1 million, but in 1946 the Secretary of the CGT reported 800,000 members, or sympathizers. See Georges Lefranc, *Histoire du mouvement syndical français*. Paris: Librairie Syndicale, 1937, p. 47; and by the same author, *Les Expériences syndicales en France de 1939 à 1950*. Paris: Aubier, 1950, pp. 365–368.

38. See Ehrmann, p. 237 and ftn. p. 288; and Edouard Dolléans and Gérard Dehove, *Histoire du travail en France des origines à nos jours*. Paris: Donat Montchrétien, 1953–1955, vol. 2, pp. 234–238.

39. In addition to the organizations already mentioned, attention should be called to the Confédération Nationale du Travail (reorganized in 1946), which is oriented toward anarchism; the Confédération Générale des Syndicats Indépendents (reorganized in 1951), which is composed mostly of white-collar workers and is charged with harboring company, or "yellow," unions; the Fédération Autonome de l'Education Nationale, a union of teachers which seceded from the CGT in 1948; and the Confédération Générale de l'Agriculture, founded in 1944, in order to organize farm workers but which is actually dominated by farm owners in a constituent body, the Fédération Nationale des Syndicats d'Exploitants Agricoles. In 1951, forty-one of the eighty-seven officers in national agricultural organizations, belonged to conservative parties and only thirteen to Leftist parties. The FNSEA claimed 700,000 in 1956. See Meynaud, *Les Groupes de pression*, p. 59; Gordon Wright, *Rural Revolution in France: The Peasantry in the Twentieth Century*. Stanford: Stanford University Press, 1964, pp. 105–109; and Jacques Fauvet and Henri Mendras (Eds.), *Les Paysans et la politique*. Paris: Armand Colin, 1958, p. 231 ff. Also *Bulletin du Ministère du Travail* for current data on membership.

40. Meynaud, p. 303.

41. The stockpile of coal was reduced by 3 million tons. *European Recovery Program: France, 1948.* Paris: ECA Special Mission to France, 1948, pp. 14–15.

42. *Programme Française pour l'accroissement de la productivité.* Paris: Commissariat Général au Plan. Groupe de Travail de la Productivité, 1948. French unions opposed profit sharing plans and compulsory arbitrations. See Joel Colton, *Compulsory Labor Arbitration in France, 1936–1939.* New York: Columbia University Press, 1951.

43. The forty-hour week was not adhered to, for additional hours were permitted if increased wage rates were paid. But this extension of working hours was not the intention of the lawmakers when the bill was passed and was not looked upon with favor by union leaders. See *International Labor Office. Hours of Work, Report 8. 42nd Session of the ILO.* Geneva: ILO, 1958, pp. 2–24. Also Dewhurst, p. 88.

44. Maddison, pp. 201–202.

45. Baum, *The French Economy and the State*, p. 344; Sheahan, *Promotion and Control of Industry in Post–War, France*, chap. 1; and Charles P. Kindleberger, "The Post-War Resurgence of the French Economy," in Stanley Hoffmann (Ed.), *In Search of France.* Cambridge, Mass.: Harvard University Press, 1963.

46. Dewhurst, pp. 762 and 778; and Wilton Dillon, *L'Aide spirituelle française peut résoudre six crises américaines.* Documents, 8. Paris: Association Française pour l'Accroissement de la Productivité, 1957, p. 9 ff.

47. Dewhurst, p. 771; and Alain Touraine and Jean Daniel Reynaud, *L'Attitude des ouvriers de la sidérurgie à l'égard des changements techniques.* Paris: Institut des Sciences Sociales du Travail, 1957.

part 2

LIBERALISM, CHRISTIANITY,

AND THE REVOLUTIONS OF 1848

The revolutions of 1848, which received their initial impulse from France, produced violent movements for constitutionalism in many of the great population centers of Europe. Unfavorable economic conditions resulting from the Industrial Revolution, poor harvests, and a growing population, as well as radical theories of social and economic reorganization, stirred discontent among urban workers and peasants. Religious movements also played a part in the outbreaks.

The Jacobin ideology of the French Revolution, among other factors, contributed to the conflict between liberalism and Christianity, which in France largely meant Catholicism. The basic rivalry of the two forces was by no means diminished following the Restoration (1814–1815). Yet reconciliation between elements of nineteenth-century liberalism and organized Christianity came to be more possible in the climate of opinion that developed during the days of the July Monarchy. After the heyday of Joseph de Maistre and Chateaubriand, Lamennais and his followers (including Lacordaire, Montalembert, and Dupanloup) not only injected vigor into nineteenth-century French Catholicism, but brought into serious consideration the possibility of reconciling liberalism and Catholicism. In France the establishment of a Second French Republic (1848–1851) produced many manifestations of the accommodation of Christianity and republicanism. The republic was strikingly more clerical than the July Monarchy had been.

During the Second Empire and the pontificate of Pius IX (1846–1878), however, the divergence between Catholicism and liberalism reappeared, and by the time of the establishment of the Third Republic the identification of clericalism and traditional monarchism had been re-established, while liberalism became increasingly secular and anticlerical. Radical republicans worked for the separation of Church and state. Frédéric Le Play, followed by Albert de Mun, who was particularly influenced by the Christian socialism of Germany, tried to reform society on a Christian basis, preserving traditional social and governmental structures, but by the 1870s monarchists and clericals reasserted the old alliance between the altar and the now vacant throne. Simultaneously, liberal Catholicism lost ground to reactionary clericalism, which sought to defend the Church against the secularizing laws of the Republic. Louis Veuillot, the militant champion of ultramontanism who had once supported the Second Republic, demonstrated this realignment with editorial blows in *l'Univers,* aimed at liberalism even within the Catholic framework. The rôle of the liberal Catholic was again extremely awkward, and remained so until the effects of Leo XIII's policies were slowly felt. The question of Church and state is certainly one of the main keys to French history, and the struggle as it took shape during the nineteenth century is particularly significant.

⤙ WILLIAM L. LANGER

William Leonard Langer is noted for his masterly
contributions to European and American diplomatic
history of the nineteenth and twentieth centuries.
Born in Boston in 1896, he received his A.B. from
Harvard in 1915, and, after service in the First World
War, obtained his A.M. and Ph.D. degrees from the
same university. A year in Vienna (1921–1922) was
the start of a career of vigorous research in modern
European history. From 1927 to 1964 Professor
Langer was a member of the department of history
at Harvard, where he appropriately occupied the
chair named for Archibald Cary Coolidge. There he
served as chairman of the Committee on Regional
Studies and as director both of the Russian Research
Center and the Center for Middle Eastern Studies.
In 1957 he was president of the American Historical
Association.

During the Second World War Professor Langer
served as chief of the Research and Analysis Branch,
Office of Strategic Services, for which he was
awarded the Presidential Medal of Merit. Immediately following the war he was appointed Special
Assistant to the Secretary of State.

Among Professor Langer's major publications are
The Franco-Russian Alliance 1890–1894 (1929),
European Alliances and Alignments (1871–1890)
(1950), *The Diplomacy of Imperialism (1890–1902)*
(1935, 1951), *Our Vichy Gamble* (1947), and, with
S. E. Gleason, *The Challenge to Isolation 1937–
1940* (1952) and *The Undeclared War* (1953). And
Professor Langer is the general editor of a twenty-
volume series entitled *The Rise of Modern Europe*,
and of *An Encyclopedia of World History* (1940,
1952) and a *Foreign Affairs Bibliography*. The
breadth and depth of his work have been universally
recognized in university circles, and he is exceptionally well qualified to present the aspects of the revolutions of 1848 treated in the following study.

The Pattern of Urban Revolution in 1848

Although the centennial celebrations of 1948 spawned many publications and brought into new relief many aspects of the European upheavals of the mid-nineteenth century, relatively little attention has been devoted to the comparative study of these revolutions. The objective of this essay is to examine the outbreaks of February and March 1848 so as to determine what, if anything, they had in common, and to raise the question whether these famous revolutions were inevitable or even beneficial.

Although there were disturbances in the countryside as well as in many cities, the events in the four great capitals, Paris, Vienna, Berlin, and London, were crucial. It is true that these government centers had been but little touched by the new industrialism and that therefore the proletariat of the factories played but a very subordinate rôle, especially in the early days of the revolutions. Yet the capitals were the seats of traditional industry, with a huge population of craftsmen, tradesmen, and specialized workers of all kinds.[1] London and Paris, in particular, harbored thousands of different industries without having much of a modern industrial proletariat.[2] The workers were mostly what might be termed *menu peuple* (lesser bourgeoisie).

This does not mean that the capital cities were less restless than the new factory towns. In all of them life had become unsettled and precarious, for everywhere the traditional artisan was exposed to the competition of machine industry, located chiefly in the provincial towns. Wages, if they did not actually decline, remained low, while employment became steadily more uncertain. The plight of the urban workers following the economic crisis of 1846–1847 is well known and its bearing on the revolutions of 1848 has been duly stressed by Professor Labrousse and others. Basically it was inevitable that the early stages of industrialization should have brought instability and hardship, but the situation in mid-century was greatly aggravated by the fantastic growth of the European

90

population; this growth entailed an unprecedented movement of rural workers to the cities, which for centuries had held the promise of opportunity.

In the years from 1800 to 1850 the growth of the European capitals was stupendous, with the result that at the end of the period a large proportion of the population was not native born. It consisted largely of immigrants, permanent or temporary, coming either from nearby areas, or from abroad. In the 1840s alone about 250,000 persons came into London, 46,000 of whom were Irishmen, who were particularly disliked and feared by the English workers because of their incredibly low standard of living. In addition, there were substantial numbers of Belgian and German workers.[3]

As for Paris, the researches of Louis Chevalier and others have thrown a flood of light on the nature of the population and the conditions of life. The number of inhabitants just about doubled between 1800 and 1850, due very largely to immigration. Thus, between 1831 and 1836 about 115,000 arrived, and from 1841 to 1846 another 98,000. Most of the newcomers were from the neighboring *départements*, but there were many foreigners as well. Accurate statistics are lacking, but there appear to have been upward of 50,000 Germans (mostly tailors, shoemakers, cabinet-makers) in Paris, to say nothing of large numbers of Belgian and Italian workers and sizable contingents of political refugees from many lands.[4]

The situation in Vienna and Berlin was much the same. The population of the Austrian capital numbered about 400,000, 125,000 of whom had been added between 1827 and 1847. In 1845 there were some 130,000 Czech, Polish, and Italian immigrants.[5] In Berlin the population rose from 180,000 to 400,000 between 1815 and 1847, due largely to the heavy immigration from the eastern provinces.[6]

In all cities the steady influx of people created an acute housing shortage. This was less true of London than of the continental capitals, for there the government offices had long since moved from the Old City to Westminster and the well-to-do had built new homes in the West End and along the main highways to the west and northwest. The 125,000 people who still lived in the Old

City were for the most part clerks, runners, cleaners, and other employees of the great banks and business houses. In the continental capitals, however, the exodus of the upper classes from the old central districts had only just begun. The new and fashionable sections of northwestern Paris were still far from complete, while the oldest part of the city was incredibly congested, "an almost impenetrable hive of tenements and shops."[7] The efforts of Rambuteau, the *préfet* of the Seine, to open up the dingiest areas by constructing larger arteries, involved the destruction of much cheap housing, little of which was replaced elsewhere. Under the circumstances, rents rose rapidly. Most immigrant workers were lucky to find even miserable quarters in the center of the town or in the workers' sections of eastern Paris. "The difficulty of finding lodgings," wrote a contemporary, "is for the worker a constant ordeal and a perpetual cause of misery."[8]

In Vienna and Berlin, as in Paris, a great many immigrant workers found refuge in the lodging houses, which enjoyed a golden age at this time. In the low-grade places men and women were housed together, and it was by no means uncommon for eight or nine persons to be crowded into one room. The old Innere Stadt of Vienna, still surrounded by its seventeenth-century walls, was so hopelessly congested that some members of the aristocracy were obliged, most reluctantly, to build new "villas" beyond the Kärntner Tor, while practically all industry, with the exception of the old-established silk trade, was compelled, by government decree, to locate in the suburbs. In Berlin, too, the rapidly developing textile and metallurgical industries were concentrated in the northern areas, while the upper classes lived mostly in the western and southwestern sections. Berlin was notorious for its wretched lodging houses and workers' barracks.[9]

Considering the great instability of the changing social order, it is not surprising that many of the newcomers in the cities failed to find the hoped-for employment. Thousands were chronically out of work, reduced to living in dank cellars or unheated garrets, and often driven by desperation into robbery or other crimes. In Paris, as in most other cities, about a quarter of the population was indigent, dependent on government or private relief. The situation thus engendered was particularly dangerous because as yet in many cities the rich and poor lived cheek-by-jowl. The Paris apartment house, whose lower floors were occupied by the well-to-do while the *petite bourgeoisie* took over the upper stories and the paupers were left the crannies under the eaves, are familiar to us from Balzac's novels, but it must be remembered that in almost every part of Paris prosperous residential areas and pockets of slums were intermingled. There was no strictly aristocratic quarter and no strictly workingmen's quarter. Even in metropolitan London fashionable streets were often backed by abandoned "rookeries." Such existed even in the West End, in the vicinity of Buckingham Palace.[10]

Overall conditions in the crowded cities of the early or mid-nineteenth century were such as to create chronic social tension. Riots by the hungry or unemployed were all too common, as were also clashes between native and foreign workers. It is obvious that these outbreaks could and at times did assume such proportions as to threaten governments, if not the entire social order.

To combat disturbances European governments had traditionally relied upon their military forces. Napoleon's "whiff of grapeshot" was an example of the use even of artillery in breaking up a hostile demonstration. More common, however, was the employment of sabre-charging cavalry. Nicholas I of Russia, though confronted with the most formidable and urgent social problem in Europe, escaped revolution in 1848 by ruthless application of these tactics. His internal defense force, quartered throughout the country, numbered some 200,000 men and beat down any threat of insurrection. The secret police and the Cossack brigades showed the world how to maintain order and vindicated Nicholas's claim to be the gendarme of Europe.[11]

But in western Europe these methods of brutal repression had by the nineteenth century become as difficult to apply as they were objectionable. To ride or shoot down unarmed citizens was hardly the answer to political or social problems, to say nothing of the fact that conscripted soldiers showed ever greater unwillingness to fire upon the people.[12] In Britain, where the problems created by the industrial revolution were most acute, the government had, before 1848, worked out a different procedure or policy. In connection with the very formidable and menacing Chartist demonstrations of 1839 and 1842 freedom of speech and assembly were generally respected, but the authorities made it perfectly clear that any effort to subvert the government or the social order would be ruthlessly suppressed. Furthermore, General Charles Napier, in charge of the forces in the industrial areas of the north, by adroitly placing his troops and by bringing additional soldiery from Ireland to ensure against defection, succeeded in creating a genuine deterrent.

As for London, much greater advances had been made in the direction of public security. In 1829 the first modern civil police force had been established, consisting of selected, uniformed, trained and well-paid constables numbering by 1848 about 5500 men. Despite much popular hostility, the London police soon made itself respected and indeed worked out the tactics of what today are called "riot control formations," that is, the organization and employment of squad or platoon wedges to penetrate mobs, arrest leaders, and break up demonstrations, and of echelons to pry rioters away from buildings and force them to move in specified directions.[13]

Chartist Demonstration in London

Some insight into the problems confronting continental governments in February and March 1848 can be gained by reviewing the great Chartist demonstration and petition scheduled for April 10 in London as the culmination of a series of disturbances in Glasgow, Manchester, and even in the capital that echoed the revolutionary events on the continent in the preceding weeks.

In the councils of the Chartist movement there were some who, as in 1839, favored revolutionary action and the use of violence in the event that the great petition were again rejected by parliament. But the majority of the leaders, long since convinced of the government's determination to suppress any attempt at insurrection, still hoped to attain their ends by peaceful demonstration. The plan then was to stage a monster meeting followed by the procession of thousands of workers to the House of Commons. The great day was to be April 10, when contingents of Chartists marched from various assembly points in the metropolis to Kennington Common, in southwestern London. When they gathered, at about 11:00 A.M., the police were already at hand. Feargus O'Connor, the leader, was warned that while the meeting itself was permissible, the law forbade large demonstrations designed to intimidate Parliament and that therefore the crowd would be permitted to recross the river only in small groups. O'Connor, a demagogue braver in words than in deeds, at once urged his followers to accept the police ruling. There was some speech-making, but presently the whole meeting was washed out by rain. The demonstrators straggled back over Blackfriars Bridge, while the petition, with its millions of signatures, was taken to Parliament by a small delegation riding in three cabs. The day ended without even a window having been broken.

There is every reason to think that the London police could by itself have dealt with the Chartist demonstration. But the government had been unwilling to take the chance and had, with the full support of the propertied classes, made preparations far beyond anything the situation called for. The aged Duke of Wellington had been put in command of the troops, which were brought in from the surrounding areas. At the same time, a call was sent out for special constables, to which all respectable elements, from peers to business and professional men, down to clerks, railroad officials, shopkeepers, and others responded in great numbers. It is said, and was so reported in the *Times*, that no less than 150,000 of these constables were enrolled. They sand-bagged and garrisoned the Bank of England, the Post-Office, India House, and other valuable properties, while the troops, which were kept out of sight as much as possible, occupied the Tower and other strong points. On the river three ships were held in readiness, with steam up, to transport troops or supplies to any threatened spot. The Chartists, as they marched to their rendezvous, could hardly fail to notice the reception that awaited them in case of serious unrest.

So much certainly was to be learned from the London experience: 1) an efficient police force was capable of dealing with even large-scale demonstrations; 2) a government acceptable to the citizenry could count on the support of huge numbers of volunteers; 3) the troops could be kept in reserve, to be used only in an emergency; 4) a clean-cut policy and adequate preparations would serve as an effective deterrent. Harriet Martineau, in her account of the Kennington Common meeting, was not far off the mark when she declared exultantly: "From that day it was a settled matter that England was safe from revolution."[14]

It is true, of course, that the British government had the advantage, in facing the Chartist threat, not only of previous experience but of the experience of the continental governments that had succumbed to revolution. Nonetheless, it will be useful to review the outbreak of insurrection in Paris, Vienna, and Berlin in the light of what could and was done in another country in what were roughly comparable circumstances. For it is probably a mistake to argue that Britain, because it had no revolution in 1848, was in some mysterious way different and therefore exempt from major social ructions. If there was a great deal of talk of revolution on the continent in the years preceding 1848, there was hardly less of such talk in England. Friedrich Engels, it will be recalled, in 1845 held that social revolution was unavoidable.

The 1848 Revolution in Paris

The events of February 1848 in Paris, which ended with the downfall of the Orleans Monarchy, were conscientiously analyzed by M. Crémieux more than fifty years ago.[15] They were far too complicated to be satisfactorily summarized in a brief essay. Certain features, however, should be highlighted. It is well known, for instance, that Louis Philippe and his chief minister, M. Guizot, were surprised by the insurrection by which they were overtaken. This surprise is at least understandable, for even though opposition to the regime had been mounting, it certainly did not suggest the possibility of a major upheaval. The opposition, insofar as it was organized and directed, was in the main a parliamentary opposition calling for very modest changes: liberalization of the electorate, limitation of political patronage, extension of civil liberties. It is hardly an exaggeration to describe this opposition as a family affair, the struggle of one faction against another within the same social framework. Its leaders did not plan revolution, nor even desire it. For months they had been carrying on a campaign of propaganda and agitation centering about a program of political banquets. But these methods, if they were not directly imitated from the British, were at any rate the counterpart of the great pressure campaigns conducted across the Channel by Daniel O'Connell and Richard Cobden, namely the campaigns that led to the emancipation of the Catholics, to the great Reform Act of 1832, and to the repeal of the Corn Laws in 1846. These victories over a well-entrenched ruling class were watched with the utmost interest by liberals all over the Continent. When Cobden in 1847 made a tour of the continental countries he was everywhere fêted by the enlightened, educated circles, all of which took heart from the British experience. Considering that in the French Chamber most of the prominent members had, by 1848, aligned themselves with the opposition, there is no reason to suppose that in the not too distant future the resistance of even Guizot and Louis Philippe would have crumbled.

Only a few words need be said in this context of the more popular opposition, that of the disfranchised writers, artists, tradesmen, and workers who, ever since their disillusionment with the July Revolution of 1830, had been organized in secret societies and some of whom, certainly, were quite prepared to rise in revolt in the name of democracy or socialism. The unemployment, want, and unrest in Paris were such that a great social uprising seemed to some, like Tocqueville, a real and immediate threat. It will be remembered that the monster opposition banquet that had been planned for the first *arrondissement* was moved to a hall in the aristocratic quarter and that, when it was prohibited by the authorities, the opposition leaders were positively relieved. Far from wanting a popular disturbance, the opposition was intent on remaining within the bounds of legality. But in actuality the popular opposition, while noisy and threatening, was so limited in numbers, so divided and weak, so unprepared as to be quite innocuous. It may be recalled that popular leaders like Louis Blanc positively dreaded an insurrection, knowing that the lower classes were bound to be defeated.[16]

The question now arises: How well equipped and prepared was the government to deal with major disorders? It had faced a series of formidable disturbances in the years 1830–1834 and a concerted attempt at insurrection in 1839. Its security forces were briefly as follows. The regular, uniformed police force (*sergents de ville*) numbered only a few hundred men, but was reinforced by an essentially military *Garde municipale*. This body, recruited largely among army veterans, consisted of sixteen companies of infantry and five squadrons of cavalry (a total of 3200 men), splendidly accoutered, thoroughly drilled, and so notorious for its brutality as to be passionately hated by the population.[17]

The *Garde municipale* was roughly the equivalent of the London metropolitan police, except that it was more pronouncedly military in character. It, in turn, was expected to rely for support on the *Garde nationale* which, again, was intended to play the same rôle as the London special constables. The *Garde nationale* was, however, a permanent force, more or less regularly trained and exercised, for the most part uniformed and armed. It consisted of one legion for each of the twelve *arrondissements*, plus one élite cavalry legion and four suburban legions—all told a force of no less than 84,000 men. All able-bodied men were liable for service in the *Garde nationale*, but actually only those who paid a certain annual tax were enrolled. It was understood that the *Garde* was an essentially bourgeois formation, designed for defense of the regime. Only after it had gone into action against insurgents was the regular garrison expected to take part. This garrison consisted of some 30,000 troops, quartered in barracks scattered throughout the city.[18]

In the July Revolution of 1830 the commander of the forces, Marshal Marmont, had been faced by the refusal of his troops to fire on the populace. The danger of defection in the event of civil strife was a continuing one and for that very reason the government relied chiefly on the *Garde nationale* to quell the disturbances of the 1830s. It proved to be a matter of prime importance, then, that the devotion of the *Garde* to the king had weakened greatly by 1848. Ever since 1835 the upper classes had evaded service, while the legions of the poorer *arrondissements* had become seriously disgruntled. The king was certainly not ignorant of these developments. Indeed, after 1840 he did not even review the *Garde*, though to show his displeasure in this way was probably unwise. The estrangement between the ruler and the formations that were supposedly the mainstay of his regime was to be the crucial factor in the events of February 22–24, 1848.

The crowd that assembled on the Place de la Madeleine on the rainy morning of February 22 was altogether nondescript and evidently moved more by curiosity than by any set purpose. It surged aimlessly to and fro until in the later morning a group of students from the Left Bank led the way to the Chamber of Deputies, where the first minor clashes took place before the crowd was pressed back over the river to the Place de la Concorde. The king and the government clearly did not take the demonstration seriously, for preparatory measures that had been decided on were countermanded, probably from fear that action by the troops would only roil the populace and possibly from uncertainty as to the reliability of the forces. In this connection it is interesting to note that on this very first day of unrest the troops tended to stand aloof. They watched idly while the crowd broke street lanterns and overturned omnibuses, and in some cases stood inactive while barricades were being thrown across the streets.[19]

From the outset the *Garde municipale* acted with its usual energy and ruthlessness and, as might be expected, enraged the populace. It might conceivably have broken up the demonstrations by its own efforts, had it been given appropriate orders. But these were not forthcoming, so the *Garde* found itself reduced to purely defensive operations. Since the disorders continued to spread, the king on the morning of February 23 reluctantly called out the *Garde nationale,* only to find, to his horror, that even the legions from the well-to-do sections had joined the opposition to the Guizot regime and insisted on immediate reforms. The effect of this revelation was to precipitate the rather unceremonious dismissal of Guizot.[20] Had the king then called at once on the opposition leaders, Thiers and Barrot, to form a ministry and had he, at the same time, accepted the modest reforms demanded by the opposition, the situation might well have been saved. But Louis Philippe disliked Thiers and was loath to accept changes. In the sequel he was to agree to a reform ministry but without consenting to reforms and, belatedly, to show a determination to resist that, at an earlier hour, might have stood him in good stead.

For the time being, both the *Garde* and the troops were left without adequate directives. In the growing disorder the officers lost confidence while the men became demoralized.[21] Meanwhile the center of disturbance shifted to the crowded *arrondissements,* where barricades went up by the hundreds.[22] On the evening of February 23 there took place the "massacre" of the Boulevard des Capucines, when a surging crowd of National Guards and people collided with a detachment of troops which, hard pressed, opened fire, leaving some fifty persons dead on the pavement. Only after this tragic episode, which raised the resentment of the populace to fever heat, did Louis Philippe entrust command of both the troops and the *Garde nationale* to Marshal Bugeaud, victor of the Algerian campaigns and a soldier renowned for his toughness, who had been itching for a chance to put the "rabble" in its place. Bugeaud started out bright and early on the morning of February 24 in an attempt to reopen communications between the key points of the city. Yet before noon he proclaimed a cease-fire. The reasons for this *volte-face* on the part of a fire-eating commander have been the subject of much debate, but need not detain us here. The fact is that the weariness and demoralization of the troops, the almost complete defection of the *Garde nationale,* and above all the hundreds of barricades must have shown him the futility of his effort.[23] The king made a last desperate but vain attempt to rally the support of at least part of the *Garde nationale,* after which he was driven to the inevitable decision to abdicate.

In review it must be reiterated that the revolution that developed in Paris was neither planned nor desired. The outbreaks were disjointed, isolated, leaderless, and utterly without plan or coordination. The king, through poor judgment, distrust, and indecision, allowed the disturbances to develop to the point at which suppression became impossible. When he failed to conciliate the *Garde nationale,* he sealed the fate not only of the regime but of the dynasty.[24]

Revolution in Vienna

The situation in Vienna was strikingly similar to that in Paris, despite the vast disparity between France and the Hapsburg Monarchy in terms of political and social development. Opposition to the Metternich system had been growing apace during the 1840s and by 1848 had reached the point at which even the old feudal estates were calling for change and, more importantly, influential officials, army officers, and intellectuals were agitating for reforms along the lines of Western liberalism. The government suffered much from the fact that the Emperor was incompetent to rule, while the imperial family was divided on questions of policy. Certainly Prince Metternich had many enemies, a situation that obliged him to acquiesce in the establishment of the *Gewerbeverein* and the *Leseverein,* organizations that soon became strongholds of the liberal, reforming factions. It is rather hard to believe that, in the natural course of events, Metternich would not soon have been forced out of office and a more liberal, progressive policy adopted.[25]

Naturally the news from Paris, the reports of the ease with which Guizot and Louis Philippe had been driven out by popular demonstration, greatly reinforced the pressure on the Vienna court. A veritable whirlwind of petitions called for an end to repression and the introduction of a liberal system. Most prominent among these was the petition submitted by the 4000 Viennese students, many of whom came from the lower classes, and all of whom suffered under the restrictions of the Metternich system. This, like other petitions, was rejected, largely because of the unwillingness of the Archduke Louis, chief of the council of state, to consider making concessions under pressure.

The Viennese government in no sense faced a threat of revolution. The loyalty of the entire population to the dynasty—even to the half-witted Emperor—was such as to astound contemporaries.[26] The opposition was, as in France, directed against the ministry, hoping that its policy of immobility or stagnation could be gotten rid of by peaceful pressure. The only real danger of upheaval lay in the workingmen of the suburbs, who like workers elsewhere in Europe were suffering, and who, by the spring of 1848, were in such ferment that the government was obliged to set up public works and open soup kitchens to alleviate the unemployment and want. But not even the workers were revolutionary in the sense of having an organization or program. The workers were desperate but knew no course of action besides wrecking the hated machines and occasionally plundering the foodshops.[27]

Besieged by deputations and all but buried under petitions, the government, fearing disturbances, ordered the garrison troops in readiness. These forces numbered about 14,000, mostly quartered in barracks just outside the walls. On these the government would have to rely in case of serious disorder, for the police forces were altogether inadequate. The civil police was almost exclusively a secret police, assigned to the surveillance of dangerous and subversive persons and organizations. Under its supervision was a *Militär-Polizeiwache* consisting of 1100 to 1200 men. On paper, at least, there stood between these police forces and the regular troops something akin to the French *Garde nationale*, namely, a *Bürgerwehr* (Citizens' Guard) that, during the French occupation in 1809 had served a useful purpose but that had since 1815 sunk to the status of a ceremonial guard, noted chiefly for the excellence of its band-music. Officially, the *Bürgerwehr* comprised 14,000 men of the upper and middle bourgeoisie, electing its own officers and serving at its own expense. Only about a third of the force was equipped with firearms.[28]

The events of March 13 in Vienna were as confused as the February days in Paris. It was a bright spring morning and many people, including elegantly-dressed ladies, assembled before the palace of the Estates of Lower Austria, because it was known that this influential body was about to proceed to the palace with yet another petition. Presently a large body of students arrived, hoping to enlist the support of the Estates for their own petition. No one knew just what to do. While waiting, some of the students began to make speeches. There was much milling about in the narrow Herrengasse and in the courtyard of the palace. Eventually, toward noon, the president of the Estates appealed to the Archduke Albert, commanding the troops, for relief from popular pressure. The soldiers had a hard time making their way to the center of disturbances. Presently, tiles and other missiles were thrown at them from roofs and windows; guns went off, no one knew how or why; there were five dead. Like the much more horrible "massacre" of the Boulevard des Capucines, this episode was enough to set off a whole series of desultory clashes between the military and the people. At the same time crowds of workers from the suburbs began to invade the Inner City until the gates were closed against them. Some remained outside the walls, howling like hungry wolves. Most of them, however, returned to the suburbs to engage in an orgy of incendiarism and plunder.[29]

Franz Grillparzer, the great Austrian dramatist, was an eye-witness of the events of March 13 and pictured the initial demonstrations at the Ständehaus as a pleasant, good-natured fracas. The whole thing, he wrote in his recollections, could have been snuffed out by two battalions of soldiers, but no troops, in fact not even the police, were to be seen.[30] The military, when at last it appeared, did too much. After the first bloodshed and after the arrival of the workers from the suburbs, the situation became much more ominous. During the afternoon the demand for Metternich's dismissal became deafening. At the same time there were violent clashes between the troops and the populace, led by the students. Efforts to storm the arsenal led to considerable bloodshed, while at the Schottentor the workers actually managed to secure control of the entrance. In the elegant suburb of Wieden the mob sacked Metternich's villa and other aristocratic homes.

In the hope that order might still be restored, a group of prominent citizens in the late afternoon persuaded the Lord Mayor, Count Czapka, to call out the *Bürgerwehr*, of which he was the commanding officer, and if possible induce the military to withdraw from the city while the *Bürgerwehr* took over. The chronology is hopelessly confused and it is hardly worthwhile trying to fix it. Archduke Albert, the commander of the forces, who himself had been badly injured by a block of wood thrown at him from a window, did in fact evacuate the inner city. For the next several, critical days, the garrison troops stood idle and useless on the parade ground just outside the walls.[31]

The *Bürgerwehr*, meanwhile, was to play the same role as that of the Paris *Garde nationale*. A deputation of *Bürgerwehr* officers at once proceeded to the palace to demand the dismissal of Metternich (allowing the court until 9:00 P.M. to make up its mind) and the arming of the students. These were hard decisions for the court to make, for the emperor was feeble-minded and his relatives were badly divided. Several of the archdukes, led by Archduke John, had long since convinced themselves that Metternich must go and that real reforms must be undertaken. On the other hand, Archduke Louis abominated reforms and was urged by Metternich and Field Marshal Prince Windischgrätz to stand firm. The whole disturbance, argued the aged chancellor, was nothing more than a riot that could be easily mastered by the police and the troops. What led to the downfall of Louis Philippe was his eagerness to dismiss Guizot. Where a policy of concessions would lead no one knew. As for Windischgrätz, he had had years of experience dealing with serious workers' outbreaks in Prague and other Bohemian cities. He was sure that energetic action by the military could quickly suppress the disturbances. To dismiss Metternich, he held, would be nothing short of shameless cowardice.[32]

In the end, "the impotent scarecrows" (Kudlich) were unable to withstand the pressure of *Bürgerwehr*, students, and members of the Estates. In the evening Metternich was obliged to resign and permission was given for the immediate arming of the students, who alone were thought to have any influence with the rampaging workers. In the course of the night thousands of muskets were dealt out to students and citizens. These, in turn, formed patrols and managed to restore some semblance of order.

No good purpose would be served by pursuing the story further. At the end of the first day the court had surrendered to the liberal elements, if only in order to master the radicalism of the workers —that is, to put an end to an unwanted revolution for which the indecision of the court was largely to blame. A few words should, however, be said of the immediate aftermath. Like Louis Philippe in his belated appointment of Marshal Bugeaud, the Viennese court made a hopeless attempt to save the situation by naming Prince Windischgrätz civil and military governor of Vienna (noon, March 14). He was to proclaim martial law, while the government was to revoke all the concessions made under popular pressure on the preceding day. The field marshal apparently thought the situation too far gone, and his efforts to assert his authority did, in fact, prove altogether futile. The court was no longer in a position to refuse the demand for the organization of a national guard, which was to include a separate student corps (*Akademische Legion*). This new national guard was intended to comprise about 10,000 reliable citizens, but popular pressure led to the enrollment of some 30,000, in addition to the 7000 students in the special legion. Windischgrätz was, for the time being, quite helpless. On the following day (March 15) the court had to agree to a constitution, with which the first phase of this rather incredible revolution was brought to a close.[33]

Revolution in Berlin

The story of the Berlin revolution—our last case study—provides a classic example of how *not* to deal with revolutionary situations. Berlin, like other capitals, was in a process of rapid economic transformation and was, in addition, a veritable hotbed of radical philosophical thought. Yet, politically, the population was strikingly inexperienced and apathetic. The rapidly developing liberal movement in Prussia had its stronghold not in Berlin, but in the Rhineland and in provincial cities such as Königsberg and Breslau. The famous United Diet of 1847 had revealed the wide divergence between the aspirations of the rising middle class and the outmoded, traditionalist notions of the ruler. But even then the liberals, for all their discontent, were far from advocating revolution. Like their counterparts elsewhere in Europe, they relied on agitation and pressure to bring about a constitutional regime. A sober evaluation of the evidence suggests that they were probably justified in their expectations. By the beginning of 1848 even so recalcitrant a prince as Frederick William IV was beginning to yield to the constitutionally-directed importunities of his ministers.[34]

Berlin is supposed to have had, in 1848, some 40,000 to 50,000 industrial workers in the textile and metallurgical trades, and certainly far more in the traditional artisan occupations. As elsewhere, the workers suffered acutely from the rapid economic changes; five-eighths of the laboring population is supposed to have been in extreme want. In the years just preceding 1848 some workers' associations had sprung up and some revolutionary groups, such as the *Zeitungshalle*, had emerged. But these were exceptional. The workers were, for the most part, illiterate and apathetic so far as politics were concerned. Class consciousness and subversive activity were practically nonexistent.[35]

It was no doubt inevitable that news of the Paris insurrection should have led to much excitement and that, somewhat later, reports of Metternich's fall should have evoked widespread enthusiasm. From March 6 on, there were many meetings, speeches, resolutions, and petitions, all advancing the familiar liberal demands. The general tone of both meetings and petitions was one of hope and good will. And rightly so, for the Prussian government, like those of the South German states, was on the verge of giving way to popular pressure. There was, to be sure, strong conservative opposition, led by Prince William of Prussia, the king's brother. But there were even stronger forces convinced that fundamental changes were inescapable and that Prussia's future position in Germany depended on leadership of the liberal movement. As early as March 12 the king, albeit reluctantly and with mental reservations, made the basic decision to accept a constitution and a responsible ministry.[36]

Had the Prussian government provided Berlin with an adequate civil police, there is no reason to suppose that the popular meetings and processions would have gotten out of hand. But, incredible though it may seem, in this city of 400,000 there was no police to speak of, nor even anything akin to a civic or national guard. Officially there was a gendarmerie consisting of 40 sergeants and 110 men, but these gendarmes were employed almost exclusively in the law courts, markets, places of amusement, and so forth. For the preservation of public order the government relied on the garrison troops (about 12,000 in number).[37] In short, the government could deal with serious disturbances only by the methods employed in Russia, methods altogether unsuited to the conditions of a large western city. This had become clear during the so-called *Potato Revolution* of April, 1847—large-scale food riots during which some barricades had been erected and severe clashes between troops and people had taken place. At that time the city authorities had petitioned for a modest constabulary, to act in the first instance. But the government had been unwilling to delegate such authority. It therefore remained dependent on the armed forces, which, because of their ruthless and brutal action, were intensely hated by the populace, and which, in turn, despised the "rabble."[38]

As popular excitement grew, the authorities brought more and more troops into the city. Clashes were almost inevitable. They began to take place on March 13 and the ensuing days, with some loss of life and much burning resentment, accompanied by insults and provocations on both sides. Already on March 9 the city authorities renewed the request for formation of a civil constabulary, which was belatedly granted on March 16. Civic guard units (*Bürgerschutzkommissionen*) were hastily enrolled. There was to be a force of 1200 men, patrolling in groups of ten to twenty, armed only with truncheons. It was, however, understood that thenceforth the military should act only if called upon by officers of the civic guard. In a word, they were expected to play the same rôle as the special constables in London.[39]

Actually this improvised constabulary played but a sorry rôle in the Berlin uprising. The men had little more than good will. Neither the military nor the populace paid much attention to them. On the contrary, their efforts met with derision. The crowds grew increasingly restless and the troops more and more eager to beat them into submission. Hence the growing demand on the part of the people for the withdrawal of the military from the city and the formation of a real national guard, which would have been tantamount to the king's putting himself at the mercy of his subjects. This he was naturally unwilling to do, but on March 18, just as a monster demonstration at the royal palace was being organized, the king issued the famous "patent" by which he promised the early convocation of the United Diet, expressed his acceptance of constitutional government, and announced his leadership of the liberal, national movement in Germany. Since this document met most of the popular demands, it called forth general enthusiasm. Huge crowds gathered in the palace square, while the recently established civic guards stood in array before the portals of the palace. Then the sight of troops massed in the courtyard of the palace led to renewed cries for withdrawal of the soldiers. The commotion became so great that the king ordered General von Prittwitz, the commander of the troops, to clear the square. The general's cavalry squadron was so hard pressed by the crowds that infantry was sent out to relieve him. In the din and confusion two rifle shots rang out. No one was hurt, but the crowds suddenly panicked. Like the Paris populace after the massacre of the Boulevard des Capucines, the Berliners were convinced that they had been betrayed: that they had been lured to the palace by promises of reforms, only to be fallen upon by the hated military. Scattering before the advancing troops, they spread all sorts of alarming stories through the city. Everywhere barricades began to go up, and before evening fighting had broken out in many sections of the metropolis.[40]

The king and his military advisers were always convinced that the insurrection of March 18–19 was instigated and planned by foreign agents—French, Swiss, Poles, 10,000 of whom were reputed to have arrived in the city. But this comfortable theory was not supported by solid evidence. No one doubts that there were a great many foreigners, mostly workers, in Berlin, nor that many German workers had spent some years in Switzerland or Paris. Furthermore, there were certainly some confirmed revolutionaries who provided what inspiration and leadership they could. But the insurrection showed little, if any, evidence of planning or organization. All strata of the Berlin population were involved in one way or another. The students played a far less significant rôle here than in Vienna, but they do seem to have been instrumental in bringing workers from the suburbs to help man the barricades. But judging from the losses, the actual fighting was carried on largely by young artisans, the traditional craftsmen of the city.[41]

Prittwitz had at his disposal a total force of about 15,000, consisting of cavalry, artillery, and infantry, with which he proceeded to act with great energy. The insurgents, on the other hand, had but few muskets or munitions and had to make do with improvised weapons. Under these circumstances they could not hope adequately to defend the barricades, many of which were but lightly constructed. Instead, they hurled paving stones and tiles from the roofs or poured boiling water from the windows. The troops invaded the houses, pursued the rebels to the garrets, and there either cut them down or dragged them away captive. The advantage throughout lay with the military, and indeed by midnight of March 18 Prittwitz had established effective control over the center of the city. This is not to say that the completion of the operation would not have been an arduous business. Prittwitz seems to have hoped that he could persuade the king to go to Potsdam, after which he would have concentrated his troops outside the city for establishment of a blockade. Eventually, if necessary, he planned to snuff out the insurrection by bombardment of the disaffected quarters. The king, however, wanted to put an end to the fighting at almost any cost. Hence his pathetic appeal "To my dear Berliners," drafted in the night, offering to discuss the situation with representatives of the people and to withdraw the troops once the barricades had been taken down.[42]

The picture at court on the morning of March 19 was one of utter confusion: The king, in a state of near collapse, was evidently unable to appreciate all the implications of his decisions or in general to provide consistent leadership. Beset on all sides by officials and deputations of citizens and, furthermore, misled by unconfirmed reports that barricades were already being dismantled, he ordered the withdrawal of the troops to their barracks except for the guards at the palace and the arsenal. Through misunderstanding even these critical places were presently abandoned. It seems likely that the king intended to leave Berlin as part of Prittwitz's plan.[43] But all arrangements for his departure were hopelessly upset when, early in the afternoon, a great procession arrived at the palace bearing the bodies of some 200 victims of the street-fighting, their wounds exposed. Eventually the crowd made its way into the courtyard of the palace. On vociferous demand of the throng the king was obliged to appear and even to doff his cap in reverence to the people's dead. Nothing, certainly, could have demonstrated more clearly the complete capitulation of the monarchy. The people, on the verge of defeat in battle, had secured not only the removal of the troops to their barracks but also the establishment of a civic guard. (The King agreed to this immediately after his humiliating appearance on the balcony.)

The *Bürgerwehr*, as the new civic guard was called, was to be organized by districts, each to have roughly 100 men. Only those who had full citizen rights (*Bürgerbrief*) were eligible for enrollment and the old traditional marksmans-guild (*Schützengilde*) was to provide the kernel of the hastily constructed force of 6000 men. Several thousand muskets were immediately supplied from the arsenal. By 6:00 P.M. on March 19 the élite *Schützengilde* and the newly recruited *Bürgerwehr* were able to take over guard duty at the palace.[44] Frederick William had placed himself entirely under the protection of his subjects. He was as defenseless, wrote the American minister in Berlin on March 21, "as the poorest malefactor of the prisons." Early in the morning of March 21 the entire Berlin garrison was withdrawn from the city. For the moment the revolution was triumphant.

Conclusion

By the mid-nineteenth century the economic and social transformation of western and much of central Europe had reached the
point at which basic political changes had become imperative.

There was much pressure on the part of the propertied middle
classes for such changes, as is shown most vividly by the fact that
in both Paris and Vienna the national guard, designed to protect
the existing regime, lent their support to the cause of reform.

Yet there was remarkably little organization or planning for
revolution. The colorful heroism of a few revolutionary leaders and
the occasional spectacular outbreaks of radical elements are apt
to be misleading.

The proponents of liberalism and reform expected to attain their
ends by peaceful organization and action. They were fascinated
by the achievements of O'Connell and greatly heartened by the
triumph of Cobden and the free-trade movement.

After 1846 the forces of liberalism were so formidable and
insistent as to be almost irresistible.

It was the unpardonable fault of the Continental princes to
have failed to gauge the strength of the opposition and to have
refused to accept the inevitable. This was particularly true of Louis
Philippe, because the reforms called for in France were of a
modest nature and the failing loyalty of the national guard must
certainly have been known to him.

Ways to avoid serious upheaval were demonstrated not only by
the preventive measures taken later in London, but also by the
timely concessions made by King Leopold of Belgium, through
which his government secured the support of the opposition which
enabled it to present a united front to efforts at radical insurrection.[45]

The alternative to concession was systematic repression, as
practiced in quite different forms in Britain and Russia. But pre-
vention of insurrection called above all for vigorous action. The
situation in the European capitals, with their dislocated artisan
economy, widespread unemployment, fluid population, and appal-
ling living conditions, was necessarily explosive. It was imperative,

therefore, to prevent ordinary assemblages of people from degenerating into mob action and eventual revolution.

Everywhere on the Continent the civil police was inadequate for the task. As of old, governments still relied on their military forces to prevent major disorders. But the use of troops for police duty, always undesirable because too drastic, had by 1848 become extremely hazardous. For even though the aristocratic officer corps might spoil for a chance to put "the rabble" in its place, the common soldier in conscript armies was understandably reluctant to shoot at unarmed citizens. In the July Revolution Marshal Marmont saw most of his forces melt away. Even in England it was sometimes thought advisable to bring troops from Ireland, lest the English troops assigned to quell disturbances in the industrial areas prove unreliable.[46]

In these circumstances it behooved governments to move promptly and energetically. In all the capitals the initial demonstrations were amorphous, aimless, unaggressive. Yet nowhere did the authorities show the required determination. Troops were left to act as best they could; higher direction was almost completely lacking.[47]

As a result, fairly innocuous aggregations of people quickly turned into bellicose mobs. Open conflict between people and troops ensued, and presently military operations in the narrow, congested quarters of the city became all but impossible. Insurrection fed on itself. Radical elements were able to take advantage of a situation that they by themselves could never have created.

Thus, by ineptitude and indecision the governments provoked revolutions that were as unexpected as they were unwanted, even by the opposition. In discussing this period stress should be laid on the failure of monarchy rather than on the forces of revolution.

To explain this failure presents something of a challenge. We must attribute it chiefly, I think, to the feeling of insecurity common to almost all princes in the period after the French Revolution. Their fear of the actually ineffectual secret societies and their dread of a world conspiracy against the throne and the altar are well-known. Moreover, they were apprehensive of the newly aroused people, the more so in view of the frightful barricade fighting in Paris in July 1830 and, in the 1840s, the growing threat of a desperate proletariat.

The liberal middle classes, too, bear a heavy responsibility for the disastrous revolutions that ensued. In retrospect, it seems almost incredible that the Paris national guard should have carried its dislike of the regime and its desire for reforms to the point of standing aside, allowing the insurrection to develop and opening the door to political and social upheaval that, in turn, provided the opportunity for a repressive dictatorship. In Vienna the *Bürgerwehr* played an equally dubious role, setting the stage for the radicalism of the summer of 1848 and the enusing counter-revolution.

Finally, one may fairly ask whether the revolutions of 1848 were necessary or even desirable. The work of reform was carried through more rapidly and more smoothly in countries such as Britain, the low countries, Scandinavia and even Russia, in which there were no revolutions. In the last analysis the Continental revolutions, while they achieved some measure of reform, led to grave political and social conflicts, to say nothing of national antagonisms and wars that might otherwise have been avoided. In view of the period of reaction that almost everywhere followed the revolutions it would seem that these upheavals actually delayed many urgently needed changes. Without the revolutions many later tensions might have been forestalled or at least attenuated, and Europe might have escaped a veritable harvest of both internal and external strains and animosities.

Notes

1. E. J. Hobsbawm, *Social Bandits and Primitive Rebels*. New York: The Free Press of Glencoe, 1959, chap. 7; George Rudé, "The Study of Popular Disturbances in the 'Pre-Industrial' Age," *Historical Studies: Australia and New Zealand*, vol. 10 (1963), pp. 457–469.

2. Some notion of the multifarious London industry may be derived from George L. Gomme, *London in the Reign of Victoria*. London: 1898, chap. 4 and appendix 2, in which the *London Directory* of 1837 is analyzed. For the industries of Paris see especially Charles Dupin, *Les forces productives et commerciales de la France*. Paris: 1827, vol. 2, pp. 196 ff.

3. Adna F. Weber, *The Growth of Cities in the 19th Century*. New York: 1899, pp. 244, 283; Arthur Redford, *Labour Migration in England, 1800– 1850.* London, 1926, chaps. 4, 8, 9; H. A. Shannon, "Migration and the Growth of London, 1841–1891," *Economic History Review*, vol. 5 (1935), pp. 79–86; J. H. Clapham, "Irish Immigration into Great Britain in the 19th Century," *Bulletin of the International Committee of the Historical Sciences*, vol. 5 (1933), pp. 596–604; Barbara W. Kerr, "Irish Seasonal Migration to Great Britain, 1800–1838," *Irish Historical Studies*, vol. 3 (1942), pp. 365– 380; John A. Jackson, *The Irish in Britain*. Cleveland: 1963.

4. Louis Desnoyers *et al.*: *Les étrangers à Paris.* Paris: 1846, pp. 163 ff., 181 ff.; Georges Manco, *Les étrangers en France.* Paris: 1932, pp. 36 ff.; Louis Chevalier, *La formation de la population parisienne au xixe siècle*. Paris: 1949, pp. 45, 48, 183; Louis Chevalier, *Classes laborieuses et classes dangereuses à Paris pendant la première moitié du xixe siècle*. Paris: 1958, pp. 267 ff. It is worth noting that contemporaries like Karl Gutzkow (*Pariser Briefe*, Leipzig: 1842, p. 276) and Arnold Ruge (*Zwei Jahre in Paris*, Leipzig: 1846, vol. 1, pp. 59, 431) estimated the German population of Paris at 80,000 to 85,000 and reported that German could be heard in almost every street.

5. Adolf Schmidl, *Wien und seine nächsten Umgebungen.* Vienna: 1847, p. 142; Fredrich Walter; *Wien: die Geschichte einer deutschen Gross-Stadt an der Grenze.* Vienna: 1944, vol. 3, pp. 105 ff.; Ernst Fischer, *Oesterreich, 1848*. Vienna: 1946, pp. 38 ff.

6. *Bericht über die Verwaltung der Stadt Berlin in den Jahren 1841 bis inclus. 1850.* Berlin: 1853, pp. 3–4; Karl Haenchen, "Zur revolutionären Unterwühlung Berlins vor den Märztagen," *Forschungen zur brandenburg-preussischen geschichte*, vol. 55, 1943, pp. 83–114; Dora Meyer, *Das öffentliche Leben in Berlin vor der Märzrevolution.* Berlin: 1912, pp. 11 ff.; Richard Dietrich, "Berlins Weg zur Industrie und Handelsstadt." In *Berlin: neun Kapitel seiner Geschichte*. Berlin: 1960, pp. 159–198.

7. David H. Pinkney, *Napoleon III and the Rebuilding of Paris.* Princeton: 1958, p. 7.

8. Théophile Lavallée, *Histoire de Paris.* Paris: 1852, p. 205.

9. According to Etienne Laspeyres, *Der Einfluss der Wohnung auf die Sittlichkeit.* Berlin: 1869, there were in Paris in 1848, 2360 chambres garnis. Of the lodgers only four percent of the men and eight percent of the women were married.
   On the Paris lodging houses see also Chevalier, *La formation de la population parisienne*, p. 102, and his *Classes laborieuses*, pp. 271 ff. For Vienna see Walter, vol. 3, p. 114; Fischer, pp. 38 ff., and for Berlin see the well-known contemporary account of Ernst Dronke, *Berlin.* Frankfurt: 1846.

10. For Paris see Chevalier, *Classes laborieuses*, pp. 267 ff., 538 ff.; Adeline Daumard, *La bourgeoisie parisienne de 1815 à 1848.* Paris: 1963, p. 181 ff.; for London see Thomas Beames, *The Rookeries of London.* London: 1851; George Godwin: *London Shadows.* London: 1854; Gomme: *London in the*

Reign of Victoria, p. 57. According to Dronke, the situation in Berlin was very similar.

11.   Nikolai I. Tourguenieff: La Russie et les Russes. Paris: 1847, chap. 7; John S. Curtiss, "The Army of Nicholas I, Its Role and Character," American Historical Review, vol. 63 (1958), pp. 880–889; A. S. Nifontov, Russland im Jahre 1848. Berlin: 1954.

12.   First Report of the Commissioners to Inquire as to the Best Means of Establishing an Official Constabulary Force in the Counties of England and Wales. London: 1839, p. 160; on the problem generally, see the excellent military analysis of Hermann Kriebel, Über die Bezwingung innerer Unruhen nach den Erfahrungen der Geschichte in der ersten Hälfte des XIX Jahrhunderts (written in 1906, published at Innsbruck in 1929).

13.   For the conditions prior to 1829 see Wade, A Treatise on the Police and Crimes of the Metropolis. London, 1829; for the rest see W. L. Melville Lee, A History of Police in England. London: 1901, chaps. 10, 12, 13; Charles Reith, A Short History of the British Police. London: 1948, chaps. 7 and 9; Douglas G. Browne, The Rise of Scotland Yard. London: 1956, chaps. 8, 9; F. C. Mather: Public Order in the Age of the Chartists. Manchester: 1959, chaps. 3, 4.

14.   Harriet Martineau, History of England, 1816–1854. Boston: 1866, vol. 4, pp. 571 ff. Among the many other accounts see especially Preston W. Slosson, The Decline of the Chartist Movement. New York: 1916, pp. 94 ff.; Julius West, A History of the Chartist Movement. Boston: 1920, chap. 8; Édouard Dolléans, Le Chartisme. Paris: 1944 (rev. ed.), 300 ff.; Albert R. Schoyen, The Chartist Challenge. New York: 1958, pp. 160 ff.

15.   Albert Crémieux, La Révolution de Février. Paris: 1912. For a more recent and much briefer account see Jean Bruhat, Les journées de février, 1848. Paris: 1948.

16.   Percy B. St. John, The French Revolution in 1848. New York: 1848, pp. 60 ff.; Sébastien Charléty, La Monarchie de Juillet. Paris: 1921, pp. 383 ff. For the intricacies of the question of the Paris banquet see John J. Baughman, "The French Banquet Campaign of 1847–1848," Journal of Modern History, vol. 31 (1959), pp. 1–15; Peter Amann, "Prelude to Insurrection: the Banquet of the People," French Historical Studies, vol. 1 (1960), pp. 436–444.

17.   Charles Simond, Les Centennales parisiennes. Paris: 1903, pp. 31 ff.; Frances Trollope, Paris and the Parisians in 1835. London: 1836, vol. 1, p. 135: "I never saw any corps of more superb appearance"; F. S. Bamberg: Geschichte der Februar Revolution. Braunschweig: 1848, p. 123: "Der reitende Theil . . . war das schönste Truppen-Corps der französischen Armée." According to St. John, 72 ff., the crowd on February 22 began to throw stones at the mounted guards whereupon "this body, detested by the Parisians as police, kept up continual charges upon the crowd until it gradually dispersed." No mercy was shown, reported this observer: "They kept galloping suddenly towards the multitude" and even used their swords. The

behavior of the mounted forces in all the capitals seems to have been uniformly ruthless, which no doubt had a lot to do with roiling the populace."

18. Edmond Téxier: *Tableau de Paris*. Paris: 1852, vol. 2, p. 319; Bamberg, p. 119; Paul Pichon, *Histoire et organisation des services de police en France*. Issoudun: 1949, pp. 88 ff. On the *Garde nationale* the recent study by Louis Girard, *La Garde nationale, 1814–1871*. Paris: 1964, supersedes all previous works. Mrs. Trollope, vol. 1, p. 139 succinctly described the National Guard in 1835 as "the industrious and orderly part of the community, organised to keep in check the idle and disorderly."

19. *Les barricades: scènes les plus saisissantes de la Révolution de 1848*. Paris: 1848; Crémieux, *La Révolution de Février*, pp. 92 ff.; Gaston Bouniols, *Histoire de la Révolution de 1848*. Paris: 1918, pp. 35 ff. See also the strictures on the military in Max Jähns, *Das französiche Heer*. Leipzig: 1873, pp. 339 ff.

20. The attitude of the various Garde legions was analyzed in detail by Crémieux, chap. 4; see also Girard, *La Garde nationale*, pp. 284 ff.; Daumard, *La bourgeoisie parisienne*, pp. 595 ff.

21. Comte de Montalivet, *Fragments et souvenirs*. Paris: 1899–1900, vol. 2, p. 119; Crémieux, p. 164; P. Chalmin, "La crise morale de l'Armée française." In *L'Armée et la Seconde République*. Paris: 1955, pp. 27–76.

22. Barricades had not played an important part in the great French Revolution, yet were positively decisive in July 1830 and prominent in other disturbances of the 1830s. In London they did not appear at all. The explanation seems to lie in the progressive paving of the city streets. In London macadamized pavement, which was quieter, was largely used, granite blocks having been introduced only in 1828. In Paris, on the other hand, the durable and relatively cheap granite blocks (at first in large sizes, six inches square by nine inches deep) were the usual thing. These blocks were, of course, the ideal material for the construction of barricades, for they were near at hand, could be easily lifted with pieces of iron railing, and provided the necessary solidity. Mrs. Trollope was undoubtedly right in remarking that if Paris streets were macadamized, real difficulties would be thrown in the way of future barricade heroes. See further S. Dupain, *Notice historique sur le pavé de Paris*. Paris: 1881, pp. 205 ff.; E. G. Love, *Pavements and Roads, their Construction and Maintenance*. New York: 1890, p. 232.

23. Bugeaud claimed that his cease-fire was demanded by the new Thiers-Barrot cabinet, which was intent on conciliation and pacification. The best detailed narrative is that of Crémieux, pp. 210 ff., but see also Comte Henry d'Ideville, *Le Maréchal Bugeaud*. Paris: 1882, vol. 3, pp. 316 ff.; Maurice Andrieux, *Le Père Bugeaud*. Paris: 1951, pp. 268 ff.

24. Crémieux, pp. 467 ff.; Charléty, p. 299, who holds that at any time during the insurrection the king could have mastered it, had he not labored under delusions which robbed him of necessary will-power.

25. Heinrich Friedjung, *Oesterreich von 1848 bis 1860*. Stuttgart: 1908, vol. 1, pp. 17–18; Heinrich von Srbik, *Metternich, der Staatsmann und der*

Mensch. Munich: 1925, vol. 2, pp. 259 ff.; Veit Valentin, *Geschichte der deutschen Revolution von 1848–1849.* Berlin: 1930, vol. 1, pp. 400 ff.; Rudolf Kiszling, *Die Revolution im Kaisertum Oesterreich, 1848–1849.* Vienna: 1948–1952, vol. 1, p. 35.

26.   Josef A. Ditscheiner, *Der Wiener Freiheitskampf.* Vienna: 1848, p. 4; Carl Graf Vitzthum von Eckstädt, *Berlin und Wien in den Jahren 1845–1852.* Stuttgart: 1886, p. 83 (letter of March 17, 1848): "Die Anhänglichkeit an das Kaiserhaus ist hier noch fabelhaft. . . ." See also Kiszling, 1, p. 41.

27.   Adolf Schmidl, *Wien und seine nächsten Umgebungen.* Vienna: 1847, p. 164; Karl Weiss, *Geschichte der Stadt Wien.* Vienna: 1872, vol. 2, pp. 176 ff.; Ernst von Zenker, *Die Wiener Revolution in ihren sozialen Voraussetzungen und Beziehungen.* Vienna: 1897, pp. 96 ff.; Ludwig Brügel, *Geschichte der oesterreichischen Sozialdemokratie.* Vienna: 1922–1925, vol. 1, pp. 15, 23, 54; Heinrich von Srbik, "Die Wiener Revolution des Jahres 1848 in sozialgeschichtlicher Beleuchtung," *Schmollers Jahrbuch,* vol. 43 (1919), pp. 19–58; Julius Marx, "Die Wirtschaftslage im deutschen Oesterreich vor dem Ausbruch der Revolution, 1848," *Vierteljahrschrift für Sozial-und Wirtschaftsgeschichte,* vol. 31 (1938), pp. 242–282. Vizthum, p. 75, reported great unrest in the suburbs as early as March 5, 1848.

28.   For an excellent contemporary account see Schmidl, pp. 162–163. See also Weiss, vol. 2, pp. 239 ff.; Viktor Bibl, *Die Wiener Polizei.* Vienna: 1927, pp. 313 ff.; Hugo Kerchnawe, *Die Überwindung der ersten Weltrevolution.* Innsbruck: 1932, pp. ii ff. Vitzthum, p. 78, speaks of 1000 more men having been recruited on March 12. Even if this is true, these latecomers could hardly have counted for much in the confusion of the ensuing days.

29.   Ernst Violand, *Die soziale Geschichte der Revolution in Oesterreich.* Leipzig: 1850, pp. 69 ff.; Zenker, pp. 112 ff. The fact that so many of the workers were non-Germans—Czechs, Italians, Poles, Swiss—gave rise to the theory, firmly held by Metternich, that the whole outbreak was instigated by foreign agents. See Srbik, *Metternich,* vol. 2, p. 280; Valentin, vol. 1, pp. 400 ff.; R. John Rath, *The Viennese Revolution of 1848.* Austin: 1957, p. 54. Good contemporary narratives of the events of March 13 are F. C. Schall, *Oestreichs glorreichste Tage.* Vienna: 1848; Josef A. Ditscheiner, *Der Wiener Freiheitskampf.* Vienna: 1848. The work of Heinrich Reschauer, *Geschichte der Wiener Revolution.* Vienna: 1872 is an almost painfully detailed chronicle which, unfortunately, is undocumented.

30.   Franz Grillparzer: "Erinnerungen aus dem Jahre 1848" in August Sauer (Ed.), *Grillparzers sämtliche Werke,* vol. 20, pp. 185–211. Later historians, such as Valentin and Jacques Droz, *Les révolutions allemandes de 1848.* Paris: 1957, p. 185 tend to agree with Grillparzer's judgment.

31.   Vitzthum, pp. 78 ff., Weiss, vol. 2, p. 310; Friedjung, vol. 1, p. 20, Kissling, vol. 1, p. 42.

32.   Srbik, *Metternich,* vol. 2, pp. 280 ff.; Paul Müller, *Feldmarschall Fürst Windischgrätz.* Vienna: 1934, pp. 66, 88–89.

33. Vitzhum, pp. 78 ff.; Paul Molisch, "Die wiener akademische Legion," pp. 64 ff.; Muller, *Windischgrätz*, pp. 90 ff. For details of the National Guard see Kerchnawe, *Die Überwindung der ersten Weltrevolution*, pp. 12, 17.

34. Veit Valentin, *Geschichte der deutschen Revolution von 1848–1849*. Berlin: 1930, vol. 1, pp. 416–417; Stadelmann, pp. 6 ff.; Droz, pp. 71–83.

35. On economic and social conditions see Pierre Benaerts, *Les origines de la grande industrie allemande*. Paris: 1934, chaps. 4, 16; Dora Meyer, *Das öffentliche Leben in Berlin im Jahr vor der Märzrevolution*. Berlin: 1912, chap. 2; Karl Obermann, *Die deutschen Arbeiter im der ersten bürgerlichen Revolution*. Berlin: 1950, p. 20. On the political immaturity and indifference of the population see Rudolf Stadelmann, *Soziale and politische Geschichte der Revolution von 1848*. Munich: 1948, p. 53; Jacques Droz, *Les révolutions allemandes de 1848*. Paris: 1957, p. 194.

36. On the early meetings see Valentin, vol. 1, pp. 416–417; Stadelmann, pp. 45, 53; Ernst Kaeber, *Berlin 1848*. Berlin: 1948, chap. 2; Alfred Herrmann, *Berliner Demokraten*. Berlin: 1948, pp. 114 ff. For an excellent discussion of the prospects for reform see Wilhelm Busch, *Die Berliner Märztage von 1848*. Munich: 1899, pp. 4, 10.

37. On the police see C. Nobiling, *Die Berliner Bürgerwehr in den Tagen vom 19ten März bis 7ten April, 1848*. Berlin: 1852, pp. 5–6; Hubert von Meyerinck, "Die Tätigkeit der Truppen während der berliner Märztage des Jahres 1848." *Beiheft 4–5 zum Militär-Wochenblatt*: 1891, pp. 99–168; Kaeber, pp. 40–41.

38. On the Potato Revolution and the resulting antagonism between the military and the populace see especially Anon., *Die berliner Märztage, vom militärischen standpunkte geschildert*. Berlin: 1850, pp. 11 ff.; Nobiling, p. 6; Meyerinck, p. 104; Meyer, *Das öffentliche Leben*, pp. 86–90; Gordon A. Craig, *The Politics of the Prussian Army, 1640–1945*. Oxford: 1955, pp. 90 ff.

39. Meyerinck, pp. 101, 104, 108; Busch, p. 6; Felix Rachfahl, *Deutschland, König Friedrich Wilhelm IV, und die berliner Märzrevolution*. Halle: 1901, p. 128; Karl Haenchen: "Aus dem Nachlass des Generals von Prittwitz," *Forschungen zur brandenburg-preussischen Geschichte*. 1933, vol. 45, pp. 99–125.

40. These events are, of course, narrated in all histories of the German revolution. In the present context the accounts of special interest are those of Meyerinck, pp. 112 ff.; Rachfahl, pp. 133, 143; Valentin, vol. 1, pp. 430 ff.; Kaeber, pp. 55 ff.; Droz, pp. 198 ff.

41. The military viewpoint is well presented in *Die Berliner Märztage*, p. 24; Busch, pp. 8, 17, and Meyerinck, p. 106; see also Rachfahl, pp. 122, 126, Valentin, vol. 1, p. 419; Herrmann, p. 121; Stadelmann, pp. 46, 57, 60; and especially the careful analysis of radical activities in Karl Haenchen, "Zur revolutionären Unterwühlung Berlins, etc." *Forschungen zur brandenburg-preussischen Geschichte*, vol. 55 (1943), pp. 83–114.

42. On the morning of March 19 the outcome of the fighting was at best a draw. Most writers consider that the military had the upper hand (see Meyerinck, p. 161; Busch, p. 21; Rachfahl, p. 164; Herrmann, p. 124; Stadelmann, p. 57). On Prittwitz's strategy and plans see Rachfahl, pp. 163, 172; Valentin, p. 437; Herrmann, p. 125; Craig, pp. 93, 99.

43. On preparations for the king's departure see especially Busch, p. 32, Stadelmann, p. 59.

44. Nobiling, *Die Berliner Bürgerwehr*, pp. 1 ff.; O. Rimpler: *Die Berliner Bürgerwehr im Jahre 1848*. Brandenburg: 1883, pp. 3 ff.

45. J. Dhondt: "La Belgique en 1848" *Actes du Congrès historique du Centenaire de la Révolution de 1848*. Paris: 1948, pp. 115–132; Jean Bartier, "1848 en Belgique." In François Fejtö (Ed.), *Le Printemps des peuples*. Paris: 1948, vol. 1, pp. 355–372; Georges Eckhout, "La réforme électoral de 1848." In Jean de Harveng (Ed.), *Histoire de la Belgique contemporaine*. Brussels: 1928–1930, vol. 1, pp. 371 ff. Brison D. Gooch, *Belgium and the February Revolution*. The Hague: 1963.

46. P. C. Mather, "The Railways, the Electric Telegraph and Public Order during the Chartist Period." *History*, n.s., vol. 38 (1953), pp. 40–53. On the July Revolution see the anonymous pamphlet *Les barricades immortelles de Paris*. Paris: 1830; *Mémoires du Maréchal Marmont, Duc de Raguse*. Paris: 1857, vol. 8, pp. 239 ff.; and on the general problem the excellent analysis of Hermann Kriebel, *Über die Bezwingung innerer Unruhen nach den Erfahrungen der Geschichte in der ersten Hälfte des XIX Jahrunderts*. Innsbruck: 1929.

47. In this connection one may appropriately quote the judgment of Michael Bakunin (surely an expert in things revolutionary) on the European insurrections of February–March, 1848: "Le révolution avait pris tout le monde à l'improviste; personne n'y était préparé. Il n'y avait pas même l'ombre d'une organisation, aucun but déterminé, rien qui ressembla à un plan." (The revolution had taken the whole world by surprise; no one was prepared. There was not even the shadow of an organization, no fixed objective, nothing that resembled a plan.) But, he adds, the rulers and governments were so frightened that the first gust of revolutionary wind brought down a harvest of concessions. (From the first draft of Bakunin's "Manifesto to the Slavs," quoted in Josef Pfitzner, *Bakuninstudien*. Prague: 1932, p. 100.)

✎ LOUIS GIRARD

Louis Girard, born in 1911, was called in 1956 to the Sorbonne as successor to Charles Pouthas. His work has been mainly in the fields of economic, intellectual, and political history of the nineteenth century, subjects he has pursued in the best orthodox French academic tradition. His carefully descriptive writing does not fit clearly into any special school of historical interpretation. His reputation was soundly established by the publication of his monumental *La Politique des travaux publiques du Second Empire* (1951), which has stimulated other studies of nineteenth-century French economic history. Professor Girard showed the real connection between the policies of the July Monarchy and the Second Empire, only briefly interrupted by the Second Republic, which provided for the national *équipement* of France by the development of public works and railroads. While the interdependence of economic questions and political evolution is brought out, there is much in the work of Professor Girard for the economist as well as the historian. In addition to this contribution, he has also written a work on *La Garde Nationale, 1814–1871* (1964). Professor Girard is especially well qualified to analyze French liberalism from 1840 to 1875, a period of economic as well as political significance.

Political Liberalism in France, 1840–1875

In January 1880 Camille Pelletan of the Radical Republican group wrote in Clemenceau's journal, *La Justice*: "The Republic has its fathers of the Church; they are the ministers of Louis Philippe."[1]* Dufaure took the same position and gave it substance without mentioning Thiers, Casimir Périer, Rémusat, or Montalivet. The idea was picked up much later by the publicist of *Action française*, Jacques Bainville, in his *Troisième République* (1935): "It is not sufficient to say that the National Assembly established the Republic when it intended to restore the monarchy. Precisely because it was monarchist, it alone was capable of drafting a constitution which would permit the Republic to last."[2] The same point is made by commentators who are separated by a half-century and who are even further apart in political thinking: the first two mean to praise, while the last is critical. But in all cases the interpretation is slanted. The fact is that these liberal monarchists, these "Orleanists," were in reality "politiques" who, believing in the principles of 1789, spent their lives in the slow discovery of the Republic, that is, of a Republic that would be as durable and as stable as a monarchy.

The Liberal Position

It must be stated at once that liberal monarchists derived from the "liberals of '89" who were royalists without being counter-revolutionaries.[3] For them the king, an hereditary moderator, would assure *legality* rather than *legitimacy*. Essential to this concept was a two-chamber parliament. Basically, they were firm on civil liberties, but might be opposed to democracy. This was as far as the conservative liberals such as Benjamin Constant, Madame de Staël, or Guizot would go. They could be monarchists and remain indifferent to the personality of the king. The Duc

---

* Translated by Joseph N. Moody, The Catholic University.

Victor de Broglie could write: "They say that the King of England, Charles I, wrote to Queen Henrietta-Maria that he had never been unfaithful, even in thought. I might say as much to the elder branch of the Bourbons but with this well-understood condition: here fidelity would be reciprocal."[4]

Another interpretation of this liberal position could be more readily conciliated with democracy. It appeared in the *Commentaire sur l'Esprit des Lois*, written by Tracy for Jefferson and published in 1819. The author declares in favor of "national" governments in which the nation participates in governing even if the office of head of the state remains hereditary, a situation he thought inevitable at that stage of European development. This was the view of Lafayette, of Voyer d'Argenson, and of Dupont de l'Eure. All of these held that constitutional liberty must be wedded to the maximum degree of democracy compatible with the level of moral and social maturity. The state belongs to all; it is the *res publica*.[5] In order to respect this potential national sovereignty, the king must reign without governing. This was the formula of Thiers, the young editor of *National* in 1830. It was "the most republican formula which had ever been put forward under a monarchy."

From 1830, Lafayette, Tracy, and Béranger thought that *in principle* a republic was the best form of government, but that in France the republic had inherited a bad name; consequently, the masses did not believe in it. Thus, the Duke of Orleans was installed because he freely admitted that the best of all constitutions was that of the United States. Besides, his only choice was exile or the throne, and he could always reflect that if he had not been there, the country would have become a republic eighteen years earlier.[6] In all this thinking there was a great indifference to the dynasty. It was monarchy without royalism.

It is a fact that the July Monarchy remained without roots. To make up for this defect, it tried to unite itself with a party of social conservatives who feared the Jacobin and the revolutionary tradition that lived on in the republicans. But as the middle class gained in importance toward 1840, republicans such as Carnot and Garnier-Pagès broke with revolutionaries like Ledru-Rollin and proclaimed themselves as constitutional, not dynastic, republicans. They renounced revolution to embrace reform.[7]

These republicans joined the groups who supported the July Monarchy but wished reform: Barrot, Tocqueville, Dufaure, Duvergier de Hauranne, Rémusat, and even Thiers. Lamartine was the most typical of this tendency. The republicans were not antimonarchical, but wanted a king who would not govern. There was some hope that the regency of the Duchess of Orleans could satisfy this demand. It was the attitude of these groups that resulted in the collusion of the reformist movement and the banquet campaign that was supported by the middle class. But by 1848, the regime was played out.[8]

The Republic

In 1848 hardly anyone defended the dynasty or regretted its passing. The liberals readily accommodated themselves to the Republic in the sense that it meant the absence of the king. The problem was, what should replace the monarchy? Rémusat put it clearly:

The Republic, among other impossibilities, or at least among other problems, presents one issue which has not been resolved up till the present. It is the structure of the executive power. Now, since it is precisely by this that republics differ from monarchy, it follows that what defines a republic is a baffling void. It lacks precisely that which the common man considers the essence of government and which gives government its name. This difficulty alone justifies its general reputation as an impossible form of government.[9]

To the liberal, the Republic presented a further difficulty in that it implied popular sovereignty and universal suffrage. If numbers ruled, was there not a danger of a legal dispossession of the upper classes? Tocqueville noted that "we have conserved the spirit of monarchy while we have lost the taste for it."[10] The apparent solution was the office of the president. But the president, elected by the people, might become a dictator since he had to contend only with a single-chamber parliament. To counteract this danger a center coalition in favor of Cavaignac was attempted. Dufaure, Tocqueville, and Rémusat collaborated with Carnot and Grévy; they announced a third party that would make the Republic legal and safe. Thiers and Rémusat did not believe in a "fusion monarchique" that would have been a condition for a restoration, and they were opposed to a seizure of personal power by Louis Bonaparte. The real dividing line between the two center groups was the social question and its correlative, universal suffrage. Even the moderate republicans wanted universal suffrage, in which they had complete confidence. Thiers and his friends continued to be disdainful of the crowd, which to them was "the vile multitude." It was this that separated them from the democrats and from President Bonaparte.

In 1851, Rémusat would regret this persistent failure to come to agreement with the moderate republicans. He would learn to appreciate the ridiculous position of favoring the Republic while remaining hostile to democracy. He, who had reproached Guizot for exploiting fear for the profit of a conservative policy, would feel humiliated by the partial complicity of the conservative liberals in the events of December 2, 1851.[11] It is revealing that among the conservative leaders only Thiers and Rémusat, along with the generals from Algeria, were expelled from France after the coup. The conservatives who did not rally to the Empire and who were not the objects of sanctions would sit on the Right Center of the Assembly of 1871; on the Left Center would be the champions of the "Conservative Republic."

The prince-president relied on universal suffrage to govern as a responsible leader, thus curtailing the role of parliament. But if his responsibility could accord with temporary power or even power for life, it no longer was suitable for a dynasty that must, if it was to last, be politically responsible to no one. The hypothesis of a natural and permanent harmony between dynastic and responsible government must be dismissed as utopian. On the other hand, by leaving the *Corps législative* prerogatives that were potential but real, the regime of Napoleon III did prepare for a conciliation between representative government and universal suffrage, which is the basic condition of a parliamentary republic.[12]

The constitutional monarchy had always exercised a restraint on universal suffrage by manipulating official candidacies.[13] But if universal suffrage were to be a governing principle, this would have to cease.

The liberals opposed to the Empire—those who were not republicans—were divided into two movements. The monarchists from Falloux to Guizot had been "fusionists," believing that a king was necessary to assure the functioning of a parliamentary government as well as to act as a brake upon universal suffrage. The other group, composed of the liberals of the *Revue des Deux Mondes* and *Débats*, did not believe fusion was possible. Hence, they doubted the likelihood of a monarchical restoration. From 1857 they had declared themselves against abstention at the polls and in favor of entering into the electoral and parliamentary life of the regime. Thus, they were in opposition to the "fusionists" of the National Assembly and the *Gazette de France*, who advised abstention. On the contrary, they drew closer to the republicans who followed the lead of the *Siècle* and the *Presse*. These republicans wanted to be elected and to take their seats in parliament even if it required taking the oath to the regime. The *Débats*, in agreement with Thiers, drew up a joint list of candidates with the democratic journals, thus forming what the *Gazette de France* called the "democratic-Orleanist coalition" or "the fusionist party of the revolution."[14] Let us say that these "fusions" are opposed to each other; no liberal of *Débats* would be elected.[15] But it is significant that some of the liberal ex-Orleanists ranged themselves with the moderate republicans in favor of a new type of constructive opposition.

These were the well-known tactics of the Liberal Union. The Count d'Haussonville conceived them and they were explained in the memoirs of his brother-in-law, Albert de Broglie:

It was impossible to think of re-entering public life or even of presenting one's name for any election, once the majority of the conservatives had passed to the support of the Empire, without the help of a fraction of the republican party. The ground for such an alliance, which fifteen years earlier would have appeared unnatural, was the demand for and the defense of liberties which had been suppressed by the imperial power. In place of an alliance of conservatives, which had seen its better days at the National Assembly, it would be necessary to substitute a new alliance of liberals of differing origins.[16]

While the liberal monarchists were always reluctant to go further than occasional electoral agreements with men from whom they were separated by both religious and political convictions, those like Thiers and Rémusat who were strangers to any religious and monarchical belief, acclimated themselves readily to the new republicans who were parliamentary liberals and enemies of radicalism or socialism—men such as Joseph Magnin, Ernest Picard, Jules Simon, or Léon Say. Conversely, these latter admired the distinguished parliamentarians and gained from their prestige.[17]

In this way an "open Left" was in the process of formation by 1867, which was rallying the moderate republicans who were opposed to the radicals. Thiers was already their virtual leader. What they lacked was mass support. But having known how to help the government of September 4, 1870 without becoming involved in its final unpopularity, having opposed Gambetta and supported the general councils in their desire for elections and peace, in which he agreed with Jules Grévy, Thiers, who had spoken of the "vile multitude," appeared from then on as the champion of universal suffrage. The elections of 1871 were an electoral triumph for Thiers and for the first time gave him an authority in the country equal to what he had enjoyed in parliament. The head of the executive power was elected by the National Assembly, but this assembly in turn was chosen by universal suffrage.

Without having any objection in principle to constitutional monarchy—except perhaps from what they knew of the character of the candidates for the throne—Thiers and his friends were convinced that the traditional solution of having a monarch as a guarantor of the social order in alliance with the upper classes was impossible. The past had bequeathed too many pretenders who were out of step with each other and with the majority of the population. On the morrow of the Commune the republicans were scarcely less divided. It was evident that universal suffrage could not be abandoned after so many years of use. It had become a vital ingredient in French society. It had replaced the principle of hereditary monarchy. Furthermore, experience had proved that monarchy in France would from now on last only for life and no longer would assure a legitimate succession.[18] What was needed was to guarantee a legal transfer of temporary power, to introduce universal suffrage into a regime of freedom, and to make certain that the life of a republic would be something quite different from a revolutionary adventure—in a word, to establish a conservative republic. The alternative was a dictatorship of social defense that would compensate for the sovereignty of the majority by its control. But this would mean the continuance of the Empire.[19]

It was true, as Dupont-White noted, that it was "a strange thing to talk to people of a Republic in the interest of order."[20] A Republic and universal suffrage would open the way to socialist hopes, "the legal Commune." For this reason, the divided ruling classes entrusted their defense to a prince. But events had shown the vanity of this trust. The Liberal Union, from the party of opposition under the Empire, was to become a party of government and was to realize social defense through the education of the democracy.[21]

The conservative Republic, instead of being a play on words comparable to the terms of an antithesis, could become a reality. It was necessary to prevent its becoming "a Republic without republicans," repelling the latter in order to combine with their enemies. Thus, there developed what the *Gazette de France* in 1857 had called the "democratic-Orleanist coalition." It was not exactly a union of centers, but a combination of Left Center with the moderate elements of the Left, so that radicalism was pushed to the periphery during the period of foundation and formation. Only the Republic could neutralize the social danger by training the democracy. In time and with experience, the radicals themselves, if they came to power, would observe legal methods in achieving such reforms as compulsory education, the separation of Church and state, and the income tax.[22]

The problem was, how create the conditions of a regime of legal liberty subject to the fluctuations of all free countries, yet obeyed and supported by all. This had to be done at a time when the popular classes, forming the majority of the republican party, had not completed their political education and when the former ruling classes had gone over to reaction.[23]

The Senate Plan

In the Left Center of the Assembly of 1871, a constitutional plan was rapidly conceived, as Dupont-White and Ernest Duvergier de Hauranne testified. Its basic ingredient was to balance a chamber elected by universal suffrage with a senate. Thus, the power of the majority would be held in check.[24] This could not have been done in 1848, when the upper house and monarchy were synonymous.[25] But after the experience of the Second Republic, there seemed to be greater danger with a president and a single chamber.

The plan was to elect a titular executive, but not by universal suffrage, for this would magnify his power, especially if there were no opposition. His election by parliament or by the lower house would be preferred. This president, conceived in the image of Thiers, would be the responsible chief of government. He could be defeated but, as in the case of constitutional sovereigns, he would have the right of dissolution with the concurrence of the Senate.[26]

The Senate was the keystone of this system. It was the moderator to arbitrate conflicts between the President and the Chamber. "It is in a republic that a second chamber is indispensable,"[27] a concept that would have astonished the republicans of 1848.

The problem was not the existence of a Senate, but its composition.[28] Since the abolition of hereditary peers in 1831, the upper house lacked political authority because it did not have independence vis-à-vis the crown. Recruitment by co-optation, which had been the plan after 1831, assured the independence but not the authority of the upper house. Nor had this arrangement been acceptable to Louis Philippe. Recruitment from the general councils was also proposed. It was not adopted under the July Monarchy because the manner of election or even the existence of these assemblies was not yet determined. This is proved by an article of Saint Marc Girardin on the peerage, which appeared in the *Revue des Deux Mondes* in 1845, when the idea of this form of recruitment revived. But in 1872 the general councils were living organisms. Their success had been demonstrated. It was on them that all the planners of decentralization leaned. The law of 1871 had added to their importance. They could provide an electorate different from that of universal suffrage but derived from it. This consideration was the genesis of the idea of electing the senators by the members of the local councils and reducing the role of the municipal councils, which were too often "unreliable." Thus was created a new "pays légal," a new political class. The Right Center, however, continued to hold to the idea of a senate of dignitaries seated by right of inheritance or appointed in the image of the imperial Senate.

Duvergier de Hauranne thought that the term of deputies should extend for three years, while that of the senators should be nine, with one-third renewed each three years. The president could be elected for six (seven was ultimately decided upon). The president would govern in the sense that Cavaignac or Thiers had done and would nominate his ministers, with whom he would share responsibility. Thus, he could be induced to retire if he had the two chambers against him or if, after dissolution, the democratic electorate sided with the Chamber of Deputies.[29]

A difficulty arose that had existed under the liberal empire: How should responsibility between the president and his ministers be divided?[30] The crisis of May 24, 1873 had drawn MacMahon close to the role of an irresponsible monarch. That of May 16, 1877 had accentuated this tendency. But in depriving the president in actual practice of the right of dissolution, the equilibrium between these institutions had been upset. On the contrary, the Senate was a success. The evolution of local institutions allowed the Third Republic to establish on a solid basis an upper chamber, an institution the monarchies had lacked. Yet, the problem that appeared after 1848 continued: The president was not the equivalent of a constitutional sovereign and he was no longer the head of state acting as executive, as the republicans of 1848 and 1871 had desired. The constitutional formula favored the transactions of the center groups dominating the Senate and discouraged the formation of two strong parties such as there were in Anglo-Saxon countries.[31]

On the whole, the thinking of these "Orleanists" of the Left, conservative republicans who were at the helm of the new republic, was "political," in the full meaning of the term.[32] Far from aiding them, the monarchists of the Right Center probably weakened the presidency by compromising its exercise. The "Left Center," formed of moderate republicans and the "constitutionals" of 1860, arranged the transition tactfully from a restricted to universal suffrage, something that had not happened in 1848. They succeeded because, lacking all faith in monarchy, they slowly and with difficulty accommodated their ideas and their feelings to entirely new situations. Abandoning the idea of monarchy, they had in the course of a decisive decade assumed for themselves the political direction of the democracy so effectively that, after their passing and the appearance of "new social strata" and new generations, their imprint remained in republican institutions and customs.

Summary

French historians have noted that the Third Republic derived its constitution from a monarchist Assembly elected in 1871. This view must be refined. To what degree were the "Orleanist" liberals, who rallied with Thiers to the Left Center to defend the "conservative republic," really monarchists? From 1830 royalty meant for them only a guarantee of a legal and national government. They were waiting for the development of attitudes and social structures that would make possible a republic, a form of government they considered preferable to arbitrary monarchy. By 1840 they had progressed to the concept of a king who would reign without governing, and they drew close to the constitutional republicans in favoring reform that would avoid revolution. In 1848 this accord forming between moderate republicans and liberals was broken. The latter accepted the Second Republic, but were frightened by universal suffrage. This predisposed them to the *coup d'état* of 1851.

From 1856 these ex-Orleanists divorced themselves from the monarchical and Catholic fusionists to draw near again to the moderate republicans in a program of liberal and parliamentary revival. This "democratic-Orleanist fusion" was an advantage to Thiers and his friends. In 1871 universal suffrage represented a victory for them as much as it did for the monarchists. Abandoning all hope of monarchy, they devoted themselves to the establishment of a "conservative republic" whose principal institution would be the senate, a balance between the elected chamber and the president chosen by parliament. The election of senators was secured by the members of the local councils, especially the general councils, a "political class" that had asserted itself since 1830. Thus, despite the misfortunes of the presidency, the transition to a parliamentary democracy was ensured.

Notes

1. January 27, 1880.

2. p. 39.

3. Rémusat, *Mémoires*, vol. 1, p. 12: "They belonged to a family of royalists rather than counterrevolutionaries." Jules Simon, *Thiers, Guizot, Rémusat*, 1885, p. 21: "He [Guizot] belonged to those whom the ultras in 1816 described as 'liberals of 1789' in order to distinguish them from the revolutionaries without admitting them to the ranks of true royalist."

4. Simon, p. 261.

5. Rémusat, vol. 4, p. 249. After February 24, 1848, Rémusat, referring to Tracy, explained why "the republic was and must be the second government of his choice."

6. Cuvillier-Fleury, *Journal*: His conversations with the King and his account of 1830. See Rémusat, vol. 2, p. 346, on the opinions of Lafayette.

7. H. Carnot, *Les Radicaux et la Charte*, 1847: "For many years they had fully understood that without going beyond the framework of the Charter but by reforming it by a strictly legal interpretation, France could be benefited by most important improvements. From that time forward the radical movement expanded without creating dismay, and the enemies of progress were deprived of a weapon which they had so frequently and impudently employed and had to renounce their habit of making a bugbear of radical doctrines."

8. Henri Guillemin, *Lamartine et la question sociale*, 1946; Duvergier de Hauranne, *De la réforme parlementaire et de la réforme électorale*, 1847.

9. Rémusat, vol. 4, p. 251.

10. *Souvenirs*, Monnier (Ed.), p. 169.

11. Rémusat, vol. 4, p. 483: "We saw then what the weakness of an opposition party in a republic is which does not have a militant people behind it."

12. E. Ollivier, *l'Empire libéral*, vol. 3, pp. 27 ff.

13. E. Tenot, *Le suffrage universel et les paysans*, 1865.

14. On this point, which the author considers essential, see the article of Saint Marc Girardin in *Débats* of June 11, 1857 and the *Gazette de France* of June 1, 3, 9, and 12, 1857. On the undercurrents provoked by the attitude of *Débats*, see *Correspondance du duc d'Aumale et de Cuvillier-Fleury*, vol. 2, p. 404, Cuvillier's letter of November 10, 1857.

15.   *Débats* placed Vavin, Lasteyrie, Cavaignac, Raynaud, and Bethmont in the foreground. It rejected Carnot, Goudchaux, Darimon, and Ollivier. Thiers was not involved, waiting to see what happened.

16.   Albert de Broglie, *Mémoires*, vol. 1, p. 317.

17.   For example, the opinions of Magnin when he entered the *Corps législative*, in Delabrousse, *Joseph Magnin*.

18.   This acknowledgment, made as early as the Second Republic to induce the monarchists to grant a presidential term of ten years to Louis Bonaparte, became more frequent after 1860. See Charles Duveyrier, *l'Avenir et les Bonapartes*. The fall of the Second Empire could only give it probative force. Dupont-White remarked in 1872 that real power in Great Britain henceforth derived from an election.

19.   For the second part of the article see Dupont-White, *La République conservatrice*, 1872; the shorter writings of the same author (1871–1875) are collected under the title *Politique actuelle*; de Marcère, *La République et les conservateurs*, 1871; Christophle, *La Solution légale*, 1872; Molinari, *Les Conditions d'existence de la République* in *Revue des Deux Mondes*, January 15, 1873; Drapeyron-Seligman, *Les Deux folies de Paris*, 1872; Michel Bréal, *Quelques mots sur l'instruction public*, 1872; and Ernest Duvergier de Hauranne, *La République conservatrice*, 1873.

20.   *La République conservatrice*, p. 9.

21.   Bréal, p. 221: "The National Assembly of 1871 was the living representation of the *Union libérale*. It was the coming into prominence of the grand party of practical and measured opposition which, since the aftermath of the elections of 1863, demanded openly the necessary liberties." Inversely, Bréal thought that "the Empire has not been anything but a long demonstration of the necessity for the French parties to come to a mutual understanding because of the impossibility of any of them alone to impose its will on the others. It was this weakness of the parties which gave birth to the Empire; it was that which made it live," p. 220.

22.   Duvergier de Hauranne, p. 87: "After many years of the Republic you will see the radicals themselves scrupulously observe the law. The parties will draw closer to each other and in place of the social war which they preach to us, we will have a regime of full liberty, subject to the fluctuations of all free countries, yet obeyed and supported by all." In pages 40–50, the author recognizes that the greater part of the reforms demanded by the radicals would be realized, but the radicals must be held on the periphery during the period of the foundation of the Republic.

23.   Duvergier, p. 160.

24.   Dupont-White, *La République conservatrice*, p. 45: "to make a republic where the executive power will be defended by a *stathouder* and by a senate, while the people will be represented and protected by a chamber chosen by

universal suffrage." Molinari, p. 52, wanted an upper house elected by the "pays légal." Since the constitutional changes of 1869 in the Second Empire, an interesting discussion had opened on the recruitment and the rôle of the senate. Marcère, p. 107, thought that the only means of avoiding Caesarism lay with the conservative classes who would "enlighten the democracy."

25.   Tocqueville, *Souvenirs*, Monnier (Ed.), pp. 166 ff.

26.   Dupont-White, *Politique actuelle*, p. 21: "Universal suffrage, introduced into elections, made the executive stronger because of its origins." Duvergier, pp. 195–202, wanted a president chosen by national representation who would govern personally, have the right of dissolution with agreement of the senate, but who could be retired before the termination of his mandate. Two chambers were necessary so that the president could not serve at the discretion of a chamber elected by universal suffrage.

27.   Duvergier, pp. 217–218.

28.   Duvergier, p. 228 ff., for the recruitment of the senate.

29.   Duvergier, p. 270 ff., for the allocation of powers.

30.   This difficulty was also found in the constitution of 1848 and was re-solved by the power of the president. A similar problem, which has remained potential, has been noted by commentators in the current French constitution of 1958.

31.   In effect, the constitution of 1875 developed from a combination of center groups against the two extreme parties. It continued to retain this characteristic, especially in the case of the Senate.

32.   Jules Simon, *Le Gouvernement de M. Thiers*, 1878, vol. 2, p. 236: "Men such as Rémusat, Casimir Périer, and Thiers himself, who had come to the republic pragmatically, first by finding it possible, then by discovering that it alone could operate, have contributed to its formation every bit as much as old-line republicans; for it was by their initiative, by their example, and under their auspices, that so many men important by their history, fortune and character have come into our ranks and who today, along with our old leaders, are the strength and light of our party."

↙ JACQUES DROZ

Jacques Droz, born in 1909, was for some years Dean of the Faculty of Letters at the University of Clermont-Ferrand before joining the faculty of the Sorbonne. He is a former president of the Société d'Histoire Moderne. In addition to being noted for the breadth and excellence of his work, he is distinguished as the outstanding French scholar of German history. His studies in this area have dealt with some of the greatest movements in European history affecting the Germanies. In many ways he has special insight with regard to German thought, particularly the relationship of ideas to political action. The scope of his approach is reflected in his extensive studies in diplomatic and intellectual history. Among his principal works are *Le Libéralisme rhénan, 1815–1848* (1940), *Histoire d'Autriche* (1946), *L'Allemagne et la Révolution française* (1949), *Histoire des doctrines politiques en France* (1948, 1956), *Restaurations et Révolutions, 1815–1871* (1953), *Histoire diplomatique de 1648 à 1919* (1952, 1959), *Les Révolutions allemagnes de 1848* (1957), and *L'Europe centrale: évolution historique de l'idée de "Mitteleuropa"* (1960). Because of his comprehensive knowledge, Professor Droz is admirably qualified to describe the religious aspects of the revolutions of 1848.

Religious Aspects of the Revolutions of 1848 in Europe

The European revolutions of 1848 have generally been interpreted in the light of national aspirations or of political and social considerations.* To contemporaries, however, these revolutions seemed to raise problems of greater importance than boundaries or forms of government: problems having to do with the basic creeds that had sustained mankind until then; problems that could mean life or death for the established churches. It was commonplace for these men to believe that science would soon bring about a reorganization of mankind. Writing on this matter in *L'Avenir de la Science* (1848) Renan says:

We shall, in all ways, proclaim the right of reason to transform society thanks to the theoretical knowledge of what is. It is no exaggeration to say that science bears in itself the future of mankind, that science alone can teach men how to reach their ends. Until now the world has not been led by reason but by whims and passions. A day will come when reason guided by experiment will recover its legitimate empire, which alone is of divine origin, and will lead the world no longer at random but with a clear view of the end to be attained.

If Positivism in another way asserted the necessity of a belief capable of rallying all spirits and putting an end to the pernicious division of creeds, this belief was sought outside of the established faiths.

Reading the best-known of the contemporary Catholic reviews, such as the *Historisch-Politische Blätter* of Munich, we feel that Western culture, threatened by a thirst for liberty and pleasure, and by contemporary materialism, is condemned to decay. This is, we read, the sad inheritance of the Reformation, which broke the bonds of Christian unity in the world, and of the Enlightenment, which led to the Revolution. To complete the work, monarchical bureaucracy followed by democratic egalitarianism have destroyed

---

* Edited by Frances S. Childs, Professor Emeritus, Brooklyn College.

the organic structure of society, reducing it to a pile of atoms. When the revolutions of 1848 broke out, the *Historisch-Politische Blätter* foresaw the end of the Christian world and the advent of a new ethic that would, under the banner of socialism and democracy, cancel out traditional values. Reading the Spaniard, Donoso Cortes, an acute observer of the revolutionary movement and the author of a well-known pamphlet, *Essai sur le Catholicisme, le libéralisme et le socialisme* (1851), we see clearly that a conflict of theologies was at stake and that Cortes was attempting to foresee the contenders' chances.

In view of the threats and anxieties to which we have but briefly alluded, historians may well ask the following questions. First, what were the religious implications of the Revolutions of 1848, and, second, what means did Catholics use to meet this danger?

Actually these revolutions had begun with an apparent reconciliation between the Church and the nations in revolt. In a different spirit than that of 1830, the revolutionaries had expressed their intention to respect established religion and its ministers, from whom, in return, they expected some help against absolutism. In Italy, for example, hopes were raised by Pius IX's attitude, while unification plans were inspired by Gioberti's neo-Guelph outlook.[1] In France, clerics themselves often blessed the so-called "trees of Liberty." In Germany, many churchmen were elected to the Frankfort Assembly as well as to other local assemblies. It was, then, permissible to believe that a new era had begun, an era that would use fundamental Christian dogmas to implement the fraternal state of the future.

For this confusion Lammenais [Abbé Félicité Robert de] was largely responsible. To him, liberty and equality were the expression of the Christian ideal in modern times. As he said, "to deny the sanctity and legitimacy of these modern tendencies is to deny the moral and social principles of Christianity, and on the whole, to deny the very work of Christianity."[2] This tendency to identify Christianity with the principles of democracy and of socialism was one of the most striking features of the kind of messianism pervading much of European thought in 1848. Supported in France by such different men as Etienne Cabet and Pierre Leroux [socialists], the same pattern of thinking can be found in the German and Swiss supporters of W. Weitling, as well as in Mazzini who invoked "God and People" in the same breath, *Dio e popolo*.

This aspect of 1848 thinking can be linked with a new interpretation by certain historians of the French Revolution. Previously, the Revolution had been used to prove the irreducible antagonism between democratic faith and fidelity to established religions. In the eyes of these historians the Revolution, at least in its Montagnard phase, was the practical implementation in modern times of the principles of Christianity. The Catholic P. Buchez, who wrote the Forewords to the volumes of the *Histoire Parlementaire de la Révolution française*[3] considered it essential to distinguish between the revolutions of 1789 and 1793: the former of rationalist and Protestant impulsion, born of the Enlightenment and therefore barren; the latter organic and Catholic in origin, therefore creative of brotherhood and love. Following the Reformation, said Buchez, the countries of Christendom, henceforth divided, experienced a long period of decay that gave birth to the materialist philosophy of the eighteenth century, a philosophy unable to give ethics "any other sanction than egotism." Constituents and Girondists were taxed by Buchez with accomplishing their work *a posteriori*; by this he meant opportunistically, in a setting of special circumstances, lacking both a general view of the nation's past and of its future promise, and consequently blind to the needs of society as a whole.

Instead of proclaiming a common aim and common social obligations, the Constituent Assembly drew up a statement of individual rights, thus cancelling out any formula capable of uniting mankind in one ideology, on the contrary, asserting what was most likely to divide and disunite them.

The Jacobins, on the other hand, were conscious of society as a whole. Robespierre and his friends formulated a "socializing principle," a "truth that could illuminate all other truths." They understood that the Revolution required "devotion and self-sacrifice." Two plans, the former elaborated by the National Convention for public instruction, the latter by Pelletier de Saint-Fargeau for the penal code, were for Buchez proof that the leaders of the 1793 revolution clearly understood the indissoluble unity of Christian revelation and moral law. "The French Revolution is the latest and most forward looking development of modern civilization, and modern civilization derives totally from the Gospel. This is an indisputable fact." And he specified, "Popular sovereignty is Catholic, in demanding that each be subject to all; it is Catholic in having a clear apprehension of the past, of the present and of the future, it is Catholic in recognizing a common nature in all mankind (subject to the law of equality); and finally it is Catholic in proceeding directly from the teaching of the Church." If, in the long run, Buchez believed, the Revolution was a failure, this meant that its leaders were not Christian enough. Had Robespierre been a Christian instead of a Deist he would have escaped the contradictions in which his moral universe was imprisoned.

The study of French Revolutionary historiography produced during the period of the July Monarchy proves that a great many historians, following Buchez's example, use this providential interpretation of history to assert that the Mountain [composed of the most extreme revolutionary faction] was God's instrument for the regeneration of mankind. In his *Histoire des Montagnards*, a well-known book of the period,[4] Esquiros also placed Providence in the midst of the historical stream, saying, "Such was indeed the splendid impetus of the French Revolution, that it did not balk at blood, terrible difficulties, or death itself; it rode over the reeking bodies of its enemies and moved as Fate itself to the end indicated by the finger of God." In the course of nature, preestablished by God, the summoning of the Estates General was to lead to the Terror that, according to Esquiros, was no less than the "Gospel itself embodied in facts."

Louis Blanc also saw a periodization in universal history, based on the three principles of authority, individualism, and brotherhood, its advent already foretold by the "thinkers of the Mountain." Indeed, he went so far as to assign the second revolution, that of 1793, to the force of the occult and secret societies which were, all through the century, able to withstand the eroding philosophy of Voltaire and the Encyclopedists.

In any case, the effort to prevent the Revolution from ending in the triumph of the middle class was due to these secret societies, which nurtured the first seeds of the enthusiasm, of the wild heroism, of the yearning for sacrifice, of the eagerness to face death, which the subsequent struggle led to a climax.

Without succumbing to such strange conclusions, Quinet, in his famous pamphlet *Le Christianisme et la Révolution* (1845), held that during the Terror the French Revolution retained a Catholic character, and was in many ways "nearer to Christianity than the Church now is."

It would be a mistake to think that the identification made by many historians, Catholic and non-Catholic, of Christianity and the principles of 1793 was admitted by everyone in 1848. The recent thesis of Paul Viallaneix on *L'Idée du peuple dans l'œuvre de Michelet*[5] shows that Michelet was always aware of the incompatibility between Christianity and the reign of justice. "Can a dead Christianity transform itself?" he wondered in his diary on November 22, 1846. "Christianity is dead in its Christian meaning; it was the religion of grace, and the problem of grace is dead, killed by the advent of justice. . . . If Christianity wants to be the same thing as justice, it is no longer Christianity." In his Introduction to the *Histoire de la Révolution française* Michelet holds the teaching of the Church responsible for mankind's long submission to injustice: "What broke my heart was the prolonged resignation, the sweetness, the patience, the effort of mankind to love the world of hatred and malediction beneath which it was crushed." He never ceased, therefore, to believe that there was an absolute divorce between the struggles of the populace and Christian dogma. Nor did he cease to condemn those among his contemporaries for whom the revolution was the fulfillment of Christianity; he had only pity for the thought of the first Christian democrats. Viallaneix clearly understands what elements in Michelet's attitude toward Christianity were somewhat pre-Nietzschean. Christianity, the religion of grace, is to Michelet the religion of slaves, and practically sustains the despotic authority of the master. A Christian must submit to a rule of violence. Viallaneix writes of Esquiros:

> I think that Christianity, the realm of the elect, based on grace, must, when viewed in the light of Esquiros' doctrine, necessarily result in the rule of the privileged. I think that the Christian world can have no logical political expression save in the salvation of the state by one man, or the monarchy. Such was the opinion of Bossuet, such the opinion of de Maistre.

The opposition between justice and religion also underlay Proudhon's thinking. The works of Père de Lubac,[6] which contain a subtle analysis of Proudhon's ideas on religious matters, indicate that the author of *La justice dans la Révolution et dans l'église* did not, in spite of his harsh words, deny the real spirit of Christianity, but that his extreme anticlericalism made him deeply distrustful of the sentimental religiosity of the "neo-Christians," who wished to be both democrats and socialists. Proudhon was, moreover, convinced that an impassable moat lay between religion, at least as Catholics have established it, and the revolution sprung from the principles of 1789. He deplored the fact that

a thick fog of religiosity today clouds the brains of all the reformers, [and went on to state] Socialism, henceforward in the hands of dreamers and declaimers, no longer a reign of justice as the Revolution expected it to be, is now sentimental, evangelical, theocratic, communist, . . . exactly what reactionaries could desire for their benefit and our shame.

Setting the reign of charity against the reign of justice in his atheistic thinking, he maintained that "religion, never able to practice its own rules and incapable of lowering itself to the level of human reality, saw no contradiction in proclaiming universal brotherhood while continuing to consider poverty a law of nature."

While Proudhon thus stigmatized the providential mysticism of his contemporaries, a rationalist tendency, born in Germany, attempted to wreck the traditional creeds and the bases of the established churches. In the name of this philosophical rationalism resulting from the breakdown of Hegelian thinking, not only the revealed religions but the political concepts founded on these creeds, such as the Christian state, were assailed. The famous theory of alienation developed by Feuerbach in his *Wesen des Christentums* (1841) was to become, in the forties in the hands of such philosophers as Stirner or the upholders of "true socialism," a weapon against the established order in the political and social areas. Karl Marx was to draw his famous doctrine of historical materialism from this theory.

The philosophical or literary pattern of this movement has been explained so often, there is no need to do so here.[7] What is important is to indicate that in Germany and in almost all the countries of central Europe ideological disunity was religious before it was political or social; that radicalism first assumed a theological character; and finally, that the confessional sects came close to setting up real fighting units in the 1848 revolutions. This is a less well-known side of the revolutionary outbreaks in 1848, and I should like now, on the basis of my own research, to sum up its most striking features.[8]

The Lichtfreunde communities were created by a number of clergymen, mostly of Saxon or Silesian extraction, with the intention of opposing Lutheran dogmatism, certain aspects of pietist reaction patronized by the minister Eichhorn, and the ideal of a Christian state envisioned by Frederick William IV. In the meetings they held from 1842 on, as for instance in Köthen, these clergymen stressed the duty of Protestantism to hold to the spirit of the early Reformation and to that of the Enlightenment. They insisted on the need for lay representation and for democratic organization within the Church. The Reverend Uhlich of Magdeburg, a most popular preacher, and the Reverend Wiscilenus of Halle, through his work *Ob Schrift, Ob Geist* (1844), became the leaders of this movement. The heart of the movement was at Halle, where K. Schwartz was Professor of Theology, M. Duncker, Professor of History, and the young R. Haym, of Philosophy, and where the review *Kirchliche Reform* was published.

The Lichtfreunde communities became the rallying point for all—rationalists, young Hegelians, followers of Schleiermacher— who fought against intellectual compulsion. The Hessian theologian, K. Hundeshagen, although he censored the destructive tendencies of atheistic radicalism in his pamphlet, *On German Protestantism* (1847), at the same time indicated that many a member of the intelligentsia was driven into irreligion by the development of absolutist states that considered the church merely as a tool in their hands. While at first religious groups, these Lichtfreunde were, as a matter of fact, likely to become political cells; hence the interdict issued against them by the Prussian government on August 10, 1845; hence, too, the strong movement of protest against this interdict in the large cities of the realm; Magdeburg, Halle, Berlin, Koenigsberg, and Breslau. This protest resulted in petitions drafted by members of all social classes, by thinkers, officials, manufacturers, landlords, and even craftsmen and workers. Clergymen who, because of their opinions, had to leave their churches, soon established "free communities" under other names; these were to play a very great part in the rising of German democracy. Besides teaching the German intelligentsia how to associate in order to fight for their liberties, these communities provided a more democratic basis for political activity than did the Landtags or the state assemblies. All distinctions in social standing as well as in class spirit disappeared in their meetings, which laid the foundation of the democratic front. These, in turn, initiated the claims of March 1848 and brought them to success. These groups were also more or less concerned with social problems. The newspaper *Der Leuchtturm* was published in the Saxon city of Zeitz from 1846 on under the auspices of the novelist Ernst Keil and in close contact with enlightened Protestant and Catholic circles. The editor, Dr. H. Semmig, a follower of "true socialism" doctrines, became one of the leaders of the Saxon democracy at the time of the actual outbreak.

In many places, the Lichtfreunde established relations with the "German Catholics." Following the exhibition of the Holy Tunic of Trier in 1844—declared false by the historian H. von Sybel— many Catholics, believing that the Roman Church promoted superstition and popular fanaticism, followed Johannes Ronge, a Saxon priest, and the Posnanian vicar, J. Czerski, and founded the so-called "German-Catholic" church whose first council was scheduled for March 1845 in Leipzig. The agreement between the two founders of this new sect did not last long and the strength of the movement suffered from their disunion. Nevertheless new members were gained in Silesia, Saxony, and all central and south Germany in the following years, and Ronge himself experienced a series of triumphal trips throughout Germany in 1845.

Before long this movement developed a political character, as had the Lichtfreunde. As early as 1845, G. G. Gervinus dedicated his booklet *Die Mission der Deutschikatholiken* to the movement, insisting on the obligation of bringing different creeds together into a national church that would be the starting point for political unity in the country. The same hope drew the radical from Baden, G. Struve, who was to play a very significant part in the 1848 outbreak, into the German Catholic movement. In Protestant circles, he was expected to give Christian faith a wider base in cooperation with the Lichtfreunde and to oppose both confessional zeal and clerical fanaticism.

Socialistic tendencies can be seen here too, and, as Iserlohn indicated in Westphalia, the movement gained large numbers of supporters in industrial cities. In the chief "Christian Catholic" (*Christkatholisch*) community of Breslau, the botanist Nees v. Esenbeck was a leader of the first rank who was to play an important part in the social-democratic working-class movement during the revolution. A professor at the university, his collectivist socialism derived from philosophic, pantheistic, and anthropocentrical tenets, due to the influence of both F. W. Schelling and L. Feuerbach. In Saxony political radicalism found its strongest supporters in these new communities. In Dresden, one such was F. Wigard, later to be a democratic deputy to the Frankfort Assembly and the publisher of its stenographic report. In Leipzig, Robert Blum, energetic, self-taught, born a humble Polish Catholic, was one of the most popular Saxon craftsmen, who had been successively a cashier, a public letter-writer, a secretary in a theater, a bookseller, and a publisher. Generally (and according to a French observer) J. Ronge was considered the pontiff of social regeneration and pantheistic reformation, while German Catholicism was clearly the most concrete and dynamic form of opposition where the parliamentary system was least developed.

It is well known that the members of these free communities played a forceful and directive part in the democratic movement. Not only did Ronge appear as a member of the Vorparlament, and of the first democratic Congress in Frankfort, traveling incessantly up-and-down Germany and Austria in order to publicize his republican and socialistic ideals, but Blum and Wigard also served as representatives of Saxon communities in the Frankfort Assembly, while Reverend Uhlich was the representative of the Lichtfreunde to the Berlin assembly. Indeed, in almost every town a member of these free communities became the leading spirit, and later, when reaction set in, the democratic ideal was preserved in the heart of these associations. Whether we should admit, as many have, that these Lichtfreunde and German Catholic movements had more political and revolutionary than religious aims, is questionable. What must be acknowledged is that in fighting for spiritual independence and for the victory of rationalism, the supporters of the free communities felt that they were fighting for political liberty as well, because, in their eyes, these causes were one.

It would be an error, however, to think that all the members of such communities shared common political and social creeds. They included supporters of constitutional monarchy as well as followers of a radical democratic ideal. The democrat Nees v. Esenbeck himself, a professor at the University of Breslau, who had formed the first Silesian workers' association and who was a member of the Berlin Assembly, protested that he was not in favor of class struggle. His main collaborators in the "Christian Catholic" communities of Breslau were liberals, who claimed only that a moral revolution, the work of the free communities, must be the prelude to social revolution. Whatever the difference in their concepts, these free communities were one of the few links between the middle class and the working class, which the free communities desired to gain for their cause. In this way the free communities contributed to the union of the revolutionary forces.[9]

The rationalist sects expanded widely in the Austrian dominions too, in close relation with the remnants of Josephism [Joseph II] and with the hostility of many clerics to the Roman hegemony. Again this sectarian movement assumed a political and social character, as Eduard Winter has clearly pointed out in his study, *Der Josefinismus*.[10] In Vienna, Anton Füster, a professor of Pedagogy at the University and a member of the German Catholic community, acted as the leader during the revolutionary days of October 1848—this in his capacity as chaplain of the Student Legion. His memoirs provide distressing evidence of the utter misery in which most of the students of the time lived, and also reveal the development of revolutionary ideas among them. In Prague, the Reverend Arnold frequently recalled the figures of Hus and Žiška in his meetings of German Catholics. In Bohemia, also, thanks to the influence of the theologian, Bolzano, there were many pro-reform priests who, without joining the German Catholic movement, yet opposed clerical celibacy and the practices of the Roman liturgy, and hoped intensely to see religion reduced to a few articles of faith open to reason.[11] The most influential of these was Bahlovski, a professor in the Slavonic seminary in Prague, who had obtained an audience in Karel Haliček's famous *Narodny Noviny*. Here it should be noted that in Bohemia such an attitude was closely identified with explicit Slavic nationalism. Moreover, it is not in the least surprising that many true Catholics were openly antagonistic to these groups, in which they believed they tasted the dregs of inveterate Josephism.

This formation of sects with both political and religious aims was a phenomenon peculiar to central Europe. Nothing of the sort occurred in Italy or in France. As regards France, however, recent studies have proved that during the revolution and especially after the June Days, anticlericalism became more and more violent, so much so as to compel pastors and vicars to leave their parishes. It is difficult indeed to measure the extent of these reactions of the working classes, who had, according to H. Vicaire,[12] organized outside of the Church and had never been subject to Christian discipline. Other recent studies on the peasantry, one by P. Vignier for the mountainous Alpine country,[13] another by Mrs. Marcilhacy for the region of Orleans,[14] have revealed the importance of anti-clericalism. Both of these works show that whatever remained of religious practice from the Old Regime was destroyed during the period from 1848 to 1851. At the same time, they indicate that the peasantry rose with violence against a clergy incapable of understanding the deep reasons for such outbreaks of fury. Moreover, to progressive thinkers at the time of the Second Republic, there was no doubt but that the established churches, no longer fit for the needs of the nation, had rather become the major impediment to the fulfillment of mankind's most legitimate yearnings. That is why, when Proudhon wrote in 1851 in his *L'Idée générale de la révolution,* "Catholicism must be resigned, the task of Revolution in the nineteenth century is to repeal it," he was simply expressing a conviction rooted deeply in a large sector of public opinion.

In the face of the assaults made upon them during the revolution of 1848 and of the increasing hostility to which they were victims, how did Catholics respond? The two most striking forms of response, religious liberalism and social Catholicism, have been carefully studied by historians. In regard to the former, the remarkable account given at the International Congress of Historical Sciences, held in Rome in 1955, by J.-B. Duroselle should be kept in mind as proving how conscious the Church was of the need to adjust to new conditions and how it took advantage of the magic word "liberty" that it expected would bring release to Catholicism from Gallicanism, Josephism, or Protestant restraints. True, Catholics did aim at taking advantage of a position they accepted halfheartedly, but one that gave them the chance to claim liberties and rights. They were able to solidify later, when reaction once more set in, by giving aid to governments against revolutionary radicalism. Thus they profited successively from the benevolence of both the democrats and the conservatives! These tactics were especially well handled in Germany, where the 1848 outbreak was the starting point for political organization in the Catholic world and the beginning of the emancipation of the Catholic church, notably in Prussia. The main lines of this evolution are well-known, but recent works, for example those of Carl Repgen, show especially clearly the important part played in the electoral field by Archbishop Geissel of Cologne.[15]

The second aspect of the Catholic reaction was due to the conviction of many Catholics that they had to rely on the religious elements in the countryside and in the towns against revolutionary forces, that is, to rely upon the popular groups in society whose faith was more genuine than that of the richer and more sophisticated circles. The year 1848 was also the point of departure for a social Catholicism that was never a very large movement and one that remained divided between a democratic and socialist wing and a more conservative one. This movement in France has been carefully studied by Professor Duroselle.[16] He has shown that it was represented by the newspaper *l'Ere Nouvelle* published by J. B. H. Lacordaire, then by Abbé Maret, with the help of Frédéric Ozanam and F. Arnaud de l'Ariège, but that after June 1848 it ran into the open disapproval of most Catholics.

In the Germanies Catholics were perhaps more disturbed than in France by the shake-up that capitalism and liberalism gave to old social structures. At the same time that Archbishop Ketteler in his sermons in the cathedral of Mainz outlined a social creed inspired by Catholicism, Buss, a militant from Baden, urged the Church to protect the workingman, abandoned by the state, and to establish a body of clergymen aware of their social responsibilities in close connection with the lower classes. Several years ago Professor Franz Schnabel[17] and his disciples pointed out the bond between the romantic movement and the first appearance of this social Catholicism. It is equally important to note that here Catholics were ahead of Protestants, who were unable to free themselves from the contemporary social hierarchy or to keep aloof from state authority.

Moreover, as is often admitted, the Catholics' desire to adapt themselves to the new order was not limited to social and liberal problems. Even the most stalwart souls recognized that Catholicism should, in view of contemporary challenges, review again the whole question of its internal organization as well as that of its teaching and spirituality. The triumph of ultramontanism in the following years with its trappings of external devotions and frequently superstitious practices should not obscure the noble effort at the time of the revolutions to revive in Catholicism the merits that would recall to the faith souls who had gone astray. It was obvious to many Catholics that the lower clergy must, with the help of the laity, again be masters of their destiny, free themselves from the heavy burden of the hierarchy, and restore a measure of self-government to the Church. If the attempt in France inspired by Abbé Clauvel to obtain canonical irremovability of vicars, studied by Professor Duroselle, bore no results, much importance must still be attributed to the synodal theory, as outlined in Germany, not only by refractory priests but also by recognized scholars. One of these was the theologian Staudenmaier from Freiburg, whose ideas were supported by Johann von Döllinger [professor of ecclesiastical history at the University of Munich] in his desire for a primate at the head of the German church, ideas Döllinger had put forward during the consistory of the German bishops held at Würzburg.

Similar attitudes existed in Italy, too, where Antonio Rosmini published in 1848 his *Five Plagues of the Church*, protesting against the separation of the clergy from the faithful during services and against the bishops' power, while, on the other hand, extolling the position of the laity and the lower clergy versus the episcopate, and passing over in silence the role of the papacy in the dogmatic and disciplinary reforms he advocated. The reconciliation of religion and liberty, so dear to the heart of Lammenais, was to become the theme of the periodicals, published by such Tuscan reformers as R. Lambruschini, G. Capponi, and B. Ricasoli, who earnestly desired to renew religious sensitivity, establish faith on a more personal basis, and "respiritualize" the Church—desires that in their opinion involved a restriction of its political power and a total renovation of its spirituality. In a different pattern close to that of N. Tommaseo, we see the continuing influence of Jansenism, deeply rooted in the religious past of Italy, not untouched by Calvin's teaching or the thinking of Sismondi, Quinet, and Vinet. All this, however, did not disturb their devotion to native Catholicism in any way. Help is available today in understanding these rather complex concepts, thanks to the work of A. Jemolo,[18] and we now know, thanks to M. Vaussard, the repercussions of Catholic thinking in France in *l'Ere Nouvelle* circles stimulated by the efforts of E. Rendu.[19]

Other thinkers were bolder in aiming to counter unbelief itself. Rosmini hoped that the regeneration of the Church would imply a philosophical revolution in order to give a firmer foundation to religious subjectivity. The most striking work in this field is that of Anton Günther, who was in close contact with the revolutionary movements of 1848. To a certain extent, Güntheranism was a vehement protest against evil Josephist legislation and a call for independence in the Austrian church, both aims to be fulfilled by the lower clergy and a laity conscious of its duty. The threat of unbelief and the spread of the German Catholic movement served to bring together all those in Vienna who feared the torpidity of an episcopate enslaved to authority. And, thus, leaders such as Häusle, Gruscha, and Brunner laid the basis for the emancipation of the Church in the Hapsburg states. In addition, Güntheranism wanted to give theology a scientific character to compel the respect of unbelievers and to allow for the expression of a truly Christian concept of the universe.

To Günther and some of his contemporaries, scholasticism was dead. One principle only was needed as a basis for his system, namely, the irreducible conflict between matter and spirit, to provide a rational interpretation of the highest mysteries, including those of the Trinity and the Incarnation. He condemned the distinctions defended by theologians between natural and supernatural truth, the former easily understood by the human mind, the latter perceptible only in the light of faith. Günther's extraor-

dinary prestige in the Church both in and even out of Germany—
E. Winter is authoritative on this point[20]—impressed even the
Curia, which refrained at that time from condemning him.

In conclusion, it becomes evident that Catholics were quite
aware that their faith was threatened during the 1848 revolutions.
Time was, however, lacking for the fulfillment of their efforts to
adjust to the practical exigencies of the modern world and, more
significantly, to rejuvenate the Church in its organization and
teaching. Instead, thanks to the quick victory of reaction, the
development of the Catholic Church under Pius IX was re-established, as was to be expected, on the basis of traditional spirituality,
sustained by the power of an imperious hierarchy. Proudhon had
clearly foreseen the defeat of the Catholic reformers. This is
evident in his *De la Création de l'ordre dans l'humanité* (reprinted
in 1849), where he says:

Some élite thinkers in our day have imagined that science, in revivify-
ing the still palpitating remains of Catholicism, would provide a happy
revolution in society and assist religion as well. They have become
convinced of the profound aversion of religion for the thinking process.
Imprudent priests who consider yourselves wise, do you want to please
the religious authorities? If so refrain from learning, keep quiet, shut
your ears, burn your books, and recite your breviary!

The consequence was, to be sure, the increasing alienation of
the European intelligentsia from the Church, and finally the "de-
Christianization" of the masses. Perhaps, one may believe, results
would have been different if the reforms planned by prominent
Catholics, founded on the faith of the people, had succeeded. In
any case, the 1848 revolutions raised serious problems for religion;
indeed it is not too much to say that the destiny of the established
churches was then at stake.

Notes

1.   R. Aubert, *Le Pontificat de Pie IX, 1846–1878.* Paris: 1952.

2.   R. Rémond, *Lamennais et la Démocratie.* Paris: 1948.

3.   P. J. B. Buchez and Roux-Lavergne. *Histoire parlementaire de la Révolution française,* Paris 1834–1838.

4. A. Esquiros, *Histoire des montagnards*. Paris: 1847.

5. P. Viallaneix, *La voie royale. Essai sur l'idée du peuple dans l'œuvre de Michelet*. Thèse: Paris, 1959.

6. P. de Lubac, *Proudhon et le christianisme*. Paris: 1945, vol. 1.

7. K. Loewith, *Von Hegel zu Nietzsche*. Stuttgart: 1953.

8. J. Droz, *Les Révolutions allemandes de 1848*. Paris: 1957; "Die religiösem Sektem und die Revolution von 1848". *Archiv für Sozialgeschichte*, 1963, vol. 3.

9. Droz, *Les Révolutions allemandes de 1848*, pp. 60–64.

10. E. Winter, *Der Josefinismus. Die Geschichte des österreichischen Reformkatholizismus 1740–1848*. Berlin: 1962.

11. E. Winter, *Bolzano und sein Kreis*. Leipzig: 1933.

12. H. Vicaire, "Les ouvriers parisiens en face du catholicisme de 1830 à 1870," *Zeitschrift für Schweiserasche Geschichte*, 1951.

13. P. Vigier, *La Seconde République dans la Région alpine: Etude sociale et politique*. Thèse: Paris, 1963.

14. C. Marcilhacy, *Le diocèse d'Orléans au milieu du XIX Siècle: Les hommes et leur mentalité*. Thèse: Paris, 1963.

15. K. Repgen, *Märzbewegung und Maiwahlen der Revolutions jahren 1848 im Rheinland*. Bonn: 1955.

16. J.-B. Duroselle, *Les débuts du catholicisme social en France, 1822–1870*. Thèse: Paris, 1955.

17. F. Schnabel, *Deutsche Geschichte im XIX Jahrhundert*, Fribourg: 1937, vol. 4.

18. A. Jemolo, *Chiesa e stato in Italia negli ultimi cente anna*. Turin: 1948.

19. M. Vaussard, *Histoire de la démocratic chrétienne*. Paris: 1956, vol. 1.

20. E. Winter, *Die geistige Entwicklung Anton Günthers und seiner Schule*. Paderborn: 1931.

Joseph N. Moody, humanitarian, Catholic educator, and scholar, is well-known for his interest in liberal Catholicism and the French urban working class. Born in New York City in 1904, educated at Saint Joseph's Seminary and Fordham University, where he obtained his A.M. and Ph.D. degrees, he has taught at Cathedral and Ladycliff Colleges and is at present professor at the Catholic University in Washington, D.C. He received the B'nai B'rith Citation for his services in behalf of human rights in 1937, and from 1941 to 1946 he served as chaplain in the United States Navy in the Pacific and African theaters. He has been associate editor of the *Catholic Historical Review*, vice-president of the American Catholic Historical Association, vice-president of the Society for French Historical Studies, president of the New York State Association of European Historians, and modern history editor of the *New Catholic Encyclopedia*. He has published a variety of studies, including *Church and Society* (1953) and *The Challenge of Mater and Magistra* (1963). He is eminently suited to present a liberal Catholic view of liberal Catholicism.

French Liberal Catholics, 1840–1875

In the chapel of the Château de la Roche en Breny in Burgundy, there is an inscription that reads:

Félix, Bishop of Orléans, distributed the bread of the Word and the bread of life to a small group of fellow Christians who had long fought for a free Church in a free state. Here they renewed the pact to consecrate the rest of their lives to God and to liberty. The 13th October

1862. Present: Alfred, le Comte de Falloux; Théophile Foisset; Auguste Cochin; Charles, Comte de Montalembert. Absent physically, but present in spirit: Albert, Prince de Broglie.

The unimpressive size of the group contrasts with a statement in a letter from the proprietor of the same chateau, on September 14, 1845, to R. P. Jean Rozaven, Jesuit assistant to France: "I have spent all my life trying to form in France a Catholic opinion that is not legitimist, and I have succeeded."[1] Why he and his associates did not succeed is the theme of this paper.

If we accept Montalembert's statement of purpose and classify as Catholic liberals those who wished to disengage the practice of their faith from adherence to a legitimist political position, we avoid a number of problems. Nineteenth-century liberalism was not a static body of doctrine nor was it interpreted alike by all who professed it.[2] Catholics who considered themselves liberals were not raising the banner of personal religious autonomy against authority in institutionalized religion, critical though they were of many papal and episcopal acts. Nor were they explicitly involved in economic liberalism, although they accepted practically all its premises.[3] They were concerned with the perennial political problem of finding the point of balance between the pursuit of individuality and the acceptance of the decisions of the group. But they were not genuinely philosophical, and their attraction to liberty was largely romantic and empirical. Their fundamental interest was expressed in a letter by Montalembert to the same correspondent on November 15, 1847. He stated that the end of the Restoration marked the final defeat of royalism. Even Austria, which seemed an exception because of Metternich, was a bloody ruin that would soon fall in decomposition. The progress of modern political forms was inevitable and it was impossible to stem the tides of the nineteenth century. Even Italy would see the establishment of a new regime. Happily, Pius IX understood the direction of events and turned the Church from hostility to contemporary conditions to a more positive course. The writer went on to advise the Jesuits that since they were identified with the Old Regime and therefore were necessarily exposed, they should rally behind Pius IX.[4]

The Bishop of Orléans, memorialized on the chateau plaque as the "breaker of the Bread," expressed the same sentiments in 1845 when he scarcely knew the others. In his *De la Pacification reli-gieuse*, Dupanloup declared that religious peace was the major aim of the Catholic liberals. This could be achieved if citizens of all religious convictions would respect one another's opinions. Un-happily, he went on, since 1789, Catholics had not been receptive to religious liberty. Since they could find no justification for this rejection in the doctrines of their faith, they should divest them-selves of the prejudices of their forebears and reconcile themselves to modern society. This could only be done on the basis of liberty, religious, civil, and political. Privilege was dead, and the Church could count only on the free assent of its members. Far from being a tragedy, this had, he believed, a positive advantage for Catholi-cism.[5]

These statements of liberal Catholics show an awareness of essential change: The closed societies which had provided but-tresses for the Church's walls were in the process of erosion. Catholicism in France had to adjust to a new situation in which it could not obtain the coercive power of the state to support its mission. Ultimately, it would have to reform into a free association of individuals of common religious convictions, legally no different, except in size, from any other religious body in the nation. That the passing of the sacral society would not be easy for committed Catholics is indicated in a remark of Archbishop Darboy at a session of the Vatican Council: "I know that the Church can rise above the support of human power; nonetheless, she has never rejected either the alliance or the help of civil society. And I do not imagine that at the time of Constantine she sighed gently for the good old days of Nero."[6] This difficulty was enhanced by a set of historical experiences that made it hard for many Catholics to believe that a secular state could be neutral. Rather, they were convinced that it would promote a dogmatic nonreligious faith.

The first Catholic effort to accept the secular state was occa-sioned by the passage of the law of February 21, 1795, the first separation of Church and State in French history. Père Emery led a movement to accept the oath to the Republic demanded by this law on the ground that it did not violate Catholic principles and was necessary for the survival of religion.[7] A move to detach Catholicism from dependence on the state was initiated by

Lamennais in the twilight of the Restoration. It survived the condemnation of *Mirari Vos* (1832) and the defection of its leader. It gained momentum in the 1840s on the more favorable terrain of a government officially anticlerical but ready for practical accommodation. This rally of the majority of Catholics on the issue of freedom of education was due more to circumstance than to conviction. It masked deep divisions on the more basic problem of the relation of the Church to the modern state. But it was a tentative grasping toward a new position that might have been consolidated in time.

The overthrow of the July Monarchy was interpreted by most Catholics as a victory and as the dawn of a better day for the Church. Evidence for this attitude is overwhelming. It is sufficient for us to summarize a letter from the Paris Provincial of the Jesuits, Ambroise Rubbillon, to the General of the Society in Rome, dated March 8, 1848: "No phase of the Revolution has had an anti-religious aspect." Neither the houses nor the novices nor scholastics, he said, had been disturbed. In fact, what happened was sufficient to efface the bloody image that the word Republic conveyed to the nation. Now he expected confidently that order and a sincere liberty could coexist.

The provincial went on to describe his interview at the Hôtel de Ville with one of Buchez's associates, a doctor and a sincere Republican liberal who expressed regret for the excesses of 1793. The Jesuit representative was promised full liberty for religious communities under the new regime. He responded that Catholics had no opposition to a republic, for in the United States and elsewhere the Church had full liberty under republican institutions; while under the July Monarchy it had struggled without success for freedom of action.

The provincial concluded that several of the fathers believed that something ought to be done to dispel the prejudice that many Frenchmen felt toward the society. If constructive action was not taken, the Jesuits might find themselves outside the law in the projected constitution. Perhaps a re-examination of the administration of the French province was in order. It would have been an advantage, he believed, if Père Ravignan, a friend of the leading Catholic liberals, were in Paris, as he could be most useful.

Lacordaire was more popular than ever and had announced a new journal to appear in April.[8]

As the crisis of 1848 unfolded, the Catholic leadership in France had several courses:

1.   It could support the aspirations of the socially dispossessed— the urban workers and the rural poor—and make some contribution toward the integration of the newly emerging proletariat into French society. A small minority of enlightened Catholics, grouped around l'Ere Nouvelle and l'Atelier, insisted on the primary importance of the social question and urged their coreligionists to enter the struggle for social justice. Contemporary social-minded French Catholics castigate the Catholics of 1848 for their failure to seize the opportunity and they insist that this was the key to the dechristianization of the French working class.[9]

However we may deplore the social blindness of the men of 1848, it is a fact that French opinion, Catholic and otherwise, in this time of crisis was in no way prepared for a serious program of social reform.[10] Democratic suffrage gave political predominance to rural and provincial France, which had little taste for social experimentation. Whatever tolerance for mild welfare proposals may have existed at the birth of the Republic was destroyed by the disturbances of May and June. The promising beginnings of Christian social thought dissolved in the atmosphere of reaction. One need not borrow Marxist criteria to conclude that a Republic at once social and democratic was more than the existing social structure of France could bear.

2.   The liberal Catholics had more modest aspirations and might be expected to have had a better chance of success. They did not aim to create a France that might be, but to accommodate the Church to a France that was. They were in tune with the social conservatism of the bulk of the French élite.[11] Their goal was to win Catholic acceptance of civil liberties and representative institutions, which had become ingredients of the French political tradition. They felt that by marrying Catholicism to the prevailing liberal creed they would serve the cause both of the Church and of social stability. That there was some substance in their view can be glimpsed from the few occasions in subsequent French history

when the combination became a reality: in the last year of the Second Empire, during the era of good feeling in the 1890s, and during the government of the Bloc National (1919–1923).

3. The view that would attract the majority of articulate French Catholics for nearly a century was a defensive one, as sometimes happens among those whose cherished institutions are threatened. This position became apparent in the debates on the Loi Falloux[12] and was consolidated by the Catholic rally to the Second Empire. It professed the impossibility of conciliating Catholicism with the principles of 1789; accordingly, only the recovery of a regime of privilege could save the situation.[13] It was the failure of the liberal Catholics to stem the movement of a majority of Catholic spokesmen to this view that is the measure of their defeat.

Montalembert was quick to recognize the new circumstances. He wrote to Orestes Brownson from Brussels on November 12, 1852: "My political career being at present closed, I am to devote myself exclusively to my former historical and humanistic studies, as much as my shattered health and fortune will allow me to do so."[14] When this forced abstention from politics had extended for nearly two decades, he wrote: "I like to believe always that I am not in revolt against the fate that God has marked out for me. I resign myself with less generosity certainly . . . but with no bitterness nor despair."[15] Yet in the same year (1869) he confessed to the Jesuit provincial that he felt some sympathy for the apostate Père Hyacinthe who had suffered the scorn of the "Janissaries of the *Civiltà* and the *Univers*."[16]

In that last phrase, Montalembert concentrated a major part of his explanation for the failure of the movement with which he was so closely identified: "Liberty reigns without religion largely because the leaders of the Christian world have allowed it to happen."[17] He would not speculate as to the degree that the question of personal infallibility had contributed to the discrediting of religion. But he was certain that the Roman Jesuits had fanned the fires of disbelief. Writing on the same day to his friend Père Matignan, S.J., Montalembert was more explicit. It was a pity, he said, that Matignan's spirit was not found in high Jesuit circles, especially among the pseudointellectuals who edited *Civiltà* and rendered orthodoxy incompatible with common sense. The writer complained that he was caught in an abyss between the government of the Church and the most natural and legitimate aspirations of nineteenth-century man.[18]

This plaint is a constant in Montalembert's correspondence with the Jesuits. In a letter to the General of the Society in 1853, he related that it was difficult for him to continue his defense of the Jesuits because of *Civiltà cattolica* "which regretfully reduces the most difficult and general questions to the narrow and exclusive terrain of Italian politics." Citing quotations in *Univers* from issue Number 83 of the Roman journal that condemned constitutionalism, elected parliaments, and liberal Catholics, he noted that the Jesuits had returned to France, England, Belgium, Holland, and Prussia under the protection of constitutionalism after having been driven out by the absolute monarchs.[19]

In the Montalembert papers there is evidence of that slow drift from ultramontanism that had previously been the hallmark of the Catholic liberals since the Restoration. Lamennais had seen the authority of the Pope as a necessary corrective to Erastianism. The early generation of liberal Catholics, anxious for the renewal of the Church, inclined toward the uniformity sought by the nineteenth-century popes as more rational in an age of improving communications and more in keeping with the centralizing tendencies of other institutions. But by the 1860s they had begun to have doubts about the desirability of pontifical centralism, since Veuillot and Rome itself had redefined ultramontanism as opposition to any accommodation with "the spirit of the age." Accordingly, rapprochement between Gallicans and liberals was occurring during those very years when the bulk of the French clergy was becoming passionately attached to the Holy See (1845–1865).[20] Pius IX used every instrument to promote ultramontanism. His willingness to admit appeals from rebellious priests, his personal charm, his capacity to cast himself in the role of a martyr, all these made him an object of personal devotion in a way none of his predecessors had enjoyed.

While the ambivalence of the liberal Catholics toward Pius IX was detaching them from the fervent, their failure to extricate themselves from support of the temporal power was making them suspect among many non-Catholics.[21] The threat to the Papal states posed a painful dilemma for nineteenth-century Catholics, nearly all of whom assumed, as did many of their opponents, that if the Pope became subject to a secular ruler, he would lose his independence and universality. Thus the temporal power was considered a necessity for the spiritual well-being of the Church at the time it had become an anachronism, for in a system of national states it could be defended only by a powerful nation, thus inevitably involving the papacy in power struggles.

This dilemma, serious for all Catholics, was more acute for Catholic liberals, who had to argue for the superiority of a system of civil liberties and parliamentary government while supporting an out-dated form of the Old Regime in Italy. Despite this incongruity, only the Left fringe of the Catholic liberals failed to defend the temporal power. Disagreeing on the issue with his American correspondent, Brownson, Montalembert writes from La Roche en Breny, October 25, 1860:

No man has the moral *right* to seek even a good end by immoral means. Now this is just what the Italians are doing: Their end may be good, as the end of the French revolution in 1789 was even more undoubtedly good; but they cared not about the *means* they employed to reach their end. Therefore God has not blessed their efforts nor indeed those of their successors. Nor do I suppose that He will do more for the Italians, for in the home of treachery, if not of cruelty, they have outdone the French.[22]

Montalembert came back to the same point in a letter from Paris, which notified Brownson that he had sent his last letter to Cavour:

I know that you do not quite agree with me on Italian affairs; but I am sure that you must be as indignant as I am against both the Piedmontese and the Napoleonic policy. We must never forget that not only Christianity but natural morality forbids *de faire le mal pour que le bien en sorte*. Granted even that a united Italy and a secularized Popedom are results to be wished for, or not to be prevented, no Christian, no honest man can approve the frightful means that are employed to bring on these results.[23]

Montalembert then went on to reveal that he had not yet grasped the mind of Pius IX:

But the point on which I most particularly wish to call to your attention is the defense of the Pope's last allocution,[24] so outrageously and
so maliciously misunderstood, not only in the revolutionary and anti-
Catholic press, but *still more* so by the ultra-Catholic papers, both
here, in Belgium, in Spain, etc. They go on asserting every day that
the Pope has declared incompatibility between the Church and
modern society, the Catholic Faith and political freedom, etc.
    Nothing can be more false. My wife, who has just returned from
Rome and whose brother, Mgr. de Merode, is perhaps the most influential man there, says that there is not the slightest foundation for
such an interpretation. But Rome's greatest mistake, which she is now
woefully ruing, is not in the antiquated wording of her public documents; it lies in the encouragement she has lavished upon the slavish
fanatics who have made her court so justly unpopular throughout the
world, and whose detestable influence has driven such men as Döllinger
and Lacordaire to become more or less averse to all secular power of
the Holy See.[25]

    In a letter of February 5, 1863, Montalembert declared that he
now accepted Brownson's views on the Roman Question as his
American correspondent had expressed them in an article entitled
Faith and Theology.[26] The letter revealed a growing bitterness:

The Emperor, having given up the plan of handing over Rome to
Victor Emmanuel, had speedily regained the confidence of the poor
credulous Catholics, who are clearly taught by their daily organ, the
Monde, to prefer any sort of despotism rather than civil and religious
liberty. Having foolishly concentrated all their energy and all their
attention on the Roman Question, they take no heed of the system
by which this once great and Christian nation has been delivered up
to this strange crew of bastards, filibusters, and renegades who are the
worthy and exclusive ministers of modern Caesarism.[27]

    If it took time for the correspondents to coordinate their views
on Italy, it was easier for them to reach agreement on the regime
in France. Montalembert labored to erase his sense of guilt for his
early support of Louis Napoléon, giving substance to the remark
of his friend de Falloux: "M. de Montalembert had twenty days of
illusion which he expiated by eighteen years of disgrace and three
political trials."[28]
    It is clear from this correspondence that Montalembert's rally
to the President of the Republic was far from complete. He wrote
to Brownson from Paris, May 14, 1851:

His (Louis Napoleon's) recent legislation on education has left but a shadow of the freedom which we had conquered in 1850, and this shadow itself is not respected as you may have seen from the arbitrary closing and re-opening of the Jesuit's College at St. Etienne last Winter in defiance of all the legal guarantees and precautions maintained even by his own decrees. Himself or his successor may deprive the Church of all she now enjoys without the slightest difficulty and without the possibility of resistance or complaint.

He then cited the arbitrary closing of a rural newspaper for an article on fertilizer, an act that revealed "the state of social and civil freedom in France." The regime eliminated all political criticism, "leaving only the safety valve of anti-religion."[29]

After his break with the empire had been final, Montalembert wrote to Brownson from Brussels on November 12, 1852:

I have stood by him [Napoleon III] *with more decision than anyone* during his quarrel with the honest but foolish majority in the Assembly and even *after* his coup d'état, as long as there appeared to be any danger of a renewed attack of socialism.[30] I thought it my duty to do all I could to ensure his victory. But since I have seen him use his omnipotence to inflict on the cause of *justice* and *property*, in the case of Orleans, an injury which the triumphant Socialists in 1848 refrained from attempting, I have felt it equally my duty to stand aside from any connection with his policy. He has on his side done nothing to bring me back. I have seen enough of him to know that he neither understands nor desires the real freedom of the Church.

Some insignificant concessions have been granted, but nothing for her permanent interests. The real gains were made prior to his accession by the free action of Catholics.[31]

Montalembert's concern for the true status of the Church mounted:

As for the religious state of this country, you may rest assured that it is very far from satisfactory and that the *outward* progress of the Church is more than counterbalanced by the formidable *reaction* which is gaining ground against her among the intellectual and superior classes. We are gradually losing all we have gained during the reign of Louis-Philippe and the Republic. The cause of this reaction is twofold: the useless and *worthless* adulation of *some* who have made themselves so conspicuous by their oratorical displays in favor of the present regime, of the Emperor and even of the Empress, who may be doubtless a pious and good married lady but who has done nothing to be compared to Ste. Hélène and Ste. Clotilde, as the Bishop of Amiens[32] did not blush to do, *parlant à sa personne*, a few months ago.

He had to be careful in publishing because "a stroke of the pen of the head-policeman at the Ministry of the Interior can put an end to the existence of the *Correspondant*, or any other independent paper, without the possibility of any judicial complaint or resistance."[33]

The Brownson papers reveal the grudging assent Montalembert came to give to "democracy," a term he used with a variety of nuances and to which he reacted according to circumstance. By July 8, 1856 he could say:

Be convinced that my friends and I are perfectly convinced that democracy is destined to dominate in our century, and we have no dreams of reconstructing an aristocracy of any sort. . . .[34] But as I have said in my book,[35] there are two democracies: and we will never cease preferring a democracy which is enlightened, honest, and liberal to a debasing and servile democracy, which is nothing more than a prelude to despotism.[36]

Montalembert's reservations in regard to democracy did not detract from his admiration for the United States, which he told Brownson "he hopes to visit to breathe more freely than is possible in continental Europe."[37] Writing in the midst of the Civil War, he stated:

Things are going badly in both hemispheres; at least, so it seems to me. But having been turned adrift in the prime of life, and living for the last ten years in downright contradiction with men and things which are uppermost in public opinion both Catholic and non-Catholic, I may be led astray by a not unnatural discontent. I see, however, that you do not judge more favorably on the course of events. Your honest patriotism does not prevent you from telling most severe truths to your countrymen and women. I am afraid that the Union will never be re-established, although all my sympathies are with the North, as I took care to state on the only public occasion I have had lately, or most likely shall have, in my speech at the Academy. . . . I cannot say how much I lament the disruption and how I detest the yells of brutal satisfaction with which all the servile egoists of Europe greet the distress of your great republic. Strange to say, except for the small group of liberal Catholics, whose mouthpiece is the *Correspondant*, the immense bulk of the clergy and Catholics agree with England (whom they have been taught by the *Univers* to loathe) in wishing well to the slaveholders.[38]

The dominant note in the Brownson papers is a deepening pessimism on the condition of the Church in France.[39] Montalembert usually connected its decline with the loss of constitutional and political freedom in France.[40] He also related it to his own political misfortunes. After predicting that "the malady of the French clergy will not be cured as speedily as it was created,"[41] he spoke of his defeat in recent elections

chiefly by the instrumentality of the clergy of my department (Doubs) who have been persuaded by *Univers* that I am a dangerous man . . . and with few exceptions have preferred a practically unknown candidate, whose only qualification in their eyes was his being a *chamberlain of the Emperor!* However, I hope you know enough of me to suppose that I can but congratulate myself on no longer belonging to that *mutum et turpum pecus* in which I have sat for five empty and tedious years where my voice knew no echo and where my speeches, few and far between, were systematically garbled and mutilated in the official *compte rendu*, while no other versions can be published under penalty of fine and imprisonment. But setting aside the painful conduct of the great bulk of the clergy in those elections, they may have given the saddest insight into the real state of French society. Nothing can equal the extent of the intimidation and corruption exercised by the immense army of government agents, except unfortunately the shameful subserviency of the rural population to this pressure from above.

Montalembert declared that the pretense to electoral freedom is more galling than the despotism. The real opposition to the regime tended to be almost exclusively socialist.

So that this far-famed *restaurateur de l'ordre et du principe de l'autorité* has not only abstained from granting to the Church any of those liberties which she seemed to long for under Louis-Philippe, but he has *not in the least diminished* the danger against which his dictatorship in 1852 was thought necessary by me and many others. He has done nothing but destroy all the personal, local, and moral influence by the help of which France was able to weather the storms in 1848 and 1849. The next outbreak of Socialism will meet with no sort of living obstacle except the army.[42]

By 1859, he was bitter that no word had been published about his recent trial[43] in a country that

Catholic prelates have dared to call the *restoration of Christian society* in the world. . . . Every bit of resistance to the Imperial will is looked upon by the blind and fanatical masses as an aristocratical protest against impersonated democracy. . . . But my dear and venerated friend, this is some comfort for Catholics like *you* and me, who see the glorious cause of the Church and faith so miserably compromised by the unnatural and dishonorable alliance between the clergy and modern Caesarism. You are quite right to be much more indignant against Louis Veuillot than Louis Napoleon. *Celui-ci fait son métier;* but the other has basely betrayed, out of sheer demogogical jealousy, the trust placed on him, and pandered, as you so justly say, to the worst and lowest inclinations of the day. Unfortunately, he has met with great encouragement at Rome,[44] where for the sake of some relatively insignificant victories on liturgical and canonical questions, they have ignored the danger and the shame which their authorized organ has brought down upon the Catholic cause, a danger ten times greater than any of those which the worst Gallicanism has ever engendered, and a *shame* which ought to call a blush on every Catholic's cheek who does not pretend to forget what perverted and exaggerated opinion on the liberal and republican side was maintained in 1848 by the very same men who now insult and deny their own former creed and all those who remain true to forsaken freedom and honor.[45]

Montalembert was not impressed by the critical attitude toward the regime engendered by the Italian war:

The French clergy are rather *déconcerté* by the conduct of him they have so faithfully built up. . . . But they are far, *very far,* from being cured of the odious Caesarism, which Veuillot and his crew have instilled into their hearts. They still dream of an orthodox Caesar, who will kindly undertake *to do their work,* or at least to keep down and gag their adversaries, so as to deliver them from all troubles or struggles here below. The bishop of Orleans is a glorious exception to this universal disposition, but he is only an exception. . . .[46]

Whether one explores the failure of the liberal Catholics from this correspondence or from a broader perspective, one has the impression that they had some theoretical chance for success. They represented the spirit of *aggiornamento* in their day and were trying to align the Church in France with the dominant forces of their time. They could have been expected to rally not merely the sympathetic interest of conservative nonbelievers, but also the vast body of nominal and moderate Catholics who certainly never succumbed to the leadership of Veuillot. They enjoyed considerable muted support even among religious congregations that are ranked among their bitterest opponents.[47] It was a combination of their own weaknesses and formidable environmental obstacles that added to the difficulty of their task and accounts for their failure.

The liberal Catholics were sincere and talented men. But neither their training nor their study prepared them for an analysis-in-depth of the problems they faced. The ecclesiastics among them were plagued by the deficiencies of clerical education, which was the bane of the Church in France during the nineteenth century.[48] The laymen—country gentlemen, lawyers, journalists—had a good general education. But they lacked the specialized knowledge to relate contemporary thought to Catholicism. Thus, they remained imprecise in their formulations, more attracted to rhetoric than scholarship and more to romantic appeal than factual demonstration.

Their interest in the renewal of the Church was genuine, but they give the impression that the world to which the faith was to be accommodated was the world of their youth, when the structure of society was still cast in the traditional mold and when Christian values, though contested, still exercised some appeal. But while they struggled, by opposition to absolute political power and aristocratic privilege, to repair the damage done by their predecessors, great transformations were in progress: The thrust of technological change, expanding population, growing urbanization, and the increasing ambit of scientific knowledge were radically modifying the France that was symbolized by the Château of La Roche en Breny. These new factors were reinforcing the hopes and illusions that had been stimulated by the expansion of Western civilization and the vision of a "brave new world."

During the active years of the liberal Catholics, these aspirations took concrete form in the demand for an expansion of popular education, the desire for wide participation in government, the quest for change in social structures, and the need for public assistance for the urban masses. To none of these did the liberal Catholics respond. Even in the rural centers, with which many of them were in contact, the drift of the local leadership toward ideas alien to Catholicism (as then presented) was not understood.[49] Unaware of the currents of change, they offered no adequate remedy. Unable to see that dissatisfaction with the positions of the Church was being nourished in secret in both rural and urban areas and was being communicated to the ordinary levels of the population, they were unprepared for the gulf that, after 1875, appeared between popular attitudes and the ancient faith. They could not believe that the more dynamic elements of the French population had come to consider Catholicism irrelevant. Hence, those who survived were surprised by a new political phenomenon in France, a parliamentary republic, basically different from its idealistic prototypes of 1793 and 1848—a republic that would be socially conservative and "radical" only in the religious sense. They remained faithful to the impossible goal of moderate monarchism. Thus their failure to reach agreement with the secular liberals and the conservative republicans of *Union libérale*, with whom they had much in common, precluded organized Catholic participation in the formation of the Third Republic.

The liberal Catholics compounded this misreading of basic trends in opinion with a lack of concern for the power factors in modern society. Essentially men of the salon and the Academy, they were generals without troops, unable to counteract the appeal of a Veuillot, who skillfully played on the emotions of rural curés and committed laymen. It was a painfully uneven contest between the plebeian vulgarizer of *Univers* and the gentlemen who broke the bread of life in the Burgundian château (that is, between Veuillot and the liberal Catholics). Stung by Veuillot's lash, the latter found no response that could win popular support.

Among their external obstacles, the most serious was opposition from Rome. This was already evident in the declarations of Pius IX before 1864; the *Quanta Cura* and *Syllabus* of that date made it obvious. Even the dialectical skill of Dupanloup could not repair the damage.[50] The events of 1870 made the aged pope more bitter. In a discourse to a French delegation on the twenty-fifth anniversary of his elevation to the papacy, he denounced Catholic liberalism as "an evil more serious than the Revolution, more dangerous than the Commune . . ."[51]

Almost as serious were the political developments after 1848. It might be said that democracy came too abruptly to France; it certainly was too sudden for most of the Catholics who wished to lead the Church to modernity. With the disappearance of genuinely representative government and the rally of Catholic voters to Louis Napoleon, what hopes there might have been for a moderate Catholic grouping on liberal lines were lost. Even if it were present, the oppressive weight of the Empire made organized legal opposition impossible.

But the liberal Catholics did make some contributions. In an unhappy period they provided a refuge for some of the more sensitive and intelligent who wished to retain their religious heritage and feel at home in the France they loved. The training they provided for some Catholics in political life was lost under the Second Empire and in the passion of the early days of the Third Republic, but was available as a model when Catholics became ready to participate positively in political life.[52] As a minority at the Vatican Council, they provided under the leadership of Dupanloup a loyal opposition that acted as a brake on the desires of the extreme ultramontanists.[53] They were pioneers in the effort to raise the level of clerical education in France.[54] In their defense of liberty of association, they showed appreciation of one aspect of pluralist society.[55]

High hopes, modest returns. But time has brought change, as it does in human affairs. Today, Church and state have been reconciled in France, and the Church has made a reasonable adjustment to the conditions under which it must do its work. It would be comforting to report that the new condition was a fruit of the labors of the Catholic liberals.

Ironically, in the case of both the Ralliement that failed in the 1880s and 1890s and the Ralliement that succeeded in the 1920s and 1930s, the major impulse toward adjustment came from Rome. In both cases, papal initiative had to struggle against descendants of Veuillot, who once had been encouraged from the Vatican. In both cases, the Popes had to depend on French Catholics who took an affirmative approach to the world in which they lived. Because the Catholic liberals pioneered in this difficult field, they may deserve a role among the minor prophets.

Notes

1.   Montalembert to Rozaven, *Archives of the Provincial of Paris of the Society of Jesus* (hereafter *APP*). Charles René Montalembert (1810–1870), the leading lay spokesman for the Catholic liberals, had joined Lamennais' staff on the newspaper *L'Avenir*. When its principles were condemned by Pope

Gregory XVI in 1832, Montalembert remained in the Church without fundamentally changing his views. He had led the campaign for the right of Catholics to operate secondary schools on the basis of liberty for all, "religious liberty under the flag of civil liberty" in Lacordaire's words. George Weill, *Histoire du catholicisme libéral en France, 1828–1908.* Paris: Alcan, 1926, p. 8, rightly sees the school issue as the genesis of liberal Catholicism.

2. All liberals, including the Catholics, professed devotion to civil liberties and parliamentary government, but there were divergencies in interpretation. Professor L. Girard's categories of Right and Left liberals in *Bulletin de la Société d'histoire moderne,* 2nd series, no. 25, pp. 6–9, could be conveniently applied to the Catholics, with Dupanloup representing the Right and Maret the Left, with Montalembert moving between.

3. Liberals, Catholic or otherwise, in the mid-nineteenth century tended to emphasize rights against the state. Only in the twentieth century did there appear an effective liberal demand for creative rights through the state, as in social security.

4. *APP.* He comes back to the same point in another letter in this correspondence, also from La Roche en Breny, dated December 2, 1847.

5. Félix Dupanloup (1802–1878) left the rectorship of the seminary of St. Nicolas-du-Chardonnet to become bishop of Orleans in 1849. He was the principal clerical spokesman for the Catholic liberals and a leader of the opposition to the definition of papal infallibility at the first Vatican Council. Similar views were expressed by Albert de Broglie, *Mémoires du duc de Broglie,* 1821–1901. Paris: Garnier Frères, 1879, vol. 1, p. 278: "We wished to maintain against *Univers,* supported by a majority of the bishops, that Catholics must continue to defend religion by means of liberty and by demanding only a generous application of the common law. They must reject absolutely an appeal to the exclusive protection of the State, and even more strongly any intolerance or persecution against those who do not share their views. Liberty in general and liberty of conscience in particular must be our banner."

6. Emile Ollivier, *L'Église et l'État au concile du Vatican.* Paris: Calmann-Lévy, 1938, vol. 2, pp. 298–299.

7. Chanoine Jean Laflon, *Monsieur Emery.* Paris: Bonne Presse, 1944 (2nd ed.), vol. 1, pp. 369–432.

8. *APP.* The Journal referred to was *L'Ere Nouvelle.*

9. H. Guillemin, *Histoire des catholiques français au XIXe siècle.* Paris: Milieu du Monde, 1947, pp. 180 ff.; Adrien Dansette, *Histoire religieuse de la France contemporaine.* Paris: Flammarion, 1948, vol. 1, pp. 351–359.

10. Adeline Daumard, *La Bourgeoisie parisienne de 1815 à 1848.* Paris: SEVPEN, 1963, has this percipient remark on the libraries of the well-to-do: "Their libraries might have inspired the men formulating the Declaration of the Rights of Man in 1789. They gave no help whatsoever in solving the

problems arising out of the birth of the contemporary world in which social differences, though perhaps no greater, were more intensely felt than in the past."

The liberal Catholics, usually products of a provincial France of a few notables and a peasant mass, were singularly unprepared to appreciate the new social mobility and the new aspirations. In his "Profession de foi électoral, 3 April 1848," in *Oeuvres complètes*, vol. 3, p. 15, Montalembert confessed having shared "not the indifference but the ignorance of the majority of politicians" concerning the sufferings of the working class.

11. The emphasis of the liberal Catholics remained pragmatic rather than theoretical.

12. The *Loi Falloux*, which gave Catholics important concessions in the field of secondary education, was made possible by an alliance of the liberal Catholics and "the party of order," notably Thiers. But it brought into the open the conflict of the liberal Catholics and the intransigents who decried any compromise with the university or the secular world it represented. Montalembert defends the *Loi Falloux* in a letter to Brownson from Paris, Easter Day (March 31) 1850. Archives of the University of Notre Dame, no. 11380. (Hereafter NDA.) Orestes Brownson (1803–1876), who had been a Universalist minister and a member of Brook Farm, became a convert to Catholicism in 1844. Until the first Vatican Council he campaigned for liberal causes in American Catholicism especially through his *Quarterly Review*. The archives of the University of Notre Dame has his papers, which contain more than a score of letters from Montalembert.

13. Louis Veuillot, *L'Illusion libérale*. Paris: 1866 (2nd ed.), p. 139 ff. Louis Veuillot (1813–1883) had been converted in Rome in 1838 and became editor of *Univers* in 1843. After 1848 his vitriolic and effective journalism promoted the most reactionary and ultramontanist positions among French Catholics. His rhetoric had the capacity to intoxicate his followers, who wanted to believe themselves right in spite of the evidence. A violent summary of his views can be found in *Univers*, November 17–18, 1852, under the title "De la Liberté sous l'absolutisme."

14. NDA, no. 11381.

15. *APP*. Letter from La Roche en Breny, January 8, 1869.

16. *APP*. To Jean Rozaven from La Roche en Breny, October 11, 1869. *Civiltà cattolica*, the Jesuit newspaper in Rome, generally expressed the views of the papacy.

17. *APP*. To Jean Rozaven from La Roche en Breny, October 11, 1869. Here Montalembert aligns himself with Archbishop Maret's opinion, which he quotes approvingly.

18. *APP*., from La Roche en Breny, October 11, 1869. Already there had been evidence that *Civiltà cattolica* and *Univers* were expressing the mind of Pius IX, at least on general lines. When Dupanloup's pastoral to his clergy

of April 19, 1852 had condemned *Univers*, the Pope replied with encyclical *Inter Multiplices* to the archbishops and bishops of France, which declared that they should encourage Catholic journalists, correcting them paternally only where necessary.

19. From La Roche en Breny, October 22, 1853, in the *Archives of the Society of Jesus*, Rome (hereafter *ASJ*.)

20. An interesting letter from Père Ravignan to the General of the Society in *ASJ*, dated Paris, October 26, 1852, analyzes this recrudescence of Gallicanism, the ancient French assertion of the freedom of the national church from the ecclesiastical authority of the papacy. A powerful opponent of Gallicanism was Felicité Lamennais (1782–1854), who had become a priest in 1816 and was the foremost apologist for religion under the Restoration. His *Des progrès de la Révolution* (1829) attacked the ascendancy of the state over the Church (Erastianism). His remedy was complete separation of Church and state and supremacy of the pope within the Church (ultramontanism). After papal condemnation of his views in 1832, he drifted from the Church.

21. While the Republicans were unanimous in their opposition to the temporal power, the secular liberals divided during the Second Empire in part because of the "revolutionary temper" of the Risorgimento, in part because French national interests might be threatened by Italian unification. Thiers is an outstanding example. But the bulk of the French population, religious and otherwise, was indifferent to the political position of the Pope.

22. *AND*, no. 12409.

23. *AND*, no. 12410, April 22, 1861. Montalembert's views led Maret to remark: "Liberals in France, absolutists in Italy." G. Bazin, *Vie de Mgr. Maret*, vol. 3, Paris: Berche et Trallin, 1891, vol. 2, p. 292. Maret was an exception on the Roman question. He accepted Louis Napoleon as an authentic heir of the Revolution and one who was sincerely desirous to collaborate with the spiritual forces of the nation.

The letter to Cavour to which Montalembert refers was *Deuxième lettre à M. le Comte de Cavour, président du conseil des ministres à Turin*, Paris: J. Lecoffre, 1861.

24. *Jamdudum*, March 10, 1861. Those Montalembert criticizes were, of course, correct. The text reveals a bitter denunciation of modern society.

25. He continues with the contention that the intransigent attitude is even more predominant in the French clergy, for "Veuillot's hateful sway has not been lost by his partial silence" (reference to the suppression of *Univers*, January 29, 1860). "The sottish *coterie* who rule the French clergy are discontented with Caesar, but not with Caesarism." In a letter of October 19, 1861 from La Roche en Breny, *AND*, no. 12413, Montalembert confesses his disagreement with Brownson on the Roman question.

26. The article is found in *Brownson's Review*, Third New York Series, vol. 4, January 1863, pp. 1–29.

27.   *AND*, no. 12414, from La Roche en Breny. Later he included Rome in his strictures: in no. 12415 from La Roche en Breny, December 17, 1869: "Above all there is the extreme danger of that centralism which is now exposing the Church to the same dangers and the same corruptions which have destroyed monarchy throughout the world."

28.   *Mémoires d'un royaliste.* Paris: Perrin, 1888, vol. 1, pp. 393–394. De Falloux adds that he had warned Montalembert. The extent of the latter's rally to Louis Napoleon is evident in the correspondence with Brownson, *AND*, no. 11380, from Paris, Easter 1850.

29.   *NDA.* For the affair at St. Étienne, Jean Maurain, *La Politique ecclésiastique du Second Empire.* Paris: Alcan, 1930, pp. 19–22.

30.   Montalembert had broken with the government, January 23, 1852, when it announced the confiscation of the Orleanist properties. In this letter, he again reveals that he was impressed by the riots but not by the social conditions which led to them.

31.   *NDA.* A longer statement of his reasons for repudiating Louis Napoleon is found in *NDA* no. 12400, from Marche-Doubs, July 8, 1856.

32.   Mgr. de Salinis.

33.   *NDA*, from Paris, December 28, 1854. Montalembert's classic expression of his disillusionment with the Second Empire is *Des Intérêts catholiques au XIXe siècle.* Paris: Lecoffre, 1852.

34.   Compare this to *NDA*, May 14, 1851: "I go so far as to admit that of all governments *aristocracy* in itself is the best, and that wherever, as in Hungary, an aristocracy has kept true to its military courage and social energy, it ought to be maintained, even at the expense of *humanitarian* theories and *so-called equality* of rights." And in *NDA*, December 28, 1854, he fears that England "is advancing with rapid strides to a *huge centralized democracy,* which centralization must sooner or later settle down into utopian despotism."

35.   *Les Intérêts catholiques au XIXe siècle.*

36.   *NDA*, no. 12400, July 8, 1856. Compare with the bitter attack in *NDA*, January 28, 1850, from Paris: "I have loved and still love liberty; but I recognize with you that I have too often confounded its cause with Revolution." Later, he would defend the right of the rural masses to vote against liberal attack, Letter to M. de Foblant in *Oeuvres complètes*, vol. 6, pp. 385–386; and he would come close to an acceptance of democracy in his address at the First Malines Congress, "L'Eglise libre dans l'état libre." Paris: Ch. Douniol, Didier et Cie, 1865.

37.   *NDA*, December 28, 1854.

38.   *NDA*, no. 12414, February 15, 1863. Montalembert was standing for election in May and would have welcomed liberal support, but did not receive

it. This election marked the complete fissure between Catholics and Republicans even when both were opposed to the government, as in the case of Montalembert, Maurain, pp. 639 ff., Albert de Broglie, "Mémoires II: Autour du Syllabus," *Revue des Deux Mondes*, November 30, 1935, pp. 135–139.

39. NDA, May 14, 1851, where he notes that in 1848, *Univers* declared royalty dead forever, in 1850, hailed Chambord as the only salvation for France, and now sees Louis Napoleon as "a preservative against Socialism." Against this tide the Catholic liberals could only cling together in the hope of better days. NDA, November 12, 1852, saw *Univers* doing harm to those "whom the events of 1848 have led to reflect on the vanity of all social institutions without religion."

40. NDA, no. 12399, November 1, 1855, from La Roche en Breny.

41. The occasion was the "appel comme d'abus" of the notorious Mgr. Dreux-Brézé, bishop of Moulins and a rabid legitimist, who refused any accommodation with the regime. See Maurain, pp. 190–196.

42. NDA, no. 12401, September 4, 1857, from Evian en Savoy. In the constituency in the Doubs, where Montalembert had three times been elected, he was able to obtain only 4378 votes, against 7134 for the democrat and 17,387 for the official candidate. See Maurain, pp. 223–224.

43. Montalembert was condemned to six months in prison for an article that appeared in *Correspondant*, October 1858, "Un débat sur l'Inde au Parlement anglais," in which he contrasted the liberal government of England with the regime in France to the detriment of the latter. He refused pardon, was tried again, and pardoned. See Maurain, p. 235, note 3.

44. For a detailed complaint, "Lettres de Montalembert à la Comtesse Sophie Apponyi," Letter of December 27, 1862, in *Revue des Deux Mondes*, vol. 83 (1913), pp. 244–245.

45. NDA, no. 12407, February 16, 1859, from La Roche en Breny.

46. NDA, no. 12409, October 25, 1860, from La Roche en Breny.

47. This is certainly true of the French Jesuits: *Etudes*, vol. 92 (1902), "L'Eglise et la liberté," and the anniversary number of *Etudes*, vol. 291 (1956), in which the subject is discussed extensively. For the background of the conflict in the Society, see Joseph Burnichon, *La Compagnie de Jésus en France; histoire d'un siècle, 1814–1914*. Paris: G. Beauchesne, 1914. In ASJ, there is a dignified letter to the Jesuit General from Père de Ravignan, from Paris, July 11, 1849; a letter to the General from Édouard de Lehen, Paris, August 22, 1850; a letter from Saint Acheul, August 9, 1851, signed Tellier; a letter to the General from Père de Ravignan, July 17, 1866, from Issenheim, all of which reveal the deep divisions in the Jesuit community in France.

48. Exceptions were Mgr. Maret and his friends, Valroger, Meignan, Vallot: J. Brugerette, *Le Prêtre français et la société contemporaine*. Paris: P. Letheil-

leux, 1935, passim and esp. vol. 3, pp. 47–57. Dupanloup's *Histoire de Notre Seigneur Jésus-Christ*. Paris: H. Plon, 1872, an attempted answer to Renan's *Life of Jesus*, is a classic instance of scholarly weakness. The intellectual sterility of the French clergy was aggravated by a tradition of moralism and pessimism inherited from Jansenism, which fitted poorly into the soaring optimism of the mid-nineteenth century.

49. Even Dupanloup, who might be termed the father of religious sociology, did not lucidly interpret the data he obtained from parish questionnaires: See Christianne Marcilhacy, *Le Diocèse d'Orléans sous l'épiscopat de Mgr. Dupanloup, 1849–1878*. Paris: Plon, 1962, esp. pp. 577–587.

50. Joseph Lecler, "Dans la Crise du catholicisme libéral," *Etudes* no. 291 (1956), pp. 199–200, with the story of how the review was moved by the Pope from Paris to Lyons because of papal suspicions of the Paris Jesuits and the Pope's belief that a series of articles by Père Matignan, one of the editors, on the historical views on liberty among the early Jesuits was an attack on the *Syllabus*. See also R. Aubert, "Monseigneur Dupanloup et le Syllabus," in *la Revue d'histoire ecclésiastique*, vol. 51 (1956), pp. 79–142, 471–512, 837–915.

51. R. Aubert, *Le Pontificat de Pie IX, 1846–1878*. Paris: Bloud and Gay, 1952.

52. There was considerable interest among young Catholics in 1910 to celebrate the centenary of Montalembert's birth, but the Modernist controversy killed it. For a short time there was a *Revue Montalembert* for university students.

53. Jean-Rémy Palanque, *Catholiques libéraux et Gallicans en France, face au concile du Vatican, 1867–1870*. Aix-en-Provence: Annales de la Faculté des Lettres, 1962, p. 191. Pius IX formally approved the restrictive interpretation of the decree of papal infallibility of Mgr. Fessler, which became the official commentary. It basically was not far from the position of the Catholic liberal bishops. Dupanloup received considerable correspondence from American prelates: *Archives Saint Sulpice*, Dupanloup Papers, for example, Whelan (Wheeling) to Dupanloup, April 24, 1870.

54. Dupanloup and Sibour were prominent in encouragement to the École des Carmes and the Chapter of Sainte Geneviève. Dupanloup was a leader in obtaining the passage of the decree of July 12, 1875 which granted Catholics the right to establish schools of higher learning; he contributed importantly to the transformation of Des Carmes to what is now the *Institut Catholique*, which ultimately provided the base for clerical scholarship.

55. Paul Nourisson, *Histoire de la liberté d'association en France depuis 1789*. Paris: Tenin (Receuil Sirey), 1920, vol. 2, pp. 349, 382.

part 3

THE FRENCH IMAGE OF RUSSIA

AND

RUSSIAN VIEWS OF FRANCE

The rôle of Russia since the Bolshevik Revolution, and especially since the Second World War, has been such that tremendous interest has been engendered in foreign views of Russia and, at least to some degree, in Russian views of various foreign countries. But France and Russia have long been engaged in this appraisal of each other. In the eighteenth century, when France was the beacon of the Enlightenment, the impact of France on the Russian court and on the intelligentsia was very great, and no one was more "enlightened" than Catherine the Great. During the days of the French Revolution and Napoleon the interaction of France and Russia could scarcely have been more powerful in some respects, nor could their mutual interest, at least in some quarters, have been keener. With the development of mid-nineteenth-century liberalism and the revolutions of 1848, mutual responses to political and cultural developments remained in high key. Continuing Russian fear of foreign revolutionary influences, especially French, however, barred closer relations between the two nations. While men like Uvarov brought France into Russian focus, the Eastern-oriented Slavophile movement damaged this association. The Crimean War, the cause of Poland, and the asylum France offered Russian revolutionaries later in the century sharpened the mutual distrust of these widely differing nations. As bourgeois France became republican, the clash of monarchical and republican ways heightened the contrasts between regimes and cultures. But even as France inclined farther to the left prior to the First World War, the alliance of 1894 between the Tsar of All the Russias and the Third Republic was consummated. After the Russian Revolution of 1917 the cycle was repeated. Initially, the reaction of France against Russian communism, together with the anti-Western attitudes of Lenin and other Bolshevik leaders, created new barriers between France and Russia. But by 1935 France leaped over her "sanitary corridor" of lesser Eastern allies to join hands once again with Russia, now a totalitarian state. The recent role of France in asserting its national might and individualism has given new significance to the Franco-Russian theme. In any case, consideration must be given to Franco-Russian mutual views in any study of the interaction between Eastern and Western ways and thought.

↗ ROGER PORTAL

Roger Portal is in the forefront among French scholars in the field of Slavic studies. Born at Ambert (Puy-de-Dôme) in 1906, he studied at Clermont-Ferrand and Strasbourg and taught at the Lycée at Colmar, then at Paris-Neuilly. In 1949 he received his doctorate at Paris and became a professor at Lille. Since 1955 he has been at the Sorbonne, where he occupies the chair of Slavic history and civilization.

Professor Portal has specialized in Russian history from the eighteenth to the twentieth centuries, stressing social and economic problems. One of his studies was on the formation of the Soviet Union, while still another dealt with Peter the Great. His dissertation was an important work on *L'Oural* [the Ural River] *au XVIIIe Siècle* (1950). In other publications he has dealt with the manufactured products and the social classes in eighteen-century Russia, the origins of the industrial bourgeoisie in the nineteenth century, and the cotton industry in the early twentieth century. Professor Portal has made five trips to the Soviet Union. He is president of the *Institut d'études slaves*, director of the *Revue d'Histoire moderne et contemporaine*, and past president of the Société d'Histoire moderne (1956–1957). He is also on the editorial board of *Cahiers du Monde russe et soviètique* and director of studies at the *Ecole practique des Hautes Etudes*. His qualifications are eminent for assessing enlightened public opinion in Russia during the eighteenth and nineteenth centuries.

Russia as Seen by the French in the Eighteenth and First Part of the Nineteenth Centuries

Perhaps the subject of this paper may seem noncontroversial and of little historical value.* When we say, "Russia as Seen by the French . . . ," we mean by a very few Frenchmen. It is true that the image of Russia was not only that developed by informed people, who, in their reading, their daily life, their travels, had direct or indirect contact with Russian reality, or that of writers who adapted that reality to the needs of their argument. It was also that of businessmen and statesmen, whose opinion varied with the fluctuations of foreign policy, national and collective interests, and the necessity of justifying their actions. This image was not necessarily true, but it disclosed a certain continuity and an evolution in opinion over and above the myths that individual accounts and personal relations tended to create.

Voltaire's flatteries of Catherine II caught people's attention. But behind the testimony of writers whose real influence was not equivalent to their personalities, there existed a more widespread opinion, derived from objective views about relations between states. The opinion of administrators and merchants often had more weight than that of philosophers and frequenters of salons. Their view counted more and more, especially after 1815, when relations between France and Russia became closer, when works about Russia became more numerous, and when the new connections between the two countries involved a greater number of people, who were obliged by their occupations to examine Russia with more attention and composure.

But if Frenchmen had ties with Russian life through their travels or through associations with Russians living in France, or formed

---

* Translated by Professor John S. Curtiss, Duke University.

judgments from travelers, historians, intelligence agents, and publicists, who overwhelmed the public with spontaneous or interested opinions, their influence on the relations between the two countries was on the whole very minimal. Their opinion was only the froth on more solid realities; it was an analysis of a state of mind, a description that certainly was picturesque, but superficial. Such are the limits of a subject that is, however, not without interest.

It should first be noted that Russia, before the eighteenth century, was almost *terra incognita* for the French, and, for that matter, for Western Europeans in general (with a relative exception made for the English). Russia entered rapidly into European consciousness from the time of Peter the Great, but always seemed distant, inaccessible, foreign because of its differences from the West. For this reason it immediately became and remained an object of continuing curiosity, even when its relations with the Western states became closer and its political power was recognized in the West, and it kept this ambiguous position of a state geographically half-European, half-Asian. Public opinion interpreted its characteristics diversely, and never completely associated it with the West.

From the reign of Peter the Great, Russia took its place in the Royal Almanach among the powers of Europe (1718). The visit of the tsar to Paris, his military successes, conquests, and reforms, forced its recognition as a great state which had more and more influence in European politics, although it remained much behind the Western powers. But the importance of Russia became evident especially under Catherine II; her armies were present in central Europe and in the Mediterranean.

It was then that political relations were really established between France and Russia, exchanges sufficiently numerous for the formation, in enlightened opinion, of a clearer image of this vast country. But in the eighteenth century these relations were rarely nourished by observation or objective information. Rare were the French travelers who visited St. Petersburg, and brief were their stays; the contacts between the two countries through diplomats or Russians residing in France were superficial. Participation in the discovery of Siberia, in the exploration of Russia under the auspices of the Academy of Sciences and of Frenchmen and

Germans (whose works, like those of Pallas, were immediately translated into French), made the geography of the country better-known than its society.

The image formed of Russia at that time was determined by two kinds of considerations:

On the one hand, Russia, which had suddenly forged ahead to the status of a European power, and made an impression on the West only because of its acquisition of "modern" ways, was used as an argument in internal politics. French philosophers and economists, for personal reasons or to justify their critical attitude toward the French monarchy, developed, curiously, the theme of Catherine II's liberalism; the efforts of the Russian government to improve the administrative system were interpreted as victories over arbitrary power, as concessions to public opinion, as steps toward a regime of justice. The deceptive appearances of the 1760s were accepted and hailed as a reality.

Certainly self-interest had a part in the praises of Voltaire and Diderot, who were received by Catherine II; and the skillful publicity of the sovereign had its effect upon many minds, blinded by or half implicated in it. But what A. Lortholary[1] calls "the Russian mirage in France in the eighteenth century" was placed in a more general perspective, that of the epoch. Behind the dithyrambes and eulogies to the glory of Catherine II, one must see in this attitude the idea that retarded Russia, thanks to an eminent sovereign, would rejoin the civilized states of the West, and would follow the same roads traced by Peter the Great; that its progress would depend on the will of its leaders, who were enlightened despots; that it would enjoy the benefits of civilization with enlightenment from the West. Russia's past, its peculiar character, were not taken into account in the judgment of writers, who appraised the future of Russia from a Western, theoretical, utopian point of view.

The work of Lortholary analyzes well this attitude of some of the great French writers of the times, Voltaire and Diderot, whose lofty views of Russian reality gave an inexact idea of the real regime. The purchase of Diderot's library by Catherine II won for the latter Dorat's famous missive, which is as mediocre in form as it is servile in content.

Tu régis cet Empire immense
dont la nuit couvre l'Orient . . .
Combien il faut que l'on t'admire,
Et qu'on répète à l'univers,
Qu'une souveraine respire
Dont les yeux sont toujours ouverts
Sur l'infortuné qui soupire . . .
Quel grand exemple pour les Rois
Poursuis, illustre Catherine,
Tu sens ces grandes vérités
Par qui sont toujours cimentés
Ces trônes que le ciel destine
À de hautes propérités.[2]

This praise addressed to the Russian sovereign was nonetheless accompanied by a feeling of superiority in respect to a country that still seemed barbarous, a sentiment that was pushed to the point of caricature by Mercier de la Rivière. According to the expression of Catherine II (who promptly got rid of him), he imagined that the Russian people were walking on all fours. Said Catherine: "He very politely took the trouble to come from Martini just to stand us on our hind legs."

The importance of these opinions depended on the personal reputation of individuals. But these judges, in spite of appearances and their relations with the sovereigns, were not in touch with political realities. Their reactions were impassioned, and if their influence on the cultivated public was great, they alone did not wholly shape public opinion.

The existence of a rather numerous Russian colony in Paris itself, at the end of the reign of Elizabeth—members of great families attracted by the social and artistic life, who remained faithful subjects of their sovereigns—helped to give the small minority of residents who frequented the salons a favorable image of Russia.[3] The solidarity of the leading aristocracies, in contact only with one another, certainly limited the knowledge of things Russian that society circles could have. It did not, however, prevent the development in Paris on the eve of the Revolution, in the atmosphere of a rapprochement between the two states, of a strong infatuation for Russia, vague and sentimental in nature, one that went far beyond the limits of "society." Such signs as café bill-boards and plays inspired by Russian history testify to this infatuation which, in aristocratic milieus, more closely knit the masonic connections of one country with the other and produced enthusiastic volunteers for the anti-Turkish crusade.

In addition to these striking and spectacular bits of evidence, one must note more thoughtful opinions which were concerned with the economy and politics. Some of them, officially suggested or directed, took the form of hostile pamphlets, very detailed and without effect on the public, such as that of Sabathier de Cabres, "Mémoire drawn up by order of the King of France and published much later by a French agent at the court of St. Petersburg."[4] This violent indictment was a demonstration of Russia's incapacity to become a good commercial partner for France and piled up the most unfavorable comments; rapacity and prodigality, manual skill and technical backwardness, servile meanness and self-conceit, and basic dishonesty seemed to him the characteristics of a people for whom "commerce will always be in its infancy unless they succeed in changing their souls, habits, and governments."

But most of the judgments in this sphere were more subtle, and became so especially in the 1780s when great hopes were harbored by French commercial circles. Certainly the remoteness of Russia, the fact that its commerce with the West was monopolized by Holland and England (even French commodities that it imported) did not facilitate the establishment of direct economic relations. Nevertheless, the extension of French trade to Russia was the leitmotiv of an abundant literature. A recent article[5] thus reveals a better-informed opinion, closer to the realities, less concerned about broad parallels established for polemic ends than about precise information about the possibility of political and commercial agreements. The treaty of 1787, after all, had been of little import; it had been an illusory step toward a political rapprochement desired for reasons of the European balance of power; moreover, its eventual effects had been swept out by the Revolution. But through the negotiations that preceded it, the treaty contributed to the ties that developed as a result of prospects for expanded outlets for French wines and manufactures. We shall limit ourselves to alluding here to some of the numerous publications of the period that contain a serious analysis of economic life in Russia.[6]

Among the works relating to the history of Russia, there stands out Levesque's five-volume *History of Russia*, edited in 1782 and completed in 1783 by a two-volume history of the various peoples under Russian domination.[7] A serious and impartial work, praised by Karamzin, its author was "the first to proclaim his confidence in the people's gifts, his faith in the future of the Russian land."[8] But the reputation of the work scarcely passed outside academic and learned circles. And if Levesque evoked the posthumous praise of Malte-Brun, (à propos of the edition of 1822), Schnitzler did not mention it, in his bibliography, where, on the contrary, one finds the mediocre *History of Russia* by Le Clerc.

After 1815 the atmosphere of Franco-Russian relations had changed. The Napoleonic conquest, the continental blockade, the war of 1812, the retreat from Russia, and the invasion of France had established close ties between a state that had been first victorious and then conquered and a power that was becoming predominant in Europe.

The emigrés returning from Russia brought a more precise image of a country where some (Richelieu at Odessa) had had a fruitful career and had mingled directly in Russian life. The officers and soldiers of the Grande Armée had experienced the military qualities of the people in regular combat and in the resistance of the partisans. The French had had a close view of the Russians in Paris after the fall of the Empire. The excesses of the invasion had been limited, and the Russian army in Paris had profited from relative sympathy. The Bourbons owed their return to the tsar, who, at the beginning of the Restoration, through the intermediary of Richelieu, exercised a *de facto* protectorate over French politics. Once the French state had been released from these bonds of dependence, enlightened opinion in large part continued to be influenced by the traumatism of defeat, which the Crimean War erased.

French and Russian aristocrats had resumed contact in the salons, where emigrating Russians were more numerous especially after 1825; they were reserved in attitude toward a country of dissipation and revolution, but found in these salons a hospitable, more liberal environment. In the first years of the Restoration feelings about Russia, depending on the milieu, were formed by secret gratitude for a state that had re-established the former social order, and by national pride wounded by defeat. But the contrast between the evolution of the two states, one toward a more authoritarian regime under Nicholas I, the other toward a more liberal and bourgeois regime, after the Revolution of 1830, modified the bases of French judgments of Russia. These varied according to prejudices, interests, and political ideas, but were all founded on a more precise knowledge of Russian reality.

In a general way, the myth of liberalism gave place to criticism of a regime that oppressed liberties. Instead of scorn for an ignorant and uncouth people, there was pity for a servile mass whose existence was an anomaly in the Europe of the nineteenth century. A new fact accentuated the force of these sentimental reactions: the Polish revolt of 1831. In great measure, Russia, after 1830, was seen through the experience of Poland. The two currents of Polish emigration, aristocratic and democratic, joined together in condemnation of a regime that took no account of national aspirations and maintained serfdom. Their influence was notable in society circles, but also among the bourgeoisie, whose criticism of Russia was not influenced by aristocratic prejudices.

The contrast between the vision of a strong state that had imposed itself on Europe and of a subject people, suffering from arbitrary rule, created a feeling of fear mixed with admiration and a still protective pity. It appeared in the famous work of Custine, where the Russian people, congenial because of their good nature, their melancholy, their poetic soul, and their manual skills (the Russian, with his axe, is "a magician"), were presented as an indistinct mass "drunk with slavery" (the Russians are "voluntary automatons"), living in an atmosphere of secrecy and constraint, passively submissive to a meddling bureaucracy and to an unjust military regime—the instrument of a power that was dangerous because of its ambitions.[9]

Dangerous on the political plane, because of its military power but also because of the strength of its nationalist feelings, its faith in a European mission and, among the Slavophils, its scorn for

Western "decadence," Russia compelled the attention of the West in this period. At the very moment when Custine wrote his indictment, the beginnings of a brilliant Russian literature became known in France in the years 1840 and 1850, thanks to Mérimée and to the translations that appeared, particularly in the *Revue des Deux Mondes*. The illusions and the ignorance of the French of the eighteenth century gave place to more extended knowledge; and views on Russia were a mixture of continuing pessimism as to the political relations of the two states, and hope arising in Marseilles circles from the creation of Odessa, the improvement of the Ukraine, and the development of Mediterranean commerce. A Russia barely emerged from barbarism, still introverted, an outlet for European products and unscrupulous adventurers, was succeeded by a powerful Russia, an exporter of wheat and literary works, a nation that was debating its place in European society and was finding in enlightened opinion the echo of its internal problems.

The multiplication of publications about Russia extended knowledge of a great country, and produced more precise, varied, and well founded judgments. Cultivated Frenchmen who had sojourned in Russia furnished justifications for these judgments, which were then supported not only by general works of an historical character in the manner of the eighteenth and nineteenth centuries,[10] but also by statistical data, which France owed to German works.[11]

Indeed, after 1815 French knowledge of Russia rested in large part on the substantial works of German statisticians published in the first quarter of the nineteenth century, and on the Strasbourger Schnitzler, who utilized these works and listed all of them with interesting commentaries in the preface of his *Essai de statistique* (1829). The bases of his *Essai* rest on the German works of Storch Hassel, to which he added some French studies.

It would be interesting to search in the Parisian and provincial publications of the first half of the nineteenth century for the reaction to these accounts, which are at the same time geographical, historical, economic, and social and are sometimes totally taken over and recopied, as in the little work that appeared at Limoges in 1851 under the signature of Prieur de Sombreuil, entitled: "The beauties and marvels of the Russias of Europe and Asia," intended for children and young people, and published with the approval of the archbishop of Bordeaux. It is a moralizing work, referring to Schnitzler for its information on the characteristics of the people and judging them severely, as was common at that time.

Civilization is not yet very advanced in Russia, and it is very unevenly distributed because of the differences in geographic conditions. The peoples of Siberia are still, at least in great part, half-savage, while the populations of the West are influenced by European enlightenment. Western Russia took its place among the civilized nations very late; it has created little, finding it easier to borrow from others the fruit of their work. The result is that the upper classes have been enlightened at very little expense and in a very short time, while the lower classes remain plunged into profound shadows. Another result is that Russian civilization has taken on a superficial, frivolous, and imitative character. (p. 12)

At the moment when this little work of vulgarization, popularizing earlier, stereotyped images, appeared, direct knowledge of Russia had made great progress, thanks to French travelers who, more and more numerous, had brought home more precise observations on Russian society: Custine, already cited, was the most celebrated, but not the most interesting; others were Ancelot,[12] Marmier;[13] Léouzon le Duc.[14] This does not take into account German travelers such as Haxthausen,[15] whose work about the structure of the agrarian community in Russia was a revelation. Of the last Herzen said, in a letter addressed to Michelet in 1851, that before it appeared the Russian people were as little known as America before Columbus.[16]

There were also accounts of travelers, slight but perceptive, in which in lieu of precision in describing society and the regime, one is struck by the impressions of discovery, resulting from the continuing astonishment of the French, even when in Russia, at this strange country. The journey of Théophile Gautier to St. Petersburg[17] adds scarcely anything to our knowledge of Russia except the description (without doubt the best we have) of the *troikas*, *drozhkis*, and other vehicles of transport. But some reflections went further. Théophile Gautier already was gaining a certain image of Russia, fixed by his childhood memories:

While still a child, Moscow preoccupied our imagination, and we often remained in ecstasy, on the Quai Voltaire, before the window of a dealer in engravings, where large panoramic aquatint views of Moscow were exhibited, colored according to the processes of Demarne or of Debucourt, as they often did in those days. These onion-shaped bell-towers, these cupolas topped with a cross with little chains, these painted houses, these personnages with long beards and wide hats, these women with their hair dressed with a *pivoinik* and wearing the short tunic belted under the arms, seemed to us to belong to the world of the moon, and the idea of ever making a trip there never entered our mind. Moreover, since Moscow had been burned, what interest could this pile of cinders offer? It took us a long time to admit that the city had been rebuilt, and that all the old monuments had not been swallowed up in the flames.[18]

But in recalling this image the poet did not engulf himself in the contemplation of the past. Admiring the theater of Moscow and its modern appointments, he made this remark: "In Russia, everything is too large and seems made for a future population."[19]

There were, however, some prudent travelers who feared to compromise themselves. Balzac, who went in 1843 to be with Madame Hanska, did not, as the Russians had hoped, write a refutation of Custine's book. He gave the reason for this in a letter to his love (January 31, 1844):

They say that I refused enormous sums for writing a certain refutation. What stupidity! Your sovereign is too shrewd not to know that a hired pen has not the least authority. . . . They will understand that I write *neither for, nor against Russia.* . . . At my age, when one is free of all political opinion, does one create antecedents for himself?

Knowledge of Russia had made progress also, because closer ties between Russia and France after 1815, on various levels—political, economic—furnished a mass of diplomatic and consular documents whose content was the basis for the conversation of the salons and for articles in French reviews.

Finally, Russia was then becoming a nation of poets and novelists, who had direct or indirect relations with French writers. People no longer held the scornful opinions of Russia which never varied in the preceding century. And it had not been necessary for this change to await the defeat of Napoleon. Already in the time of the Consulate, Prince Bielozersky, a cosmopolitan Russian nobleman, writing in French, published in Moscow in 1802 his second *Epistle to the French,* in which he evoked this new climate of equality. After saluting the rebirth of France following the revolutionary horrors, he exclaimed:

> Freed tigers, sublime madmen, great men
> I write again to you: at last we are on the same level.[20]

A climate of equality existed but was certainly unstable. The situation had reached the point at which Russia inspired some fear, at which its regime, weighing on oppressed nationalities such as Poland, was condemned without appeal, at which the memory of defeat inspired rancor and passionate reactions. A man like Ancelot struggled against this feeling, but when passing near the triumphal gate at Tsarskoe-Selo, near St. Petersburg, which commemorated the victories of Alexander I, he could not restrain himself from crying out: "Let us not stay near this monument, whose appearance makes such recent wounds in the heart of a Frenchman bleed." And on the road back, stopping on Sparrow Hills and viewing Moscow, as Napoleon had done fifteen years earlier, he sought in a poem with a singular ending a sort of revenge for past humiliations:

Ainsi, sur la montagne, aux rayons du matin, Vers un temps qui n'est
    plus, égarant ma pensée,
O France, O mon pays de ta gloire passée, je réveillais l'écho lointain.
Peut-être de tes fils, au fond de ces vallées, ma voix consolera les
    ombres exilées:
Loin de ton doux soleil, de tes fertiles champs, ton nom seul à mon
    luth arracha quelques chants;
Et quand de la Moskva parcourant les rivages d'un peuple sans passé
    j'épiais l'avenir
Dans ses vastes cités, dans ses forêts sauvages, j'interrogeais ton
    souvenir,
Je t'ai trouvé partout . . . aux portes de l'Asie, il veille, il parle seul aux
    mortels inspirés;
Et sur ces bords longtemps des Muses ignorés, il a semé la poésie.[21]

The memory of the defeat, but also the Polish question, determined the severity of the judgments and perpetuated this traditional image, in part exact, but too black, of a Russia scarcely worthy of being numbered among civilized countries. The criticism reached the point of pure and simple calumny in the attacks of Michelet (profoundly moved by the misfortunes of Poland), which

Herzen raised again, and which he took the trouble to refute in a long rebuttal.

In an article that appeared from August 18 to September 17, 1851, in the revue *l'Evénement,* entitled "The legend of Kosciusko," Michelet described the Russian people and, carried away by his Polonophile sentiments, brought up earlier affirmations of the lying and dishonest spirit, the absence of a moral sense, that, he said, characterized them.

Herzen, in a letter of September 22, 1851, replied to these unjust accusations. His argument, which carefully distinguished between official Russia and the Russian people, and explained the apparent failings of the latter by the regime of oppression, had no effect on the general public. The "Legend of Kosciusko" duly took its place in the collection of *Democratic Legends* that was later published, and that the reputation of the author assured a wide influence.

But parallel to this current of opinion supported by great talents, which again raised polemics, a more complete and objective knowledge of Russia became widespread. One must mention again these travelers such as Ancelot, even Marmier, who, in spite of the brevity of their contacts with the Russians, had been able to observe and analyze Russian reality with much intelligence and impartiality.

Ancelot had certainly been, more than Custine, one of the most remarkable observers of Russia and, in particular, of the Russian people. If one reflects that he wrote in 1827, at a moment when, in the West, they were scarcely fathoming the diverse conditions of the peasant mass, which, from a distance, seemed uniform in its servitude, one cannot fail to be struck by his penetration. Among other things he recognized that these serfs, these "slaves," lived under widely differing conditions, that some of them had even been authorized by their lords to possess serfs themselves: "Is it not a strange spectacle, my dear Xavier," he wrote, to his correspondent, "—to find men who are at once serfs and despots?" Ancelot understood that for peasants to be free meant for them to possess, and he made a distinction, very remarkable for a Westerner, between fertile and infertile domains, between the serfs on desmesne lands and the serfs on *obrok* [rent]. (The eventual emancipation of both, following natural and social conditions, placed the landowners in very different situations.)

He described without passion and with fairness the character of the Russian people and the cosmopolitanism of its aristocracy, who spoke foreign languages rather than their own and were singularly separated from the masses. He criticized the system of private tutors of foreign origin, who could not bring up Russians. "To meet," he said, "real patriotism, one must seek it among the people." And he exclaimed, with Béranger: "I like a Russian to be Russian and an Englishman to be English."

In reality, this cosmopolitanism was on the surface. Ancelot recognized, moreover, that the nobility was transformed by the educational system "into an innumerable regiment, and the Empire into a vast barracks." At this time, moreover, the private tutor was beginning to disappear; except in the greatest families, the young nobles generally received public education.

Well before Custine, Ancelot sensed the dangerous strength of a people, full of vigor, cleverness, and endurance, who were the instrument of an ambitious state and on the path of progress. Like the Occidentals, and in this period, like the greater part of the cultivated Russians, who considered themselves the heirs of Peter the Great rather than the descendants of Ivan the Terrible, he recognized only modern Russia. Standing before the Church of St. Basil the Blessed at Moscow, he could not prevent himself from condemning "this bizarre creation of a disordered imagination, the product of an epoch of barbarism."

On the eve of the Crimean War, at the moment of tension between the two countries, the image of Russia presented to the French for propaganda purposes resembled the most severe traditional judgments; but even in the work of a Léouzon le Duc (*La Russie contemporaine*), published in 1853, the pamphlet revealed truths that evidenced a deeper knowledge of certain aspects of Russian life. Without doubt Léouzon le Duc denounced what he called "the permanent imposture of Nicholas I," of whom he said: "And there is the puritanical monarch who was so strongly scandalized by the accession of Louis-Philippe, who for so long refused to recognize Leopold, who today rejects the Queen of Spain, and who consented to deal with the nephew of Napoleon, now on the throne, only as a good friend." He reproached him for his autocracy, which he distinguished from monarchy and despotism. He reproached Russia for its conquests, its policy toward the subject peoples, and in particular, in the wake of Michelet, for its anti-Polish attitude. He rejected the Russian people as Asiatics, accused them of fanaticism, of barbarism, of lack of creativity. The defects traditionally attributed to the Russians appear once more in his description: obstinacy, fatalism, carelessness, laziness, lying, a proneness to theft. "Let us say it frankly, no, Russia is not a civilizing power."

Despite the excessive or inexact statements in this pamphlet, certain remarks do not lack penetration, in particular those that concern the interior development of the country, the contrasts between the reforming activity of the tsar and the effective results of the measures taken and between the image of the country that Russian propaganda imposed on the foreign world and its real aspect. Thus the reign of Nicholas I had been marked by a certain progress in public education, but the creation of numerous scholastic establishments did not disguise the fact that the school system was still backward. Léouzon le Duc showed clearly that he had not let himself be taken in "by this great bustle of academies, schools, institutes of every kind," when at most 350,000 to 400,000 persons participated in the benefits of instruction (a quarter of the above were still Poles). And he accused Russia of throwing "dust in the eyes" of a Europe that remained very superior to it.

One might find similarly interesting comments in the work of Marmier,[22] whose travels date from 1849. Marmier started from the Polish situation to describe and judge Russia. And after showing the weight of Russian repression at Warsaw following the insurrection of 1831, the silence imposed on Poland, the efforts at Russification, he reproached Russia for its ambition to be a Western power, when its mission, according to him, was Asiatic.

In his very harsh critique of Russian society, where he rightly marked the contrast between a privileged minority and an uncultivated and superstitious mass, the fear of a development toward progress that would give Russia invincible power cropped up. For him, the "barbarism" of the Russian people—a common term—was only outward.

Let us observe with impartiality all the natural gifts, physical strength, patience and neglected seeds in this people, to whom we still daily apply the epithet of barbarous; let us think of the development that even the most restricted instruction could give them, and I leave it to be guessed how far they will go when they have put their hand to the tree of knowledge and steeped their minds in the living spring of civilization.[23]

Russia was, however, less frightening than it appeared from afar, because of internal weaknesses that the despotism had not succeeded in concealing.

Russia is in reality much less frightening than we imagine from afar, when we observe it only on the surface and in its external manifestations. Sooner or later, the twenty millions of serfs who still can only follow compliantly the law that is imposed on them in the ranks of the army or in the anti-chambers of their masters, will attain these ideas of intellectual development which awaken the pride of man, and then will the despotic power that has ruled them for so long be strong enough to maintain them in their passive obedience? This we cannot logically admit.

Judgment leveled against the political regime against the arbitrariness of power, polarized criticism upon the sovereign, upon the state. What was troublesome in the popular condition appeared to be the result of obsolete or excessive regimentation imposed by the tsar, and not the expression of the relations of social categories. From this so many tendentious allegations and inexact interpretations developed.

It was Ancelot (p. 70) who showed the connection between the Russian spirit of servitude and the fact that the coachmen of St. Petersburg had a number on their clothing and not on their carriages.

It was Marmier (p. 107), who declared, in a judgment completely contrary to reality, "It can be said that the peasants of the lords, although subject to the most severe working conditions and taxes, are in general in a better condition than those of the crown, because they are closer to the lord's justice."

These notations, which smack of reporting, and betray very superficial observation, did not prevent these travelers, in general, from seeing Russia as it really was.

The French in high society had other means of information. As in the eighteenth century Russia was, in fact, to a certain degree represented in Paris by numerous aristocrats, elegant and refined, whom one met in the salons of Mesdames Récamier, Ancelot, Cuvier, and Guizot. Not all of them were of the type of singular persons who were said to be so eccentric that, scarcely arrived in Paris, they offered to modistes and to ballet-dancers their hands, their fortunes, and their slaves.[24]

Some of them were in the foreground, such as Nicholas Alexander Melgunov (1804–1857), essayist and bibliophil, Alexander Ivan Turgeniev (1774–1886), historian, brother of the Decembrist Nicholas Turgeniev, with whom he exchanged a voluminous correspondence, and his friend Peter André Viazemsky, critic and poet; and such as the writers Vasilii André Zhukovsky (1783–1852) and Eugène Abram Boratinsky (1820–1845). These very Parisian Russians also appeared in two Russian salons frequented by French businessmen, diplomats, military men, writers, those of Madame Svechina and Princess Mecherskaia. Without doubt they helped to give the French aristocracy and upper bourgeoisie some idea of the Russian nobility, but in this they did not add anything new. For the type of magnanimous Russian noble, open and generous, ostentatious and lavish with money and with his emotions, was a classic image.

What was new was that these nobles then represented a bond between two cultures, and that through them, little by little, the first great writers in Russian literature became known in France. In this respect progress was rapid from the years 1820–1830, when the only names mentioned in France were those of Pushkin and the historian Karamzin, to the 1850s, the period of "Russian fervor," when knowledge of the literary works translated from the Russian became fuller, more precise. But in the meantime—especially after 1840—all sorts of activity went on in translation, in the publication of works in the reviews, in the salons. Beginning in 1844, Louis Viardot made Gogol known. Prince Elim Mechersky (1808–1844), about whom the recent work of André Mazon adds so many interesting facts, who had lived in Paris for a long time, and who from 1833 until his death had been more or less officially charged with a diplomatic mission by Uvarov, Minister of Public Instruction, had veritably set himself the task of making Russia known to Europe and in particular to France. He frequented the Parisian salons and also received in the salon of his wife, Princess Mecherskaia, the greatest living French writers, Alfred de Vigny, and Alexandre Dumas père, to whom, very oddly, he had given the taste for Russian tobacco. He translated the Russian writers for the French: Pushkin, Zhukovsky, Krylov, Countess Rostopchin, and these translations were published in collections in the 1840s.

Prince Mechersky was in correspondence with Victor Hugo, to whom he sent a piece of verse written by the Countess Rostopchin, dedicated "to Victor Hugo," who had not yet been elected to the Académie Française (August 14, 1840). Recalling a conversation that he had with Victor Hugo a year earlier, he added: "Public opinion in Russia, in order to make you understand its shocked admiration, has chosen one of the prettiest mouths in the world, one of the prettiest women of St. Petersburg society, and one of the best Russian poets. She has done only what was owing to you. May the immortals pardon her for being more French than the Académie Française."

Victor Hugo replied on August 27, 1840: "All the Academies in the world are not worth two pages written by this charming and noble hand."

The activity of Prince Elim Mechersky was not centered only in Paris. His movements throughout France revealed the existence of provincial centers that were very much interested in Russia. On June 28, 1830, he gave a lecture at Marseilles on Russian poetry. Traveling salesman of literature, he also did the same for a certain form of rather conciliatory patriotic orthodoxy which he compared with the forms of militant Catholicism. He went to Strasbourg, where he had a conversation in 1833 with Abbé Beautin, whose researches appeared to him to be "the source for a Christian science that would reconcile . . . the Occident and the Orient" and would "merge the different churches into a single church of science." An exchange of letters ensued, which lasted three years (1834–1837).[25]

Knowledge of this recent Russian literature could not go beyond the narrow circles of the salons and the few readers of the reviews. It would be interesting to measure this audience in the 1850s, when it was rather extensive, but held judgments that were not always favorable.

Literary Russia was in fact appreciated universally by persons of taste for the aesthetic value of its works. But the greater number appreciated it from a very narrowly national point of view: The Boeotians of critcism did not feel the enthusiasm of the habitués of the salons where the works of Russian writers were presented— an enthusiasm in which there was an element of snobbery. They saw in this young literature an imitation, a reflection of the West, although they admitted the existence of original talents and of recent, but "praiseworthy" accomplishments. This is the term used by Léouzon le Duc who, in *la Russie contemporaine* (1853), with much nimbleness depicted Lomonosov, a man of the Renaissance, Karamzin, who patterned himself after France, and Pushkin, understudy of Lord Byron. After citing the names of some contemporary Russian writers, who he thought bore some evidence of national talent, he completed the balance-sheet in these terms:

Four great names figure in its literary Olympus: Lomonosov, Karamzin, Zhukovsky, and Pushkin. What are their titles to glory? Lomonosov is the man of the Renaissance; he presents himself adorned with Greek and Latin: he is the translator of Homer, Plato, Horace, and Ovid. Karamzin patterns himself after France, Zhukovsky after Germany. As for Pushkin, is it incorrect to describe him as the understudy of Lord Byron? This is not to say, assuredly, that in some writings of these authors some reflections of pure nationality do not spring forth here and there; but, in short, such is not at all the general, dominant, characteristic tone. But that is what counts above all, when it is a question of representing the literary genius of a country.

However, a sort of reaction seems to have appeared, in recent years, against a tendency that has prevailed so long. At first this reaction was manifested by excesses; works emerged, inspired by a jealous hatred of foreign lands rather than by a sincere love of nationality. But, aside from these crises of delirium, it can already boast of rather praiseworthy results. Krylov has fables that owe nothing either to Phèdre or to Lafontaine; Kamakov, some tragedies and some lyric bits freed of all imitation. Furthermore I shall cite Gogol, the unfortunate Gogol, who died disavowing himself, whose original novels and biting satires MM. Prosper Merimée, Louis Viardot and Philippe Douhaire made known; Venevitinov and Viasemsky, melancholic poets; Madame Pavlov and Countess Rostopchin, gracious muses as well as charming women. Let us add the eccentric and profound Lermontov, miserably killed in a duel in the Caucasus; the novelists Muraviev, Batushkov, and Sagoshkin, the novelist philosopher Odoevsky and Count Sologub, who handles the most varied subjects with the verve of a man of letters and the grace of a great lord. There are those who also include among the national literary men of Russia MM. Bulgarin and Nicholas Grech: The first has, in truth, distinguished himself by some very interesting novels of manners and by a remarkable talent as a journalist; the second, by his numerous editions of learned grammars, brilliant contributions to the national language.

Such is then the balance-sheet of Russian literature; such are, at least, its most important figures. Doubtless its richness will appear as very poor. It is certain that much better things could be expected from a power so ambitious and so haughty toward the West. What are, then, its twenty or thirty literary men, compared to those brilliant phalanxes with which the other countries of Europe are honored? The contrast will appear even more striking if one fixes his attention on their works. Let us suppress Karamzin's histories, which, incomplete as they are, form, however, the chief serious monument of Russian literature; let us suppress some poems of Pushkin, Derzhavin's ode to God, some fables by Krylov, some romances or novels of Lermontov or of Gogol, finally some more or less brilliant productions of five or six other authors, cited or not in the preceding enumeration— what will remain to Russia to justify its right of citizenship among literary nations?[26]

Finally, as in the eighteenth century, the business world was interested in Russia. The projects and attempts to develop southern Russia were coming to fruition; new hopes were rising, but also new fears. These hopes were soon disappointed, but they gave rise to an abundant literature that has not yet been much studied by investigators.

France of the Restoration and the July Monarchy considered seriously the development of a new realm of commercial exploitation in southern Russia, which, after the creation of the port of Odessa at the beginning of the century, was becoming a wheat-exporting region, and, even more important, a zone for intermediary exchanges between the interior of the country and the Mediterranean. It was out of the question for France to have anything but a modest role in the Baltic, where commerce was in the hands of the English, Dutch, and Hamburg merchants and where French merchandise was transported almost entirely in foreign ships.

The Black Sea raised hopes of an increased trade, and also of the effective participation of a French merchant marine in this trade. Marseilles circles were particularly interested in projects in which in general they had the initiative and which they considered above all from the point of view of the exportation of Mediterranean products (such as wines, fruits, oil, and pickled olives) to Odessa. But this commerce was tied to the exportation of Russian products and in particular of Ukrainian wheat, and the Marseilles schemes very quickly collided with the protectionist policy of France in respect to foreign grain and with the resistance of agricultural interests. Moreover, in spite of the development of commerce on the Black Sea, where Odessa became the second port of the Empire, and the increase in trade between France and Russia, the presence of the French merchant marine in the Black Sea remained insignificant: In 1844, six French ships of 1744 tons, against 53 Russian vessels of 18,210 tons, and 219 ships of other countries (chiefly Greek), of 66,837 tons.

These projects, however, instigated numerous reports from French consuls in Odessa; they entailed a serious study of Russia, of the condition of the southern provinces, of the activity of the Black Sea ports, and they evoked a response in the French press, where commentaries appeared inspired by fear of the agricultural power of Russia. Systematic research would be necessary here. From a mere sampling let us take this interesting article, which was printed in the *Moniteur Industriel,* entitled: "Why the French farmer cannot compete with the Russian farmer."[27]

The arguments given here are based on a serious examination of economic and social conditions in Ukrainian agriculture and of the wheat trade in the Ukraine, where the net price was low, the article said, because of the use of servile labor in production and transportation. To open French ports to Ukrainian wheat would be to ruin French agriculture. And following the article, a farmer added some lines expressing the idea that the development of the Ukraine was limited by the lack of export markets, that the opportunity to import grain into France would triple its commerce and would dangerously reinforce the economic potential of Russia.

These were doubtless oversimplified and traditional arguments. But they were at once refuted and discussed, and in this debate between merchants and agricultural proprietors a much more precise image of Russia appeared, which, to be sure, applied to one part of Russia, to the recently developed southern provinces, in this respect different from the country as a whole. But the debate touched as much on more general problems, particularly on the rôle of serfdom. This was, it is true, the eve of its abolition, and it made much ink flow in Russia and abroad. Russian peasant society was then much better known in the West. The discussions about serfdom, however, forced reconsideration of the totality of economic conditions in Russia. The latter no longer appeared powerful because of this institution that gave it unpaid labor, but on the contrary seemed hampered by it, inasmuch as this labor was quite unproductive.

In regard to the Ukraine, Molinari's letters on Russia, published in 1861, show conclusively that the corvée in the Ukrainian lands exporting wheat was not very heavy, that paid labor was more and more widespread, and that low net prices were the result of other causes. But the idea of Russian power based on agriculture was erased on the eve of the Crimean War. Reports of consuls and travelers proved the difficulty of developing the Ukraine, the slowness of its growth, and emphasized the permanent causes for the economic backwardness of Russia.

Would other Frenchmen have been able to make Russia known to France: those who resided in Russia and took part in its activity over long periods? For Russia was still, in the first half of the nineteenth century, a country of adventure; but it was a bourgeois adventure, offering sure opportunities for enrichment, without risk, to the skilled technicians it needed.

We know that after the protective tariff of 1822 the textile industry, particularly that of printed cotton, where traditional block-printing gradually was replaced by cylinder printing, made great progress in Russia. The role of the French of Alsace, of Mulhouse, had been considerable in the modernization of printing and dyeing. Numerous mills in the Moscow region owed their organization to them. One should not be astonished at the advantageous contracts that were granted to them; in comparison with these, the contracts of the technicians recruited by Peter the Great at the beginning of the eighteenth century cut a poor figure.

Thus one George Steinbach, in 1833, signed a contract for four years giving him the right to twenty-five percent of the profits realized annually by the firm and to free quarters, food, and a carriage. Moreover, whatever might be a result of the transaction, a minimum of 14,000 [rubles] was assured to him. A chemist,

Léonard Schwartz, had worked in Moscow, for Titov, under almost analogous conditions. He earned 20,000 rubles (perhaps 23,000 francs) per year and was able to save 4000 rubles in three months. The Mulhouse industrial community unceasingly supplied technicians, most of whom returned home upon the expiration of their contracts and often were replaced by other members of their families. They knew Russia, then, or at least certain aspects of Russian life in these spheres. But on reading the letters sent by these specialists, one perceives that this knowledge was very limited, that it was not sustained by a general culture or by an interest in the country and in the people. Without doubt, a study of the relations between industrial Alsace and Russia has not been made. Only a few investigations have been attempted by local scholars, dealing with a limited number of cases.[28]

It certainly appears that these Frenchmen had penetrated little into Russian life, that they had been absorbed by their work, that they had, moreover, deliberately avoided mingling in polite society, and that their judgments reflected their power of observation less than their prejudices. Their opinion of the Russian worker was scarcely different from that of French employers of their own workers in the same period. Let us listen to what the chemist Schwartz wrote in 1843 to his compatriot Camille Koechkin, who was about to leave for Russia:

Here is the rule of conduct that my instinct prescribed for me in Russia regarding the workers and the nation in general: The worker is lazy by nature, dirty and without self-respect; make up your mind to it; *never get angry with them;* rather have pity on them and try to stimulate them by the fondness that they have for you, to make yourself obeyed by the intellectual superiority that they recognize in you.

Society in Russia is rare, and you will be more or less reduced to yourself, above all for learning. The society of nobles is very expensive; gambling and pleasures are their chief occupations; they spend much money without enjoying it.

Do not mix in politics, *not at all;* the police know everything, even your letters if they suspect you. Moreover, in Russia politics can bring you only disagreements, never satisfaction.

Thus French residents in Russia, insofar as we know their reactions, do not seem to have brought much knowledge of Russia to France.

Do these samplings of opinions, touching on very varied spheres of activities, lead to some general observations?

The sources that permitted soundings of French opinion about Russia and the Russian people, were, of course, more and more abundant to the extent that political and commercial relations developed and that Russia further asserted itself as a powerful state. But their abundance should not create an illusion. The serious, documented studies descriptive of Russia of the period, that were sources of knowledge, but at the same time bore or implied value judgments, were in great part of German origin. Their content, utilized, commented on, was found in French works devoted to Russia in the first half of the nineteenth century. But apart from the serious works, which had very few readers, most descriptions of Russia, without getting far from the reality, perpetuated, through omission, a deformed, stereotyped image, in which the elements of progress were concealed or projected into a distant future. It was not the Russia of the present that was evoked, but a Russia of the past, immobile under its Western clothing.

This false image appeared in popular opinion through works of vulgarization, always a decade or more behind, and it still lived at the very moment when the great turning-point of the 1850s and 1860s occurred in the knowledge of Russia. An élite of Russian writers then emerged, which excited the interest and the admiration of the cultivated French public. The brutal shock of the Crimean War, the great reforms of the 1860s in Russia, all at once brought about the disappearance of the 1812 defeat complex and inspired a literature, better informed, if not more objective in its interpretations. The discussions concerning Russia's role in the world, the characteristics of its people, its views of the future, that until then had been centered around some very celebrated works (Custine, Haxthausen), developed in the current press.

The exploitation of these sources has only begun; it must be pursued in the provinces, in order to collect scattered documents: textbooks, articles in reviews and newspapers, brochures. Marseilles and Mulhouse circles were not the only provincial centers interested in Russia. A complete study of this kind must be made.

One can say that the knowledge that the French *could* have of Russia was solid, that the means to obtain this knowledge existed, but that the traditional image (in part exact) of a barbarous people and of a backward country influenced every judgment more or less. Progress was felt, but scarcely accepted; for the reaction of enlightened French opinion was dominated by the memory of defeat, fear of a powerful state, and also by a feeling of time-honored superiority (originating in the seventeenth century?), which later flat contradictions never succeeded in dispelling. A simplistic reaction of bad humor and pride was the most ordinary one. The opinion of businessmen and of all those for whom Russia had economic value, was more objective, but made less noise. It was difficult to ascertain, even though it was that of a by no means negligible number of Frenchmen.

In a word, the opinion that cultivated Frenchmen had of Russia had no effect upon the state of relations between the two countries, whether this opinion was true or false. It tells more about the French than about Russia. This basic contrast between information that was very often valid and enduring national prejudices, between a scarcely perceived, almost subterranean truth, and judgments inspired by present interest alone, enables us to clarify certain traits of French mentality and feeling rather than to give an account of Russian reality.

Notes

1.   Albert Lortholary, *Le mirage russe en France au XVIIIᵉ siècle* (1952)— an excellent study, limited, however, to some enlightened minds, above all Voltaire and Diderot. This work is especially useful for its bibliography, which permits one to go beyond the somewhat narrow point of view of the author.

2.   You rule over this immense Empire,
Whose night covers the Orient . . .
How much must one admire you
And repeat to the universe,
That a sovereign breathes
Whose eyes are always open
On the unfortunate one who sighs . . .
What a great example for Kings
You set, illustrious Catherine.

You sense these great truths
By which those thrones
That Heaven destines for great prosperity
Are always reinforced.
(C. J. Dorat, *Épître à Catherine II*. Paris, 1765).

3.   See Léonce Pingaud. *Les Français en Russie et les Russes en France*. Paris: 1886.

4.   Sabathier de Cabres, *Catherine II; sa cour et la Russie en 1772*. Paris: 1862.

5.   Van Regemorter, "Commerce et politique: Préparation et négociation du traité Franco-russe de 1787," *Cahiers du monde russe et soviétique*, July–September, 1963.

6.   Marbault, *Essai sur le commerce de la Russie*, 1777; Leclerc, *Atlas du commerce*, 1787; Schérer, *Histoire du commerce*, 1788.

7.   P. C. Levesque, *Histoire de la Russie*. Paris: 1782.

8.   André Mazon, "Pierre-Charles Levesque, humaniste, historien, et moraliste," *Revue des Études slaves*, 1963, pp. 7–66.

9.   Marquis de Custine, *Voyage en Russie: La Russie en 1839*. Paris: 1843.

10.   Comte de Ségur, *L'Histoire de la Russie et de Pierre le Grand*. Paris: 1829.

11.   J. H. Schnitzler, *Essai d'une statistique générale de l'Empire de Russie, accompagnée d'aperçus historiques*. Paris: 1829; and *L'Empire des tsars, un 7e des terres du globe, au point actuel de la Science*. Paris: 1856–1869; with the bibliography given in his *Essai de statistique*, cited on the page following.

12.   F. Ancelot, *Six mois en Russie. Lettres écrites à M. X. B. Saintine*, 1827.

13.   X. Marmier, *Lettres sur la Russie, la Finlande, et la Pologne*, 1866. His travels date from 1849.

14.   L. Léouzon le Duc, *La question russe* 1853; see also his *La Russie et la révolution européenne*, 1854.

15.   Auguste de Haxthausen, Baron, *Etudes sur la situation intérieure, la vie nationale, et les institutions rurales de la Russie*. Berlin: 1847, 1848, 1853.

16.   A. I. Hertsen, *Polnoe sobranie sochinenii i pisem* (complete collection of works and letters. Published by heirs of the author, n.d., vol. 6 (1850–1851). Letter to Michelet: "Russkii narod i sotsializm [The Russian people and socialism]." See p. 189.

17.   Théophile Gautier, *Voyage en Russie*, 1866.

18. *Voyage*, vol. 2, p. 22.

19. *Voyage*, vol. 2, pp. 141–142.

20. André Mazon, *Deux écrivains russes en France*. Paris: 1964.

21.   Thus, on the mount, in the morning rays,
             Letting my thought wander to a past that is no more,
             O France, my country, of thy past glory
             I awakened the distant echo.
             Perhaps of thy sons, deep in these valleys,
             My voice will console the exiled shades:
             Far from thy soft sun, from thy fertile fields,
             Thy name alone will tear from my lute some songs:
             And when, the Moskva's banks traversing,
             Of a people without a past I espied the future,
             In its vast cities, in its savage forests,
             I consulted thy memory,
             I found thee everywhere. . . .at the gates of Asia,
             France watches, it alone speaks to inspired mortals;
             And on these borders, long ignored by the muses,
             It has sowed the seed of poetry. (Ancelot, pp. 421–422.)

22. Marmier, *Lettres sur la Russie*, p. 259.

23. *Lettres*, p. 125.

24. Novel of Saint-Aguet, *Sous les marroniers*, which appeared in the *Salon littéraire*, March 17, 1842.

25. For all that concerns the activity of Prince Elim Metchersky, see André Mazon, *Deux écrivains russes en France*. Paris: 1964.

26. Léouzon le Duc, *La Russie contemporaine*, 1853, pp. 183–187.

27. *Moniteur Industriel*, September, 1851 (*Arch, Nat.*, F. 122286), information communicated by M. Ph. Van Regemorter.

28. André Brandt, "Essai sur les Mulhousiens en Russie au XIXe siècle," *Bulletin du Musée historique de Mulhouse*, vol. 67 (1959), pp. 77–97.

⤳ ROBERT F. BYRNES

Robert F. Byrnes, born in 1917 in Waterville, New York, received a B.A. from Amherst (1939) and a Ph.D. from Harvard (1947). He has taught at Swarthmore, Rutgers, and the University of Indiana, where he is professor of history and director of the International Affairs Center. His earlier studies dealt with modern France, while his later work has involved Russian history, the Slavic world, and international relations. He has been president of the American Catholic Historical Association, chairman of the American Historical Association Committee on Reproduction of Slavic Documents, and an editor of the *Slavic Review*. He is the author of *Antisemitism in Modern France: Vol. I: The Prologue of the Dreyfus Affair,* and is at present preparing the second volume. He has published a *Bibliography of American Publications on East Central Europe, 1945–1957,* and is general editor of a series entitled *East Central Europe under the Communists.* A major interest of his is Konstantin Pobedonostsev, a nineteenth-century Russian jurist and state official, about whom he has written various essays. Professor Byrnes is now completing a full-length biography of Pobedonostsev. The nature of his research places Professor Byrnes in an ideal position to discuss Russian views of France in the nineteenth century.

Some Russian Views of France in the Nineteenth Century

As Russia became a more integral part of Europe in the nineteenth century, the knowledge that educated Russians had of France and of other parts of Western Europe inevitably increased. Russians—in particular members of the nobility—began to develop clearly defined views of France. This was so despite the backwardness of Russian culture, the low level of Russian education generally, and the rest of the world's ignorance about that vast Russian group described by the seventeenth-century archpriest Avvakum as a ". . . self-sufficient majority untouched by any cultural influence." Even the best-educated Russians, however, often were poorly or inaccurately informed, so that their views on occasion were both shallow and indefinite and changed in remarkable ways from time to time.

Russian interest in France, or more accurately the interest some educated Russians developed concerning France, began in medieval times, but it was only in the middle of the eighteenth century that a handful of educated Russians (most of them in the aristocracy and residents of Moscow or St. Petersburg) began to develop a serious interest and to acquire the kinds of knowledge from travel and study that enabled them to create a coherent view of France and of French culture. The apogee of French influence within Russia was probably the period from 1780 to 1815, but French influence grew remarkably beginning about 1740 and remained high throughout the nineteenth century.[1]

The reign of Catherine the Great is, of course, the great landmark for intellectual relations between Russia and France, and the age of the Enlightenment in France therefore occupies a central position. It has been estimated that three-quarters of the books imported and read in Russia in the last third of the eighteenth century were published in France and that most of these books dealt with France itself. Thus, by the beginning of the nineteenth century, the established tradition as reflected in reading and travel made France the principal subject of study by both aristocrats and bureaucrats in the Russian empire.

Basically, Russia was afflicted with "idol worship" in regard to France throughout the last part of the eighteenth century. This enthusiasm about every aspect of French culture survived the powerful waves of disenchantment produced by the violence of 1793 and even by the invasion of Napoleon in 1812.[2] During the French Revolutionary period several journals that translated articles of all kinds from French newspapers and magazines and selections from the classics of the age of Louis XIV and those of the eighteenth century were published in St. Petersburg and in Moscow. Even during the period of strictest censorship, Russian journals carried great quantities of information about France translated from French books and journals. Indeed, a high proportion of the material published in Russia even during these critical years was French.[3]

Perhaps the most revealing demonstration of this attitude is the immense work carried on between 1796 and 1835 by Professor Peter Pobedonostsev, the father of the celebrated Constantine Petrovich Pobedonostsev, the civilian head of the Russian Orthodox Church from 1880 to 1905, who is known in history as the grand inquisitor, or the conservative evil genius of the last years of the Old Regime. Professor Pobedonostsev, who graduated from a Russian Orthodox seminary in 1796 but chose not to remain a priest, served as a teacher in a private school and later as a professor of Russian literature at Moscow University, where he was a member of the faculty from 1812 until 1835. Even though Professor Pobedonostsev was a pious member of the Orthodox Church, a nationalistic Russian, a professor of Russian literature, and a founder of the Society of the Lovers of Russian Literature, he devoted a good part of his time and energy to publishing journals whose main function was the translation of materials from French books, journals, and newspapers. In fact, even during the Napoleonic wars, the journals edited and published by Professor Pobedonostsev served to make available selections of eighteenth-century French literature that had in fact contributed to the coming of the French Revolution and that, through the hands of Professor Pobedonostsev and others like him, helped to increase Russian knowledge of things French.

The journals of Professor Pobedonostsev serve to demonstrate that Russian intellectuals early in the nineteenth century considered France the standard-bearer of the highest levels of European culture. A mark of one of the changes in the Russian view of France that unfolded as the nineteenth century progressed was the contrast between Professor Pobedonostsev and his distinguished son. The latter, unlike his father, learned to read French at an early age and as an adult read the *Revue des Deux Mondes* regularly; nevertheless, he refused to visit Paris and turned to England, Germany, and the classics rather than to those whose works his father had published or to French writers of his own era.[4]

It is important to note that there is apparently little connection between Russia's official foreign policy toward France and the views that Russians had of France. In fact, the years during which French cultural influence was greatest in Russia were years in which France and Russia were usually hostile toward or at war with each other. Russian opinion of France did, however, reflect Russian foreign policy in that many educated Russians in the last third of the nineteenth century paid little attention to France because they were obsessed by German power and policy. In other words, the Russian view of France changed to some degree during the course of the nineteenth century, because Russian foreign policy tended to concentrate ever more on Germany.

Throughout the nineteenth century, particularly during the period labeled by Russians as "from Napoleon to Napoleon," the Russian court played an important part in shaping the Russian view of other countries and of other parts of the world. The court in St. Petersburg was basically a German institution, most of the Russian tsars had German wives, and Germans, usually from the Baltic area, occupied many important state positions. In fact, almost all of the princesses whom Russian state leaders married after the time of Peter the Great were German. Moreover, the education of the court was German throughout the eighteenth and nineteenth centuries, and the German state system very often served as the court's model. In other words, when the court looked westward to Europe, it tended to concentrate on Germany, whereas the aristocracy, looking in the same direction, tended to see only France.[5]

The court's attitude toward France was inevitably shaped by the French Revolution and by the invasion of Napoleon as much as it was by family relations. During the era of reaction after 1815, both Alexander I and Nicholas I tightened censorship to a degree beyond that practiced even during the French Revolution. In 1830 Nicholas I was prepared to invade France and to crush the revolution that broke out in that year, and he abandoned this intention only because it was impossible to fulfill. Even so, the Revolution of 1830 had a great influence on the official Russian view of France and became one of the most important and curious developments in Russian cultural history. So alarmed by developments in France and so frightened by the fear that the infection would spread from Paris to other parts of Europe, Nicholas I in effect closed Paris and all of France to Russian tourists and students. He began to send Russian students to Berlin for their studies, particularly after 1840. It was in Berlin that young Russians encountered the doctrines first of Hegel and later of Marx. Ironically, therefore, the policies of Nicholas I led to the importation of doctrines into Russia from Berlin that turned out to be far more dangerous and destructive than the ideas Russian scholars would have received in Paris.[6]

The censorship of Nicholas I and his efforts to isolate Russia from France failed for many reasons. The whole culture of the aristocracy of that time was so French that he could not divert this great stream. In addition, the libraries that had been imported into Russia in the eighteenth century and that continued to grow in the nineteenth century included a large number of French books, particularly the classics of the age of the Enlightenment. These libraries in the great homes of the aristocracy were in fact time bombs, because the Herzens and the Kropotkins absorbed these volumes when they were youngsters and in the 1830s and 1840s imbibed doctrines and information from them that Nicholas I was trying to obliterate and destroy. These libraries, accumulated in the eighteenth and early nineteenth century, therefore, had influences in the nineteenth century far beyond what the Russian government of Nicholas I could have envisaged.[7]

Nicholas I and his chief administrator in cultural affairs, S. S. Uvarov, the Minister of Education, were not hostile to Europe and France, but only to a particular definition of Europe and France. Uvarov, for example, the symbol of the repressive policy toward culture and education in the thirties and forties, considered himself a true European. He spoke several European languages, including French, and had himself received the kind of education that Nicholas I considered dangerous for other Russians. He was a great admirer of France, but of the France before 1789. He feared the French Revolution with its secularism and liberalism and its effort to destroy the old France that he considered the soul of Europe. Consequently, Uvarov in all his policies tried to preserve the France that he and others like him had cherished; but to destroy the France of the first half of the nineteenth century, which he considered a perversion of French history and tradition.

France was central in the thinking of the cultivated aristocracy of St. Petersburg and Moscow, and occupied quite a different position from that held at the court. Of course, most of the Russian nobility in the first half of the nineteenth century, and even in the first part of the twentieth century, were no more cultivated or educated than the English gentry whom Thomas Macaulay ridiculed in the famous third chapter of his *History of England*. The educated aristocrats, who tended to spend their winters at least in St. Petersburg and Moscow, were, however, highly educated people, in many ways more French than Russian. Almost all of them spoke French; they had traveled often in France; most of their reading was in French books, journals, and newspapers; and they traditionally had their children educated by French tutors.[8]

For them, as for Uvarov, France was the France of the eighteenth century, of the Enlightenment. For them, France was not just a country or a people, but a number of ideas that they thought should affect the lives of all men. For them, France represented the belief in the excellence of natural man, the importance of the individual and of the individual's rights, and the power of reason. It also meant the great literature of the eighteenth century, Paris as the City of Light, and, perhaps above all, the fashions and luxuries for which Paris was known throughout all Europe. Their readings and travel, their ideals and sympathy, and their definition of France in general therefore produced a quite different view of France and Europe from that held by Nicholas I, Uvarov, and the court. For the nobility, the West began west of Berlin and Vienna, while for the court and the state officials Berlin and Vienna were the centers of the Western world. For the nobility, Victor Hugo, George Sand, and Father Felicité de Lamennais represented the Western giants of the nineteenth century, standing on the shoulders of the great Frenchmen of the eighteenth century.[9]

The cultivated aristocracy of Russia in the nineteenth century was thus in some ways more French than Russian: They had no real roots in Russian society; their main cultural influences came from abroad; their eyes were always directed abroad; they often had no real understanding of Russia or sympathy for Russia; and their whole tradition and upbringing had destroyed many of the beliefs that the aristocracy had held in earlier years. This helps to account for the "betrayal" of Russian tradition by the nobility: A handful of nobles turned in revolt against the regime in 1825, and others helped to lead the revolutionary movement later in the nineteenth century.

Probably the most critical period in shaping the view of educated Russians of France in the nineteenth century was the 1840s, when the celebrated debate or discussion took place between the Slavophils and the Westerners, a debate about the nature of Russia and about Russia's position in the world which is still being fought. This discussion goes back, of course, at least to Peter the Great and his impact on Russia. It was launched by the publication in French in a Russian journal of the *Philosophical Letters* of Peter Chaadaiev. This important treatise argued that Russia had no past, no present, and no future, and that Russia had to become a part of Europe if it were to make any significant contribution in world history. This series of essays ignited a vigorous debate in Russia and led to the creation of two schools of the philosophy of history that have had a profound impact on Russian intellectual history; they also led to definitions of Russia and of Russia's attitude towards the rest of the world that still remain lively and vital.

The Slavophils, who were much influenced by the German romantics, particularly Schlegel and Schilling, in effect tended to glorify Russia, emphasizing the qualities that separated it from other peoples and other countries and arguing that Russia should remain true to its historical traditions. Alexis Khomiakov, the Kireevskys, and the Aksakovs became convinced that Russia had a mission to the rest of the world and that the outstanding qualities that had characterized the history of the Russian people and of the Russian state should be recognized and adopted by others.

The Slavophils therefore began to glorify the Russian Orthodox Church, the saintly quality of the Russian people, the peace and tranquility that, they assumed, prevailed in Russian social and political relations, and what they believed to be the kind of Christian, peasant kingdom that the Russian autocracy had always been. This glorification of rural Russia and of the old regime also reflected the view of the Slavophils that Russia should remain isolated from other cultures and that Russia in borrowing from other cultures would only poison the springs of its very peculiar and distinctive civilization.

The Slavophils had a great admiration for England, partly because Aleksei Khomiakov and his associates believed that the England of the first half of the nineteenth century shared some of the fine qualities they found in Russia. Khomiakov, who had studied in England and who knew rural England quite well, was a scholar of Shakespeare, was able to quote long passages of Byron, and was a great admirer of English history and literature. In fact, he found in England a kind of advanced or progressive Russia, a society that had established and respected conservative institutions, the kind of peaceful relations between the classes that he thought also existed in Russia, and a proper respect for the past and for authority.[10]

The view the Slavophils held of France was quite different. They thought France an artificial, overly rational, abstract, depraved, and cruel society, one ruled on occasion by a fierce Catholicism and at other times by what they called a bureaucratic and parliamentary despotism. They were convinced that the French people, or at least their rulers, were the prisoners of an abstract rationalism that led them to glorify materialism and cruel despotic rule. One of the Aksakovs [a family of Russian writers] even said that France was "the miserable land called to warn by her fate the rest of mankind, a country flinging herself about between papacy and atheism, between superstition and disbelief, between slavery and revolt."[11] In short, the Slavophils despised France and feared French influence in Russia. The only two Frenchmen of their generation they admired were Tocqueville and Montalembert, both of whom they called "Western Slavophils" and whom they considered almost English in their view of the state and society.[12]

The Westerners naturally had a different view of France and of Russia. Led by Vissarion Belinsky, the celebrated critic of the 1840s, Alexander Herzen, and N. P. Ogarev, they developed the view that Russia was a backward and underdeveloped country and could progress only if it recognized that it was a part of a larger civilization and borrowed effectively from the institutions and achievements of other European countries. The Westerners were, in general, great admirers of France, particularly of the French Enlightenment and of the socialist ideas that appeared in France in the 1820s and 1830s. They were much influenced by Fourier and Louis Blanc, and were great admirers of the French writers of that time, particularly of Victor Hugo and George Sand, whom Belinsky called "the first poetic glory of the contemporary world" and "the Joan of Arc of our time." While they were on occasion critical of particular French institutions, they were in general great admirers of the French as "an heroic and noble people." They thought that Russia could progress only if it continued to revise its institutions and values along the lines established clearly by France.[13]

Belinsky reflected some of the principal changes that occurred in the Russian view of France in the second quarter of the nineteenth century. He represents what Vladimir Weidlé has called "the coming of the clerks" because he was of the nonnoble class, did not complete his formal education, read French poorly and did not speak it at all, and was more attracted by the French socialist and radical thought of the nineteenth century than by the writers of the Enlightenment. He reflected the group of "clerks," which included sons of priests, expelled students, and censored journalists, who began to have a powerful impact on Russian thinking by the middle of the nineteenth century.[14]

An important turning point in the Russian view of France occurred between 1848 and 1870. The official point of view, that is that of the court, of the leading statesmen, and of those who were part of the then Russian establishment, became even more sharply anti-French during these years than before. The 1848 revolution in France, which spread into other countries in western and central Europe, alarmed Russian conservatives, and the rise to power of Napoleon III frightened them even more, both because the name of Napoleon meant invasion and difficulty for Russia and because of the radical social policy and the reorganization of Europe that Napoleon III advocated. Russian failure in the Crimean War, the ensuing "thaw" and reforms, and the unsuccessful revolt of the Poles in 1863 pushed the official Russian view of France even further toward hostility, particularly because of the diplomatic support Napoleon III gave the Poles and because of the traditional Russian fear of the Catholic powers, Poland, and France.[15]

Consequently, Russian foreign policy during the years before the Franco-Prussian War helped Bismarck to create the situation in which he was able to isolate and attack France, and the Russian court and most Russian leaders supported Germany in the war. So far as can be determined, most of the educated people not involved in the court or official activities provided sentimental support for France in 1870, and popular sympathy as well seemed to be for the French against the Germans. It is also clear, however, that this popular support for France, which had no effect whatsoever on Russian policy, was for the "ideal, imaginary France" of the eighteenth century and first part of the nineteenth century and not for the France of Napoleon III, for which there was little affection or sympathy.

While the court and the government were becoming more clearly critical of France during the years between 1848 and 1870, an important change was also occurring during these years among the educated members of the aristocracy and of the new class, the intelligentsia, almost all of whom had a view of France quite different from that of the educated aristocracy of the first part of the nineteenth century. One splendid example of this is Alexander Herzen, who left Russia in 1847 but who had a powerful influence on Russian thought and political development during the next quarter-century because of his journalistic and other activities in France and in England. Herzen had been brought up to believe in

the France of the great century, but his residence in Western
Europe after 1847 quite clearly disillusioned him, and by 1854
he was almost as critical of France as was Nicholas I, though for
quite different reasons. Herzen's letters, particularly those written
between 1847 and 1854, reveal his growing disillusionment with
France and his growing conviction that the salvation of Russia
had to reflect Russian history and tradition and must be found
within Russia itself.[16]

Herzen became convinced that France had little to offer Russia,
because he was appalled by the rôle that the petty bourgeoisie
played in France, because the power of Catholicism as an organized religion filled him with alarm, because parliamentary government as he saw it practiced by Napoleon III in France and by
Palmerston in England gave him no confidence, and because his
residence abroad persuaded him that his own country must have
a splendid future. He was so dismayed by economic developments
in France that he denounced "the small, dirty milieu of petty
bourgeoisie, which covers all of France like a green slime." He
remarked as early as the 1850s that he had begun "the moral return
to my own country." Herzen began to have great faith in Russian
man and in the likelihood that the Russians might form some new
kind of society superior to anything with which he was familiar
in Western Europe. It is no doubt symbolic that Herzen wrote
most of his letters in French in 1847, that he began then to write
some in German, and that he usually wrote in Russian after
1854.[17]

The Populists, or the *narodniki*, whose writings and ideas dominated the Russian social movement in the 1860s, also were critical
of France. One of the leading Populists, Peter Lavrov, referred to
France as "the republic of humbug." The Populists were much
impressed by peasant institutions and began to believe that the
future of socialism could be built on native Russian institutions.
They were also more influenced by philosophers from England and
from Germany than they were by those of France. For example,
Herbert Spencer and Charles Darwin had a profound influence
on Populist thinking in the 1860s, much more than that of the
earlier French philosophers or that of the French Socialists who
had had such great effect in the thirties and forties, or even than

that of Hippolyte Taine, August Comte, and Ernest Renan, then among the most popular writers in Paris.

As one moves further to the right in the Russian political spectrum, one encounters a view of France that is even more critical and hostile. The Panslavs, the great Russian nationalists, who in the sixties and seventies began to advocate that "big brother" Russia should help lead the other Slavic peoples to independence and to some form of federation in which Russia would have the leadership, were even more critical of France than were the Populists. In addition, they were more influenced by England and by Germany than they were by France. The celebrated conservative journalist, Michael Katkov, in his outpourings between 1860 and 1885 reflected great admiration for prereform England and great hostility toward Germany. As Khomiakov had been, earlier, Katkov was an Anglophil with a great admiration for the way the English lived, for their established institutions, for the power of prescription in England, for English agricultural life, and for the extraordinary way in which he thought they managed to preserve their political and social system while at the same time modernizing the country.[18]

At the same time, Katkov and other Panslavs were so mesmerized by the rise of German power and by what they considered the threat of Germany or the Germans in the Balkans that France almost ceased to exist for them. Count Nicholas Ignatiev, the celebrated Russian ambassador to Constantinople during most of the 1870s, for example, devoted most of his attention to England and Germany and thought that France was an unimportant power in European politics. Nicholas Danilevsky, who in 1869 wrote an important volume entitled *Russia and Europe,* so concentrated on Germany as the enemy of Russia that other European states to some degree ceased to exist. General Rostislav Fadeiev dismissed France as a power of no importance and wrote that "Russia's chief enemy is by no means western Europe, but the German race and its enormous pretensions." A final illustration of a Panslav who paid little attention to France and relegated it to a second role was the poet, Fedor Tiutchev, who lived twenty years in Germany, whose two wives were German, who wrote very often in French, and who did not even speak Russian with fluency, but who was so consumed by the German problem that he thought France of little importance either politically or culturally.[19]

The great novelist, Dostoevsky, illustrates another attitude or view of France that fits quite well into this general pattern. Dostoevsky was a great admirer of French literature, read Fourier, George Sand, and Hugo, and was much influenced by Balzac in particular. At the same time, he lived much more in Germany than in France, and he was more impressed by German thought and German power than he was by those of the French. For Dostoevsky, Paris was *Nineveh*, a dying power. In 1868 he even criticized a niece who sought a French governess for her daughter, because he thought French would no longer be spoken in Russia and because the little girl would learn "vile things" from such a governess. Moreover, France to him also represented Roman Catholicism and the idea of force in religion, while Russia represented Orthodoxy and unity in freedom. Dostoevsky saw Catholicism, socialism, the corrupting power of the bourgeoisie, and Western civilization in general as the principal threats to Russia. France was the main culprit in these developments, although Dostoevsky was more concerned with the rising political power of Germany and of German ideas than he was with those of France.[20]

Count Leo Tolstoy, another of Russia's great novelists, represents still another view of France but one that is also a part of this same scheme. As a young man, Tolstoy often read French literature, and he was much impressed by Stendhal in particular. He was so influenced by Rousseau that he carried Rousseau's picture in a locket around his neck when he was still in his teens. Tolstoy visited Paris only twice, however, in 1857 and in 1860. In 1870 he wrote that "civilization and progress are on the side of the Prussians" in the Franco-Prussian war. Although he did remain interested and informed about French literature and culture, he became more and more possessed by Russian problems and turned more and more to the Russian peasant and the Russian people for the solutions of the issues that Russia and the world faced. As a consequence, France has little significance in the last forty or fifty years of Tolstoy's life and thought, thus reflecting in part the great change that had come over the Russian view of France in the course of the nineteenth century.[21]

When one turns to the period after 1870 and to the Third Republic, one finds that Russian views of France again underwent a significant turn. For the court and those involved in guiding the Russian state, the Third Republic was even more dismal and even disgusting than the France of Napoleon III. In fact, it is clear from the Russian press before the formation of the Russian-French alliance in 1894 that the Third Republic was considered a "hotbed of republicism, atheism, and anarchy" by those who were engaged in directing Russian destinies. Alexander III, who ruled Russia from 1881 to 1894, once defined France as "nothing but atheists and radicals." In the two decades of history before the alliance was formed in 1894 there was more friction than friendship between the two countries. Moreover, the outstanding French intellectuals of the time, men such as Taine and Renan, had remarkably little influence in Russia because most Russians from every level of society were more concerned with English and German political thought and actions than they were with those of France.[22]

At the very end of the nineteenth century, however, a new and important view of France began to emerge in Russia, among Russian artists and writers in particular. In the Silver Age of Russian literature and art a new appreciation of France and of French art and literature appeared among important Russian painters and artists. Between 1899 and 1904, for example, Sergei Diaghilev edited a very important journal, *Mir iskustva* (*The World of Art*), which reflected a great admiration for French art and literature as well as great French influence. Consequently, in the decade or two before the First World War there were very close ties between French and Russian literature, and the important poets and painters of Russia—men such as Constantine Balmont, Valerii Briusov, and the group known as "Scorpions,"—had great admiration for earlier French poets, such as Théophile Gautier, Charles Baudelaire, and Jean Rimbaud. In addition, Russian painters such as Marc Chagall and Vasilli Kandinsky had a great appreciation for the French impressionists and symbolists, and were indeed both influenced by them and much appreciated by them. In fact, it is impossible to separate the Russian art and literature of this period from literary and artistic developments within France. Three of the great purchasers of French art during these years, Savva Morozov and S. J. and D. J. Shchuikin, provide a most appropriate demonstration of this, for they displayed a very early appreciation of the French symbolists and of Picasso. Their purchases have given Russia the splendid collections of French painters of that time which are now among the glories of the art museums in Moscow and Leningrad.[23]

At this level of artistic endeavor, a new view of France began to emerge in Russia, one that would clearly have much affected the Russian view of France except for the overwhelming role that other forces of an economic and political character played. The individuals who became particularly important in Russian political life held quite different views of France from those of the intellectuals of the Silver Age. Perhaps four or five of the outstanding Russians of the quarter-century before the First World War can be used to identify the changes that had taken place and to characterize the view of France held by the rising leaders.

One of these important leaders was Count Sergei Witte, who began the massive industrialization of Russia in the eighteen nineties and who represented the new businessmen's spirit at the very highest levels of the Russian government. The career of Witte represents the new attitude toward Russia and toward France and the world. Witte, for example, was born in Tblisi—whose rise illustrates the growing significance of areas remote from Moscow and St. Petersburg and from French influences. His early career was based on important achievements in the railroad industry, particularly in Odessa. As Witte rose to power over the railroad system and then to a commanding position over Russian finances and economic development, his view of Europe began to be impressed upon the Russian state.

Uvarov, who had sought to resist European influence, was in many ways more European in culture than Witte, who spoke no foreign languages, did not read easily or well in any foreign language, and did not travel extensively. Yet Witte was interested in making Russia a modern European power and in borrowing from the new Europe as effectively as he could to achive this. The Europe from which he borrowed, however, was industrial Germany.

For many members of the educated aristocracy in the first third of the nineteenth century, Berlin was on the easternmost fringe of the frontiers of Europe. Nevertheless, for Witte, Berlin and all of Germany were the very heart of Europe, even though France became an ally of Russia and French funds provided a good part of the investments Witte poured into the industrialization of Russia. To him, France was *in* but not *of* Europe, while German industrial power constituted the heart and the future of Europe.[24]

Peter Stolypin, who was the principal political leader in Russia from 1906 until his death in 1911, represents in many ways the same kind of development. Born in Dresden and resident throughout most of his adult life in a part of the Russian empire very close to eastern Prussia, Stolypin's view of Europe concentrated on Germany. He was particularly influenced by the agricultural progress of eastern Prussia when he set out to "wager on the strong" in Russia by abolishing the mir and by seeking to establish an independent farming class. Stolypin, in other words, looked first of all to Germany, and to a lesser degree to the United States, when he thought of reorganizing the Russian economy and the Russian state system. France was a very minor power indeed, so far as Stolypin and his generation of those remaking Russia were concerned, and the qualities that had attracted the attention and affection of earlier generations of Russians did not fascinate him.

Another great man of quite a different character and position in Russia at this time was Vasilli O. Kliuchevsky, who was born in Penza, southeast of Moscow, and who spent the last fifty years of his life in Moscow teaching Russian history and writing his celebrated volumes. When Kliuchevsky came to Moscow early in the 1860s, he was especially interested in French history, and some of his earliest teaching was concerned with the French Revolution and with the history of France between 1789 and 1848. Kliuchevsky quickly turned away from the history of France, however, and devoted his scholarly life to the history of early Russia. He was a Russian nationalist. Even though he was an important scholar in an age of great Russian historical scholarship, he never left the Russian Empire. The parts of Europe he hoped to visit did not even include France. His view of Europe and the world tended to concentrate above all on Russia itself and then on her neighboring states, particularly on the Turks and the Germans, and France and its qualities played no significant role in his thought.

The final example of this generation of Russians who tended to neglect France and to place her in a minor position was Vladimir Lenin. Lenin was born in Simbirsk, northeast of Penza on the Volga, an area even more remote from Moscow and from Paris than Kluichevsky's native city. Both French and German were read and spoken in his family. He was well educated and spent an important part of his life outside of Russia, being as much at home in London, Paris, Capri, and Cracow as he was in Moscow or St. Petersburg. Lenin had very little regard for France, however, and was very little influenced by French thought or French policy. As a disciple of Marx, he was especially learned in German thought, and he declared Germany "the classical country of capitalism and of socialism." While Lenin was European in knowledge and outlook, Germany was the center of his world. France had indeed fallen to a very low state.

With some exceptions and with some degrees of change, most of Lenin's highly educated associates shared his views. Thus, Leon Trotsky, Maksim Litvinov, Georgi Chicherin, Christian Rakovsky, and Nikolai Bukharin all shared Lenin's view of Germany and of the role of France in modern and future European politics. Germany was the land of industry and of socialism, while France for them was the country of the bourgeois republic and of luxuries. The capital of Europe had therefore moved east from Paris, where it had existed for most educated Russians earlier in the century.

The changing views of France held by Russians in the nineteenth century, as even this brief review indicates, derive from the changes that occurred within France and Russia in the nineteenth century, from the general Russian view of the West as it was revised during the course of the century, and from economic, social, and political developments in other countries, particularly Germany.

One is impressed by the relative unimportance of foreign policy and of the diplomacy of the nineteenth century as factors affecting Russian views of France. The degree of tension or strain between the two countries seems to have had very little effect. The relative decline of France's traditional allies in Eastern Europe, the Swedes, the Poles, and the Turks, however, and the relative decline of France itself in the course of the century did have a very profound effect upon the Russian view of France, if only because the position of France declined so very sharply while that of England and Germany rose. In fact, France to many Russians in 1900 or 1914 was far more remote than it had been in 1800 or 1815, even though France and Russia were allied in the more recent period and were generally at war in the first period. In fact, the revolution in transportation and the industrial revolution in general did not bring France and Russia closer together in the course of the nineteenth century.

One measure of the declining number of contacts between France and Russia and the rising influence of Germany is reflected in important statistics. For example, the 1897 census indicated there were 605,500 foreign residents in Russia, of whom only 9500 were French and 158,000 were German. Moreover, that same census revealed that 1.75 million permanent residents or citizens of the Russian Empire spoke German as their native language, while only a handful spoke French.[25] These facts reflect, of course, the large number of Germans who had lived in the Baltic area since the eighteenth century and before, the thousands of Germans who lived along the Volga River, and those who resided in the two principal cities of the country. In the course of the nineteenth century, many Germans occupied important positions in the Russian state, particularly in the army and in the diplomatic service. B. H. Sumner, for example, noted that four of the nine ambassadors who served Russia at the Court of St. James in London between the time of Napoleon and the Russian Revolution in 1917 were German, and that these four representatives accounted for 83 of the 105 years.[26]

Trade statistics reflect also the considerable rise of German contact with Russia during the nineteenth century. For example, German trade with Russia increased 11.5 times in the course of the second half of the nineteenth century, while French trade grew only three times. France accounted for less than five percent of Russia's imports during the thirteen years before the outbreak of the First World War, while German exports amounted to 35.8

percent of Russia's imports from 1901 through 1905, and to 52.7 percent of Russian imports in 1913.

Thus, the relationships between Germany and Russia and between France and Russia changed considerably during the course of the nineteenth century. For most educated Russians, France remained "old France" and had less intellectual and political impact and effect than did "new Germany." The rise of Germany and its place in the Russian view of Europe is also naturally reflected in philosophy and in statecraft. For example, Hegel had replaced Voltaire by the middle of the nineteenth century in Russian political thought. Bismarck clearly had more influence on the Russian state and on Russian politics in the latter part of the nineteenth century than did Napoleon III or any of the statesmen of the Third Republic. Consequently, when the modernization of Russia was begun, particularly under Count Witte, and when Russia's army and industry and state system in general were reorganized during the course of the last part of the nineteenth century, the Russians almost inevitably turned to Germany rather than to France, this step reflecting one of the important changes in the view of France that had occurred during the course of the century.

This changing attitude is represented clearly in the Russian state structure and in institutional developments. The Napoleonic Code had considerable influence outside of France during the first part of the nineteenth century, even in Russia, and Mikhail Speransky, to whom Alexander I assigned the responsibility for planning the reorganization of the central government in the first decade of Alexander I's reign, turned to French institutions as his models. The institute established by Prince Peter Oldenburg in St. Petersburg in 1836 to provide training in law for future Russian bureaucrats paid as much attention to the Napoleonic Code as it did to Roman law. By the middle of the nineteenth century, however, Russian law professors were studying under Savigny in Berlin, and it was German and English influence rather than French that helped to shape the judicial reform of 1864 and the legal institutions and attitudes that developed in Russia following that momentous change. These institutional changes reflect the view of many Russians that France was "old" and that modernization meant looking more to Germany and England than to the country that had dominated the intellectual scene earlier in the century.[27]

This new view of France was a result of a number of changes within Russia, particularly the decline of the aristocracy and the various waves of social revolution that swept over the country. As the nobility lost its influence and power, the view of France it had traditionally held ceased to have influence. At the same time, the new radical view of the West that began to develop after the 1840s and the increasing effort to modernize Russia led to a quite critical view of France as a bourgeois country and one which possessed very little dynamism. Even the court, especially the men with power in the higher levels of government, such as Witte and Stolypin, had a low regard for France, particularly as a model for Russia, and turned more to Germany and even to the United States as patterns of development that Russia ought to follow.

This change to some degree derived from changes that occurred within France during the course of the century. The Old Regime and the Enlightenment had a clear and powerful attraction for Russians, but it diminished as France became less stable and more bourgeois. The rise to power of the middle class in France occurred at the same time that the antibourgeois tradition in Russia increased in strength, both among the nobles and among the lower classes as they achieved intellectual and political significance.

The position of France in the view of Russians also declined to some degree because of the great achievements of the French in introducing Western European culture into Russian circles. In a sense, France served as a translator or interpreter for other countries, such as Sweden or Italy. One of the great achievements of the French during the eighteenth and nineteenth centuries was to widen the vision of Russians and to give them a greater range of interest and knowledge of western Europe as a whole. This was done to some degree at the cost of France. France declined in the view of Russians in part because of the growing understanding which Russians acquired concerning the rest of Europe.

Louis XIV once remarked that nations meet only at the top and that the ambassadors and others at high state and social levels serve as interpreters or translators of one society for another. This was clearly the case during his age, but was less true as the eighteenth and nineteenth centuries unfolded. Moreover, it is clear that the general Russian view of France in the nineteenth century tended to emphasize Paris and the things for which Paris generally stood, rather than the countryside or the great bulk of the French people. There were very few Russians in the nineteenth century who had any substantial knowledge of France or any real understanding of the French people. No one interpreter of France ever emerged in Russia (comparable, for eaxmple, to Tocqueville's interpretation of the United States for France in the middle of the nineteenth century). Most Russians, even those who were relatively well informed, had little understanding of the peasantry, of the French political system, of French life outside Paris, or indeed of the essentials of France. The Russians in general serve as illustrations of the supreme difficulty any citizen of one culture or society has in understanding another country or civilization.

Thus, the understanding of France in Russia had filtered down gradually from the upper level of the state and the aristocracy to a larger and wider class of educated people. The views of this new group were changed significantly by developments within both France and Russia and by the rise of German power, German industry, and German philosophy. Consequently, the views of France held in Russia at the end of the nineteenth century were very different from those that had prevailed a hundred years earlier. Marx, Hegel, and Bismarck generally prevailed over Voltaire, Fourier, and Comte, just as industry overwhelmed luxuries and fashion.

Notes

1.   Abel Mansuy, *Le Monde slav et les classiques français au* XVIe–XVIIe *siècles*. Paris: 1912, pp. 1–2; Emile Haumant, *La Culture française en Russie, 1700–1900*. Paris: 1913, pp. 11–68, 130–170; Renato Poggioli, *The Poets of Russia, 1890–1930*. Cambridge: 1960, pp. 9–13.

2.   Mikhail Mikhailovich Shtrange, *La Révolution française et la société russe*. Moscow: 1960, pp. 47–48, 53, 183–185.

3.   Haumant, pp. 171–319; Shtrange, pp. 66, 77–86.

4.   Robert F. Byrnes, "The Pobedonoscev Family," *Indiana Slavic Studies*, vol. 2 (1958), pp. 63–78.

5.   Wladimir Weidlé, *Russia: Absent and Present*. New York: 1952, pp. 48–49; B. H. Sumner, *Peter the Great and the Emergence of Russia*. New York: 1962, pp. 5, 84, 190.

6.   Stepan Stepanovich Volk, "Dekabristy o burzhuaznom Zapade," *Izvestiia Akademii Nauk SSSR. Seriia istorii i filosofii*, vol. 7 (1951), pp. 78–81; A. Molok, "Tsarskaia Rossiia i iiul'skaia revoliutsiia 1830 g.," *Literaturnoe Nasledstvo*, vols. 29–30 (1937), pp. 734–740, 750–755; Poggioli, pp. 43–45.

7.   Sydney Monas, *The Third Section: Police and Society in Russia under Nicholas I*. Cambridge: 1961, pp. 135–140, 190–196.

8.   Alexander von Schelting, *Russland und Europa im russischen Geschichts-denken*. Bern: 1948, pp. 25–26, 319; B. H. Sumner, "Russia and Europe," *Oxford Slavonic Papers*, vol. 2 (1951), p. 4; Haumant, pp. 69–118.

9.   Haumant, pp. 320–403.

10.   Albert Gratieux, *A. S. Khomiakov et le mouvement slavophile*. Paris: 1939, vol. 1, pp. 115–126; vol. 2, pp. 33–34; William J. Birkbeck, *Russia and the English Church in the Last Fifty Years*. London: 1895, Sergei Bolshakoff, *Russian Noncomformity*. Philadelphia: 1950, pp. 8–18, 110–112.

11.   Quoted by Nicholas Riasanovsky, *Russia and the West in the Teaching of the Slavophiles*. Cambridge, Mass.: 1952, p. 108.

12.   Vasilii V. Zenkovsky, *Russian Thinkers and Europe*. Ann Arbor, Mich., 1953, pp. 27–32; Iurii F. Samarin, *Sochineniia*. Moscow: 1911, vol. 1, p. 394; Riasanovsky, pp. 29–33, 100–108; Weidlé, p. 56; Poggioli, pp. 33–35.

13.   Kyra Sanine, *Les Annales de la patrie et la diffusion de la pensée française en Russie, 1868–1884*. Paris: 1953, pp. 12, 45–46; Herbert Bowman, *Vissarion Belinski, 1811–1848*. Cambridge: 1954, pp. 37–38, 141, 145–146.

14.   Weidlé, p. 2.

15.   P. V. Annenkov, *Literaturnie vospominaniia*. Leningrad: 1928, p. 291; Haumant, pp. 417–432, 472–483.

16.   Alexander Herzen, *My Past and My Thoughts*. London: 1924–1927, vol. 1, pp. 50–54; Martin Malia, *Alexander Herzen and the Birth of Russian Socialism, 1812–1855*. Cambridge: 1961, pp. 9–37.

17.   Alexander Herzen, *Pis'ma iz Frantsii i Italii*. Moscow: 1934, p. 284; Franco Venturi, *Roots of Revolution*. New York: 1960, pp. 1–35; Sanine, pp. 28–30, 35–37, 100–102; Haumant, p. 359; Malia, pp. 99–133, 313–368; Zenkovsky, pp. 62–67.

18.   S. Nevedenskii, *Katkov i ego vremia*. St. Petersburg: 1888, pp. 323, 403; Marc Raeff, "A Reactionary Liberal: M. N. Katkov," *Russian Review*, vol. 11 (1952), pp. 160–167.

19. B. H. Sumner, *Russia and the Balkans, 1870–1880*. Oxford: 1937, pp. 37–43.

20. Ernest J. Simmons, *Dostoevsky: The Making of a Novelist*. New York: 1962, pp. 289–290, 319–332; Riasanovsky, pp. 206–207; Haumant, pp. 437–439, 461–462, 489–490.

21. Zenkovsky, pp. 120, 126, 197; Haumant, pp. 422, 442.

22. William L. Langer, *The Franco-Russian Alliance, 1890–1894*. Cambridge, Mass.: 1929, pp. 10, 90–92, 253–255, 270–271.

23. Poggioli, pp. 4, 58–68, 89–92, 101, 107.

24. For the career of Count Witte, see Theodore von Laue, *Sergei Witte and the Industrialization of Russia*. New York: 1963.

25. Grigorii Aleksinskii, *Russia and Europe*. New York: 1917, pp. 50–51, 58–60.

26. B. H. Sumner, *A Short History of Russia*. New York: 1943, pp. 331.

27. Frederick Barghoorn, "Some Russian Images of the West," in Cyril E. Black (Ed.), *The Transformation of Russian Society*. Cambridge: 1960, pp. 574–587; Haumant, pp. 513–529; Sanine, pp. 46–60.

⤳ *CRANE BRINTON*

Crane Brinton, McLean Professor of Ancient and Modern History at Harvard University, is an authority on Western intellectual history and the patterns of revolution. Born in Winsted, Connecticut in 1898, he was a Rhodes Scholar from Harvard (1919), received his Ph.D. degree from Oxford in 1923, and returned to Harvard to teach, where, except for special appointments and service as Special Assistant to the Office of Strategic Services, European Theater of Operations (1942–1945), he has remained. He has explored many subjects and published widely, not only in professional journals, but in literary reviews as well. He is a fellow of the Royal Historical Society and a Chevalier in the Legion of Honor. A member of many learned societies, he was elected president of the American Historical Association in 1963, and he has been a recent president of the Society for French Historical Studies. His many works include *The Political Ideas of the English Romanticists* (1926), *The Jacobins* (1930), *English Political Thought in the Nineteenth Century* (1933), *A Decade of Revolution (1789–1799)* (1934), *French Revolutionary Legislation on Illegitimacy* (1936), *The Lives of Talleyrand* (1936), *The Anatomy of Revolution* (1938), *Nietzsche* (1941), *The United States and Britain* (1945, revised 1948), *From Many One* (1948), *Ideas and Men: the Story of Western Thought* (1950), *The Temper of Western Europe* (1953), *A History of Western Morals* (1959), and *The Fate of Man* (1961). He is editor of the *American Foreign Policy Library* (Harvard University Press), and is at present preparing a volume on France. It would be difficult to find a person with qualifications comparable to Professor Brinton's to present in a broad sweep the links between different revolutionary traditions.

The French Revolution: Its Relation to Contemporary Revolutions

Let me begin what I half hope and half fear will be a controversial paper with the saving statement that I fully agree with the optimistic page that prefaces Leo Gershoy's revised bibliography in the 1964 edition of his *The French Revolution and Napoleon*. There is indeed a sense in which the study even of events so stirring as those of the great French Revolution—stirring not only in the literary and romantic sense but also in a not wholly unrelated sense, physiologically stimulating on the adrenals—a sense in which this study is a slowly cumulative one that comes closer and closer to what we may innocently call truth. The cumulation is not merely one of greater factual accuracy, but also of greater objectivity, more subtle interpretation, less intolerant partisan zeal.

Yet there is a limit to this process, especially if the goal is held to be complete agreement even among scholars, specialists, and experts. I do not intend to dwell on the subject of historical methodology. Suffice it to say that there are still great areas of disagreement among experts on important problems of interpretation of the events of the French and American Revolutions. One such area I propose to discuss this afternoon.

To borrow from our colleague R. R. Palmer, this area may be roughly defined as that of the *associationist* as against the *dissociationist* view of the relationship between the revolutions of the later eighteenth century and the Communist revolutions of our own century, and, in particular, between the French Revolution and the Russian Bolshevik Revolution of 1917. Two firm antithetical positions are marked out by Palmer and Arnold Toynbee. Palmer writes:

> The exact relationship of the Russian to the French Revolution has in recent decades been the subject of much careful examination. Two tendencies may be perceived: the one to associate, the other to dissociate, the two revolutions. By an "associationist" view . . . I would mean . . . a view in which the French Revolution is seen as a kind of origin, partial cause, or distant prefigurement of the Russian Revolution, which insists upon "Jacobinism" as the "communism" of the eighteenth century, or sees a kind of continuing linear process in which the Russian Revolution is in some way a consequence of the French, or presents a more highly developed stage of the same process.[1]

More simply, "dissociation" is a denial of any genetic, or if you prefer, causal, relation between the French and Russian Revolutions.

As for Toynbee, the titles alone of some of his lectures are *pronunciamentos*: "The Shot Heard Round the World," "The Handicap of Affluence," "Can America Re-join Her Own Revolution?" But perhaps a quotation is needed:

> The United States has become the arch-conservative power instead of the arch-revolutionary one. . . . She has made a present of her glorious discarded revolution to the country which was the arch-conservative power in the nineteenth century. . . . America has presented her historic revolutionary role to Russia.[2]

We are, he says in a very characteristic fashion, choosing the role of Metternich rather than that of Mazzini.

In terms of intellectual history, no doubt unacceptable to many of you, the problem may be put simply as what, if any, is the relation between the "principles of 1776 and 1789" and the principles that the triumphant Bolsheviks of 1917 appealed to, and that their successors still appeal to.

I shall not now attempt to give any answer to this problem. What I am now concerned with is an attempt to explain why there are such diverse, indeed antithetical, answers given to such a question. I shall be concerned solely with American and British answers, though I may later give some tentative and hesitant explanations of why this problem does not loom as large, and certainly does not take the same form, in France as in the United States.

I shall largely confine myself in this paper to the attitudes—the basic ambivalences—of American intellectuals, liberals of the non-Communist left, men and women of good will. No single word or phrase will block these out for the clear understanding of all of us, and instead of using worn and vague labels, let me be specific. Some Americans, some indeed in very high places, like the late General Douglas MacArthur, do fit some of Toynbee's reproachful simplicities: They are Metternichian conservatives, willing and eager to use force to repress revolutionists of Communist or even Socialist stripe, supporters, if I may use a Near-Eastern term in a wider sense, of the *effendi* class all over the world. Some, like the minions of Henry Luce [the publisher of *Time* and *Life* magazines], are most certainly American imperialists, current American versions of the nineteenth-century British imperialists of the school of Cecil Rhodes and Lord Milner, not quite foolish or daring enough to use unfashionable terms such as "the white man's burden," but still at bottom taking substantially this position. Then there are the millions of good conventional patriotic Americans for whom our revolution has quite simply become part of the dead past of history-as-museum, has become the American non-Revolution of the Daughters of the American Revolution. For all these people, the American Revolution is simply, if I may borrow a phrase from that familiar historical masterpiece *1066 and All That*, A Good Thing, the French Revolution something that started out to be A Good Thing but became for a time A Bad Thing, and the Russian Revolution, the Chinese Revolution, the Cuban Revolution, all unmitigatedly Bad Things, utterly unrelated to the American Revolution.

A good many of the Americans I am here lumping together no doubt sympathized with the Irish Revolution, and to a degree even with the Algerian Revolution, largely because as good Americans they tend to sympathize with underdogs, or at least with underdogs beneath such top dogs as the British or the French. In fact, I think it clear that there is among most classes in the United States a strong current of sympathy for anticolonialist movements even when they turn to violence. To that extent at least, Americans are for the most part really nearer Mazzini, even Garibaldi, than they are to Metternich.

Certainly, however, the classes or groups I shall here call intellectuals of the non-Communist left do not want this country to play the role of a Metternich, are positively sympathetic not merely with anticolonialist revolutions, but with the whole great current Professor Cyril Black calls "the worldwide process that is variously known as Europeanization, Westernization, social change, the revolution of rising expectations, and modernization."[3] Incidentally, Black prefers the word "modernization," which I find too vague and too innocently based on an American version of the economic interpretation of everything. "Revolution of widespread rising mass-expectations" seems to me better, though paradoxically, or merely ambivalently, one might use the term "Americanization." For though much American policy and American influence in the world today run against this world revolution, most of the revolutionists would like very much indeed to lead the kind of life most Americans manage to lead, with all its slavery to "the Machine."

The ambivalent attitude I wish here to emphasize is, however, that of Americans—let me again be specific—like most of us. We feel, it seems to me, that those who today claim inspiration from the Russian October or Bolshevik Revolutions are a different breed, having different ideas and ideals, behaving differently, from us and from our spiritual ancestors of the eighteenth-century Enlightenment, the men—I use Palmer's familiar phrase—of the "age of the democratic revolutions"; and yet we feel that somehow or other the masses in countries led by men of this different breed—

some even of the leaders of this breed—are seeking social justice, are rebelling or have recently rebelled justifiably against their own variety of privileged aristocrats. Many of us in the 1930s, I suspect, would have sympathized with a good liberal friend of mine who used to say that he felt toward both communism and fascism as did Mercutio in Shakespeare's "Romeo and Juliet" to the warring Montagues and Capulets, "a plague o' both your houses," but if he had to choose, he'd have to choose communism.

Yielding briefly to a temptation to discuss methodology, I admit that such statements lack social-scientific precision and rigor, both as to those included in the group generalized about, and as to the nature of their sentiments. Nonetheless I insist I am at least groping toward something that does exist, well summarized by the feelings of my friend just mentioned. For many of us, dislike communism as we may, feel that in contrast with fascism, nazism, falangism, and other totalitarian systems, communism is in intent at least on the side of the angels—good freethinking, anticlerical angels, of course.

A nice easy rationalization of such a feeling is obvious: Marxism-Leninism is essentially a perversion of democracy, a democratic heresy. But even a perversion or a heresy is at bottom a relation, and will not satisfy the really determined "dissociationist," who will object even to such a nice neutral pseudo-scientific front as can be achieved by distinguishing between Western democracy of the Jefferson variety and Eastern democracy of the Lenin variety. Moreover, there is a current of thought among historians today, well represented by J. L. Talmon, which very specifically finds the origins of *"democratic* totalitarianism"—a phrase that gives great offense to many good democrats, a phrase that seems to them no mere rhetorical oxymoron, but just damned nonsense, offensive nonsense—not just in Marx and his successors, but right back there in the century of Enlightenment, in the age of the democratic revolutions. Talmon finds the source of his democratic totalitarianism in ideas in Rousseau, in practice in Robespierre, and in the movement led, more or less, by Gracchus Babeuf, the "Conspiracy of the Equals."

This Talmonian position, less rigorously held, is to be found in one phrasing or another ever since the great French Revolution. The distrust of the "tyranny of the majority" shared by John

Stuart Mill and Tocqueville has in our time appeared as an element of such familiar attitudes as Ortega y Gasset's alarm over the behavior of the masses, the horrid anti-Utopias of Aldous Huxley or George Orwell, the shocking inference to be drawn from the work of such reputable historians of the United States as Richard Hofstadter that such progressives as the three La Follettes and such extreme conservatives as Senator Joseph Mc-Carthy are not to be *entirely* dissociated. For the basic ambivalence that lies behind radical dissociation of the late eighteenth-century revolutions and the great Russian Revolution is surely a deep emotional adherence to the good democratic principles of 1776 and 1789, of the preamble to our Declaration of Independence, of the French Declaration of the Rights of Man and the Citizen, on the one hand, and, on the other hand, distrust of, dislike or even contempt for, most human beings—at any rate as political animals. Something seems to have gone wrong since France was

> . . . standing on the top of golden hours,
> And human nature seeming born again.
> . . . .
>
> Bliss was it in that dawn to be alive,
> But to be young was very heaven.

> (William Wordsworth, "The Prelude," Book XI)

Whoever, whatever, was and is to blame for what's gone wrong, it can't have been the founding fathers, it can't even have been Rousseau, and surely it can't be the bourgeoisie, not even in its Menckenian form of the "booboisie." Nor—since Wordsworth's poetic lines do conceal what an unfeeling mind might describe as unconscious metaphoric references to meteorology ("that dawn") and to biology ("to be young")—can our good democrat lapse into historicism and admit that the storms of our nocturnal era, the old age of our existentialist despair, were "determined" by the events of the late eighteenth century.

That term "historicism" can, however, give us a start toward a deeper probing than is afforded by the somewhat vague, though I think important, generalization that good classical democrats today are unwilling to find in the beliefs and sentiments of classical democracy any explanation for the evils of today, any relation between the two, in fact. The term "historicism" is for most of us historians a bad word, reeking of philosophy, and even in Meinecke's German use as *Historismus* at best a rather heavy reminder that historians should deal with individuals and groups of individuals who are alive, who change, and who are indeed unique. Here, for example, is a passage from a recent book by Jeffrey Kaplow on Elbeuf during the revolutionary period:

> Now it seems to me that any appeal to human nature and its so-called inalienable qualities as a principle of historical explanation is a sign of intellectual bankruptcy. Beyond the desire to survive that they hold in common, men change from generation to generation and from year to year. Their problems, and therefore their conflicts, are specific to the time in which they live and to the society of which they are a part.[4]

I will not go so far as my colleague Sorokin and coin the word "unique-icist"; it is sufficient to note that if you hold vigorously the concept of the past as in some sense finished, separate from us, only to be recaptured, and that imperfectly, by the exercise of the historian's imagination or empathy, plus of course pure source material, you will dissociate the eighteenth and the twentieth centuries entirely. To be fair, I must admit that most of those who hold to this view of history do not go quite so far in dissociationism as this, but hold that the past does somehow live on in the present. But I should like to emphasize that commonplace word "somehow," which does not here include the concept of cause, or even that of genetic relationship. Indeed I'm afraid— one bit of Wordsworth brings on another—that the confirmed believer in the uniqueness of historical events will not even admit that the "child is father to the man."

In the specific case that concerns us, there is, I think, an even deeper reason why an American liberal historian should reject association of the eighteenth-century American and French Revolutions with the twentieth-century Russian Revolution, and have some qualms about associating these democratic revolutions with anticolonialist revolutions of our time. They don't seem to be paying much attention to the Rights of Man in Ghana or, for that matter, in Algeria. The good democrat finds it difficult to admit that democratic principles and practices, being true and good, won't work except under certain definite and relatively rare conditions. The good American liberal democrat has his full share of our national impatience. He wants the present series of world-wide revolutions to come out fairly quickly—even in the American South—the way he wants them to come out. He wants to be on the side of the underdog; but the underdogs are not today very good democrats.

This last is a restatement in another form of the basic ambivalence I spoke of a few minutes ago. In this form, however, it brings up once again the Toynbeean oversimplification: America *has* perhaps deserted her own revolution: has abandoned Jefferson, has taken on the unhappy and hopeless role of Metternich's Austria. The good liberal American democrat half fears that this is true, and yet has great difficulty adjusting his principles and his hopes to actual conditions. He can and does blame the wicked men and their misguided followers who clearly want the United States to take on successfully the role Metternich once took on unsuccessfully, and shape the world into a contented acceptance of a United States doing what no state has ever yet done—ruling the world, not in mere rhetoric, but really ruling, as Rome and Britain ruled their inferior empires. Such men have no difficulty with the problem of association or dissociation of the revolutions of two hundred years ago and those of today. They are just out to hold together their own coalition and beat the opposing coalition, West versus East, a colossal collective Octavian against a colossal collective Mark Anthony. Cleopatra, alas, is missing, though I hate to think of a collective Cleopatra.

This world of ours today is obviously not the world of Condorcet's tenth epoch. May I say incidentally that I do not think Condorcet was a bumbling old fool like Bronson Alcott, for instance, or that he failed to know how evil, how imperfect, human beings and human institutions were in 1794. But I *do* think his tenth epoch is a Utopia, and not an anti-Utopia. I think he meant it when he wrote:

Nos espérances sur l'état à venir de l'espèce humaine peuvent se réduire à ces trois points importants: la destruction de l'inégalité entre les nations; les progrès de l'égalité dans un même peuple; enfin, le perfectionnement réel de l'homme. Toutes les nations doivent-elles se rapprocher un jour de l'état de civilisation où sont parvenus les peuples les plus éclairés, les plus libres, les plus affranchis de préjugés, tels que les Français et les Anglo-Américains . . . ?

En répondant à ces trois questions, nous trouverons, dans l'expérience du passé, dans l'observation des progrès que les sciences, que la civilisation ont faits jusqu'ici, dans l'analyse de la marche de l'esprit humain et du développement de ses facultés, les motifs les plus forts de croire que la nature n'a mis aucun terme à nos espérances.[5]

I must not be sidetracked into trying to describe those hopes—it is enough to note that they were very high indeed, and have not yet been realized.

I come back to the theme of "something went wrong." Burke of course thought something was going wrong already in 1789, but neither in this country nor in France has Burke had standing with any but a conservative minority of intellectuals. Perhaps I may be permitted in closing to abandon my position of mere analyst of how we liberals think and feel in this matter, a position I am sure most of you hold is mere pretense on my part, and take a stand. To the extent that the principles of 1776 and 1789 were and still are taken to mean that sometime soon everything will go right, those who deeply and sincerely so take them are going to be unhappy, uncertain, and neurotic when, as *clercs*, members of a clerisy, intellectuals who don't want to betray, they face the world we live in.

But, you may insist, the principles of 1776 and 1789 really ought not to be taken in any Utopian sense, let alone as a charter for what that outdated prophet Carl Becker called the *Heavenly City of the Eighteenth-Century Philosophers*. The revolutions of the late eighteenth century, you may continue, were made by political realists who happened, luckily, to be men of good will. If the widespread circulation among the many of such phrases as: "We hold these truths to be self-evident, that all men are created equal, that they are endowed by their Creator with certain unalienable Rights, that among these are Life, Liberty and the pursuit of Happiness"; and that marvelous slogan, *Liberté, Egalité, Fraternité* (remember how dull the Vichy trinity, *Travail, Famille, Patrie* sounded in comparison!)—if these phrases stirred many to believe that for them the pursuit of happiness would be the complete, unspotted achievement of happiness here on earth now, or soon, the fault surely did not lie with Jefferson, Rousseau, Condorcet, Tom

Paine, and the rest. Perhaps most men are really too sensible to want such happiness. Even more surely, mistaken men like Marx, men in a hurry like Lenin, bad men like Napoleon, Hitler, and Stalin could in no sense have found their way prepared for them by these good political realists of the eighteenth century. Our revolutions of rising expectations—all modern revolutions of rising expectations—do not stem from expectations first widely spread among ordinary human beings in the Enlightenment.

Well, perhaps not. But where on earth do they come from? Technological improvements, economic growth, the good hard, no-nonsense facts of life among rational human beings quite unaddicted to ideas, ideals, heavenly cities—in short to sources clear in the work of those realists of the economic interpretation of history, Karl Marx and Friedrich Engels? Perhaps. We humans have invented, among many other trinities, that of past, present, and future. No other animal, presumably, copied that invention; none has our trouble with time. This trinity is as much a mystery to the mere practical and rational understanding as any other. For past, present, and future are also one—one stream, to use a very worn figure. In this stream Socrates and Jesus, Voltaire and Jefferson, Robespierre and Babeuf still flow on, here, in France—and in Russia. If this be associationism, make the most of it.

Notes

1.   R. R. Palmer, *The Age of the Democratic Revolution.* Princeton: Princeton University Press, 1959, p. 11.

2.   Arnold J. Toynbee, *America and the World Revolution.* New York: Oxford University Press, 1962, p. 102.

3.   Cyril E. Black and Thomas P. Thornton (Eds.), *Communism and Revolution.* Princeton: Princeton University Press, 1964, p. 8.

4.   Jeffry Kaplow, *Elbeuf during the Revolutionary Period: History and Social Structure.* Baltimore: 1964, p. 9.

5.   "Our hopes for the future state of the human spirit can be reduced to these three important points: the destruction of inequality between nations; the advancement of equality within a nation; finally, the real perfection of man. Must not all nations themselves one day approach a state of civilization

in which the people have become the most enlightened, the most free, the most unprejudiced, such as the French and the Anglo-Americans . . . ?

"In answering these three questions, we shall find, in the exeprience of the past, in the observation of scientific progress, that civilization has up to now given us, in the analysis of the march of the human spirit and of the development of its faculties, the strongest reasons to believe that nature has put no limit to our hopes." (Condorcet, *Esquisse d'un Tableau Historique des Progrès de l'Esprit Humain.* Paris: 1933, pp. 203–204, 205.)

part 4

FRANCE AND THE SECOND

WORLD WAR

The coming of the Second World War was feared and perhaps foreseen by many Frenchmen, even before the dust of the First World War had settled. The Maginot Line was testimony to this fear. Although France occupied a major place in the plans of the League of Nations proponents of collective security, France never placed full trust in the international movement for world peace in the 1920s. On the contrary, she made alliances with Belgium, Poland, Czechoslovakia, Rumania, and Yugoslavia, and during the 1920s tried to replace Russia with a Little Entente orientation. Yet this "sanitary corridor" against Communist Russia did not give full satisfaction, and in 1935 France re-established her 1894 alignment as protection against the growing power of Nazi Germany, just then rearming. Returning to conscription and naval rearmament in 1935, Germany did indeed seem a special menace, and the crisis of March 1936, when Germany reoccupied the Rhineland, indicated that the time for countermeasures to check aggression had come. The rôle of the Nazis in the Spanish Civil War, the annexation of Austria, the seizure of the Sudetenland, the liquidation of Czechoslovakia, and the pressures on the Polish Corridor made the rearmament of France the question of the day. But at a time when cavalry was not yet altogether a thing of the past, armor and aviation became more and more the essential weapons, whose development and procurement was France's special concern. In spite of great technical advances in France, mass production of the means of modern warfare, including warplanes, posed great problems, with which men like Jean Monnet had to come to grips. With the unleashing of the *Blitzkrieg* against Poland, a *Sitzkrieg* lasting several months developed in Western Europe. Even this respite availed France little, and one cannot avoid weighing the question as to how deeply ingrained was the blind hope that the Maginot-Line solution inspired by the experiences of the First World War would suffice. Since France had really been saved quite miraculously by the ingenuity of the taxicab tactics at the First Battle of the Marne, it is difficult also not to speculate as to the degree to which subconscious expectancy of a military miracle may have influenced not only the French public, but even some in high office and command. In 1940 the victory of the Germans was in part the result of the tremendous advances in the development of offensive over defensive weapons. Moreover, the Germans had taken the initiative against an only partially prepared France. Men like Monnet had seen the needs of France, but those needs had not been filled. The high-water mark of a triumphant Hitler's advance was the conquest of France, and the drifting of France into that sad position has an inescapable fascination.

↶ JEAN-BAPTISTE DUROSELLE

Jean-Baptiste Duroselle, born in 1917 in Paris, was educated at the Ecole Normale Supérieure and the University of Paris. After some years as a professor at the University of the Sarre and the University of Lille, he returned to Paris, where he is Director of the *Centre d'Étude des Relations Internationales* and also, since 1964, professor of contemporary history at the Sorbonne. His interest in closer Franco-American intellectual relations is reflected in his position as director of the *Commission Franco-Américaine d'Exchanges Universitaires*. He has been visiting professor at several American universities (Notre Dame, Brandeis, and Harvard), and also in Mexico. Well known for his work, *Les Débuts du Catholicisme social en France, 1822–1870* (1951), he has more recently specialized in twentieth-century diplomacy. Among his books are his *Histoire diplomatique de 1919 à nos jours* (1953, 3rd edition, 1962), *De Wilson à Roosevelt: Politique extérieure des États-Unis de 1913 à 1945* (1960), *L'idée de Europe: Origines et évolution* (1964), *Le conflit de Trieste, 1945–1954* (1965), and, with Pierre Renouvin, *Introduction à l'histoire des relations internationales* (1964). Fortified by this intensive and extensive knowledge of the field, Professor Duroselle authoritatively discusses France and the crisis of March 1936.

France and the Crisis
of March 1936

Articles 42 and 43 of the Treaty of Versailles established that the left bank of the Rhine and a strip fifty kilometers wide on the right bank could not be fortified nor occupied by military forces, even on a temporary basis.* Germany, which had been forced to accept this arrangement as part of the "dictated peace" in 1919, later accepted it freely by its participation in the Locarno Pact, October 16, 1925. The five signatories of the Locarno Pact— Germany, Belgium, France, Great Britain, and Italy—decided to guarantee "individually and collectively" both the territorial *status quo* obtaining between Germany and Belgium and between Germany and France respectively, and the maintenance of Articles 42 and 43 pertaining to the demilitarized zone.

Article 4 of the Locarno Pact was particularly important, in that it distinguished between a case in which one of the high contracting parties "considered" that the treaty had been violated and a case of "flagrant violation" of the treaty. In the former case, the question was to be taken immediately to the Council of the League of Nations, and as soon as that body had "ascertained" that a violation had occurred, the signatory powers were to give aid "immediately" to the state against which the violation had been directed. In the latter case, without waiting for a decision by the League Council, each of the other contracting powers committed itself,

from now on, to give its immediate assistance to the party against which the violation or infringement has been directed, as soon as [each party to the agreement] has been able to determine that the violation was an unprovoked act of aggression and that immediate action is necessary, either because the frontier has been crossed or because hostilities have begun or armed forces have been assembled in the demilitarized zone.

---

* Translated by Professor Nancy L. Roelker, Tufts University.

244

It is known that Hitler considered odious the limitation of German sovereignty by the existence of the demilitarized zone and that as early as the publication of *Mein Kampf* (1926) its abolition was one of his objectives. In a speech to the Reichstag on May 21, 1935, Hitler declared that the Franco-Soviet Mutual Assistance Pact (signed on May 2, 1935) constituted a tampering with the Locarno Treaty. German jurists argued that the Locarno Treaty prohibited France from crossing German frontiers unless Germany attacked Poland or Czechoslovakia, which were allied with France. (This was not mentioned in the Locarno text, except very indirectly in Article 6.) They reasoned that the introduction of the Soviet Union as a new ally of France constituted, *ipso facto*, a violation of the pact. These legalistic subtleties are not important, however. We learned at the Nuremberg trials that on May 2, 1935 Hitler had given orders for the preparation of plans for the reoccupation of the Rhineland "by lightning surprise."[1] We also know that on February 27, 1936, the Franco-Soviet Pact was ratified in the French Chamber of Deputies by 353 votes to 164, that on March 1 Hitler decided to act, and that the German Minister of War, General von Blomberg, gave the necessary orders on March 2.[2]

All these are well-known facts I do not need to stress. My purpose is rather to try to explain the French attitude, at the government level and also at the level of public opinion, as reflected in various communiqués issued before and immediately after Hitler's coup and in the press. The publication of a large volume of *Documents diplomatiques français*[3] makes this analysis timely and permits us to correct on several points information available in the memoirs and in *Les événements survenus en France de 1933 à 1945.*

The Level of Government Policy

There are three problems to be considered: The extent of advance information; the extent of preparations for a response to possible German action; the decisions taken.

INFORMATION. In his speech of May 21, 1935, Hitler confined himself to denouncing the Franco-Soviet Pact as a violation of

Locarno and in no way implied that Germany would take advantage of it to remilitarize the Rhineland. The German press subsequently followed this line. The French ambassador in Berlin, André François-Poncet, tells us that after an interview with Hitler on November 21, 1935 he warned the French government of the possibility of remilitarization.[4] We have no documents to confirm this statement and we can begin our analysis only with January 1, 1936. The documents reveal that, in fact, François-Poncet hesitated greatly in his evaluation of the situation. On January 1, for instance, he said that Hitler had reiterated "what he had already told me often, namely that he did not intend to challenge the agreements of 1925."[5] In the long report on the general situation and outlook for the future that François-Poncet drew up on January 2, only two lines (out of 241) allude to the Locarno Pact.[6] In the following weeks François-Poncet returned to this theme from time to time,[7] but in general he did not seem to expect immediate action.

On January 10, he merely warned the German Secretary of State, Von Bülow, against the use of force in the demilitarized zone: "In such case, I must warn you that the situation will immediately become very serious."[8] After a conversation with Von Bülow on January 13, his basic conclusion was that "Germany does not intend to denounce the Locarno Pact nor to break it suddenly and face us with a *fait accompli*. . . . *At the moment* there is no such intention, but the future remains uncertain."[9] On January 22, he took satisfaction in the fact that the campaign in the German press had been completely stopped and assumes that Germany "will . . . proceed by the method of friendly negotiation" in settling the problem.[10] Again on January 27, he said that despite the ratification of the Franco-Soviet agreement, Germany

will *probably* avoid the irrevocable, that is [action] that would risk war, which it does not at present feel in a position to undertake. It will not openly violate the Locarno Pact. It will not make a sudden military move to reoccupy the Rhineland zone. More likely, it will protest.[11]

It is known that on February 21 Hitler granted an interview to Bertrand de Jouvenel in which he repeated conciliatory statements, with the aim of encouraging certain French deputies not to ratify the Franco-Soviet Pact. But the interview was not published in *Paris-Midi* until February 28, *after* the favorable vote of the Chamber of Deputies.

When Hitler received François-Poncet on March 2, he did not fail to protest the ratification, but he reassured the French ambassador by proposing negotiations.[12] Moreover, François-Poncet on the morning of March 6, one day before the catastrophic act, cites an informant who "does not believe that Hitler is preparing to reoccupy the zone at a date in the very near future."[13] The ambassador repeated this opinion in a telegram sent at 9:25 P.M.[14]

If the principal informant of the French government remained so vague and was anxious to believe that a forceful coup was improbable, this was not the case with the French consuls in Cologne, (Jean Dobler) and Düsseldorf (Noël Henry), the French ambassador in Berne, Count de Clauzel, or the French military attaché in Germany. On the other hand, French Ambassador Laroche wrote from Brussels on March 2, "information in the hands of the Belgian government does not indicate that we should consider that the German government plans a threatening move for the moment."[15] A note from the General Staff of the army, dated March 7—the day of the occupation—furnishes three bulletins, two from the French Intelligence announcing the reoccupation for March 12 or 15 and for April 1, respectively, and one issued by the press announcing it for March 7.[16] (Parenthetically, this is no credit to the French Intelligence.)

In any case, whatever the hesitations and uncertainties, the French government could not avoid foreseeing the *possibility* of German reoccupation of the Rhineland in the near future. Moreover, Foreign Minister Flandin, who succeeded Laval on January 24, was perfectly conscious of the fact, as was the Deputy Director for Political Affairs at the Quai d'Orsay, René Massigli, to whose role we shall later return. Flandin says so in his memoirs.[17] The *Documents diplomatiques français* confirm his allegations. As early as January 27 a note from the political section of the Foreign Ministry referred to the risk:

Germany, realizing that the French government is not inclined to close its eyes to the violation of the Rhineland statute, might be tempted to precipitate a resolution and to adopt openly an attitude of defiance.[18]

This leads us to pose a second problem. If the risk was clear, well-known, even studied, what preparations had the French government made to deal with it?

PREPARATIONS. The account of the weeks preceding March 7 in the diplomatic and military documents is extremely disillusioning. It reveals that, while the Quai d'Orsay was aware of the problem, General Maurin, Minister of War, and the high military authorities generally, had not made a single preparation worthy of the name and obstinately refused to envisage a response to possible German action. The interim government of Albert Sarraut, which was in power between Laval's Rightest cabinet (resigned January 22) and the beginning of the Popular Front (June 1936), either did not know of or was unwilling to be concerned with the problem.

As early as January 21, Laval had written to the then Minister of War, Jean Fabry, to inform him of the threat of German action, but he did not ask anything about what French forces could do to oppose it. The Minister of War and, especially, the General Staff were blindly hostile to the ratification of the Franco-Soviet Pact. A note of January 27,[19] found in the war archives shows that they foresaw the results of ratification would be: 1) to furnish Hitler "a pretext to abandon the commitments of Locarno"; 2) to drive Germany and Poland together—"the military alliance with Poland seems incompatible with the Russian alliance. We must choose."; and 3) to push Belgium into a policy of neutrality.

In his correspondence with Flandin, General Maurin seems to have done everything possible to avoid answering precise questions. On January 29 he confined himself to a declaration that the demilitarization of the Rhineland was imposed by the treaties. This was news to nobody. On February 1[20] the Foreign Ministry prepared a note saying

[we should] determine what measures of precaution or response we should resort to with minimum delay in case of any German initiative undertaken with a view to unilateral abrogation of the status of the demilitarized zone. This poses a technical problem on which it is the business of the Ministry of War to offer suggestions.

Only after such propositions were adopted could conversations be opened with London and would France be able to send "a clear warning" to Germany and, eventually, begin negotiations with Germany—if the Germans took the initiative—"to obtain a consolidation of the Rhineland regime on essential points, (for instance, stationing of troops, fortifications, and so forth) by means of concessions on secondary matters." On February 6[21] a note to the Ministry of War made explicit that in case of the entry of German troops into the demilitarized zone, the French government

even while apprising the Council of the League of Nations, is free to act by military means if such measures appear necessary. Each of the signatory powers is indeed obliged to intervene, without waiting for the decision of the League council, if it considers that an act of unprovoked aggression has occurred and that immediate action is necessary. Nothing in the Treaty obliges the French government to subordinate its own moves to an exchange of views with London or Rome.

Nevertheless, of course it must make sure "in advance, that the nature of the decision is understood, at least in London."

Armed with this precise plan, to which he adhered without reservations, Flandin attended a meeting on February 7[22] at the Ministry of War. Present were General Maurin, François Piétri, Minister of the Navy, and Marcel Déat, Minister of Air, attended respectively by General Gamelin, Admiral Durand-Viel, and Generals Pujo and Picard. It should be noted that the High Military Commission (created in June 1935 and composed of approximately the same people) had met on January 18[23] and that the then Minister of War, Fabry, had proposed at the close of the meeting that the High Commission study the agenda for its next meeting. The February 7 meeting was the equivalent of one of the High Military Commission.

After long discussion of relatively minor matters, Flandin put the question: "It is time," he said, "to define in a very clear manner the probable means of remilitarization, and, on the other hand, what countermeasures we can assume we should take." According to minutes in the archives of the Navy, the military ministers merely changed the subject—an elegant way of refusing to answer without saying so.

In his memoirs[24] Flandin is more precise.

My statement was received with much reticence by the Ministers of National Defense and their colleagues. I had asked a specific question . . . the Minister of War declared, to my great surprise, that the mission of the French army was conceived entirely in terms of the defensive, that it had nothing in preparation and was still less ready for use in a military intervention.

General Gamelin said that it was up to the French government to decide.

I then asked, in anticipation that the Government might decide on armed resistance, that measures of implementation be prepared in advance and that a new meeting of the High Military Commission be planned to this end.

Flandin says that he transmitted his wishes to the next meeting of the Cabinet. He was about to go to Geneva for a meeting of the Council of the League of Nations, where he would meet British Foreign Secretary Eden, to whom he wished to submit a precise plan. The Cabinet merely authorized him to declare "that the French Government would put its military forces (including Navy and Air) at the disposition of the League of Nations in order to oppose by force a violation of the Treaties." This vague decision seemed to rule out unilateral action by France. In any case, a meeting of the High Military Commission would be held "in order to translate the decision taken by the Government into acts."

On February 12[25] General Maurin wrote to Flandin, describing the measures he envisaged. They were ridiculous. "The sudden reoccupation of all or part of the demilitarized zone would necessarily involve certain precautionary measures on our part." Precautions, because reoccupation might be followed by a German attack. No direct response to reoccupation itself was planned. On the contrary, General Maurin seemed so afraid of attack that he envisaged "the reduction to a minimum of the number of measures actually planned in the case of the threat of a sudden attack, so as to avoid any valid pretext for a clash." Hence, no recall of available troops or reservists.

Flandin replied to this letter on February 14.[26] "The operations you list," he said, "are incomplete, and you confine yourself to mere allusions to the most important measures, which are to be reserved for government decision, pending further notice." "I agree with you," he added, "on the necessity of this decision. But what measures are we talking about? The government should decide the principle behind these measures, their implementation being reserved for further deliberation."

What was Maurin's answer, in a letter dated February 17?[27] He seemed to pretend not to understand. First, his general attitude was wholly negative. "It would seem that to use our right to occupy the demilitarized zone runs the risk of being contrary to French interests. . . . We risk appearing as the aggressor and finding ourselves left to face Germany alone." This last phrase is pregnant with meaning and we shall return to it. Then Maurin replied obliquely to the question. Flandin had asked him to outline precise measures of eventual *response,* but he replied in the abstract with a list of *precautionary* measures: warning, stronger warning, security, reliance on protection forces. Nothing is said of possible intervention.

Furthermore, the military chiefs met without the ministers on February 19[28] and the decisive word was pronounced by Gamelin. He considered that "it is not proper to envisage that France alone could occupy the demilitarized zone, but precautionary measures would be called for." He then said "everything must be done to maintain the causes of the Treaty of Versailles relative to the demilitarized zone, at least until such time as the influence of the depletion of our military reserves ceases to make itself felt, that is, until about 1940 or 1942." Do anything, that is, except the most essential thing.

The Quai d'Orsay was not satisfied. With great clarity, Massigli, in a note relating to the letter of February 17,[29] remarked that "the Minister of War does not reply exactly to the questions asked him." The real problem is as follows: "Are we concerned with simple precautionary measures or should we envisage a positive response?"

Did Flandin continue the correspondence with Maurin? No trace has been found. Déat, Minister of Air, wrote to Piétri, Minister of the Navy, on March 2 to inform him of measures that should be taken, but again they were only precautionary ones.[30]

It is abundantly clear that, through blindness or unwillingness, the leaders in charge of national defense had not, before March 7, planned a single measure or prepared a single move toward a response in terms of force by France to an imminent German move using force. Even the idea of general mobilization, which from March 7 on was to be used as a bugbear, was never mentioned before that date. Although it was fairly well warned, the French government was absolutely unprepared for action.

Hence, finally, the decision not to act.

THE LACK OF DECISION. First, let us outline, as far as possible, the timetable of official steps taken by the French government between March 7 and March 11.

On March 7, François-Poncet, who learned of the German decision at 10:30 in the morning, protested solemnly while awaiting "the evaluation and decision of the government of the Republic."[31] He sent another telegram at three o'clock in the afternoon[32] concluding, "personally, it seems to me difficult for the French government to accept the *fait accompli* deliberately created by the German government without a vigorous reaction." But what could this reaction have been?

On the same day there was no meeting of the whole Cabinet in Paris but there were two meetings attended by some members of the Cabinet. One, late in the morning, was attended by Premier Sarraut, Foreign Minister Flandin, Minister for League of Nations Affairs, Paul-Boncour, Minister for Colonies, Georges Mandel, and Generals Gamelin and Georges. Paul-Boncour and Mandel declared themselves resolutely in favor of decisive measures. But, wrote General Gamelin,[33] "we stayed in the realm of generalities." Paul-Boncour said to him, "I'd like to see you in Mayence as soon as possible." Gamelin replied, "That is another matter. I ask nothing better, but I must have the means." Sarraut asked Gamelin if France could act alone. Gamelin replied that at first "we would have the advantage," but that a long war would bring out German superiority.

Flandin then met with the ambassadors of Great Britain, Sir George Clark, Italy, Vittorio Cerruti, and Belgium, Baron Kerchove de Dauterghem.[34]

At three o'clock in General Maurin's office, Generals Gamelin, Georges, and Colson, together with those in charge of equipment, decided on the disposition of matériel.

At five o'clock, Gamelin saw the Secretary-General of the Quai d'Orsay, Alexis Léger, who "is still of the opinion that we should react and act energetically. The British and the Belgians will be inclined to yield, but they will be obliged to follow us."[35]

At six o'clock there was another meeting in Flandin's office, with Déat, Piétri, and their staff leaders, Pujo and Durand-Viel, in addition to those who had been present at the morning meeting. "Renewed theoretical discussion, but we did not seem to be planning firm solutions, at least not immediately." The only decision taken was to move two divisions from the Rhône Valley toward the Maginot Line by truck and railroad.

The next morning, Sunday, March 8, the Cabinet met. It is very difficult to know exactly what was said, because in the first-hand accounts there is great confusion between the Cabinet meeting of March 8 and that of March 9. We know for certain that Flandin spoke and that it was decided 1) to send a message to the Secretary-General of the League of Nations[36] and 2) to call a meeting of the signatories of the Locarno Pact—excluding Germany—in Paris the next day. When Foreign Secretary Eden let it be known that he had to make a statement of general policy in the House of Commons, however,[37] the meeting was postponed to Tuesday, March 10.

What is also certain is that at the Cabinet meeting of March 8 the government took no decision to act at once. Nevertheless, the atmosphere seemed to favor firmness, which permitted Premier Sarraut to make his famous radio speech that night, in which he declared that France would not negotiate under pressure. Notably, he said, "we are not disposed to leave Strasbourg exposed to German guns." It is known[38] that this speech had been drawn up at the Quai d'Orsay. Massigli formulated the phrase. He had underlined it. He and Flandin had pointed out its implications to the Premier. The fact that Sarraut agreed to read it seemed to indicate that he expected to galvanize public opinion and that the Cabinet had not yet debated the heart of the problem: Was France going to intervene alone and at once?

There is therefore reason to believe that the Cabinet meeting of Monday, March 9 was of capital importance. Would France decide on immediate intervention, or would she wait for the meeting of the Locarno powers? The first-hand accounts of the debate (those of Flandin, Paul-Boncour, Sarraut, and Maurin) are contradictory.

According to Flandin[39] and Paul-Boncour,[40] after Flandin had asked what military measures were planned,

the Minister of War, then indicated, to my profound stupification, that all that had been planned was to place in position the security troops of the Maginot Line and to move two divisions stationed in the valley of the Rhône toward the eastern frontier. And he added that in order to intervene with military force in the Rhineland, the General Staff demanded general mobilization. General mobilization, within six weeks of election would be a crazy move!

Paul-Boncour, Minister in charge of League of Nations Affairs, also expressed surprise.[41] According to his account, Mandel, Flandin, and he himself

declared ourselves very clearly in favor of military action; two others present, messieurs Guernut and Stern, agreed. The rest showed by their statements, their reservations, or their silence either that they were opposed or that they felt it had serious disadvantages.

Flandin thought that Premier Sarraut was also in favor of immediate military action.

Then the debate "continued, conscientious, but painful and without enthusiasm." And, reports Paul-Boncour, Flandin then concluded, "I see, Monsieur le Président, that one must not press the point." Sarraut himself[42] thought Paul-Boncour was wrong in saying ten years later that the decisive opportunity had been lost through weakness.

The interpretation of General Maurin was more significant. An intimate friend of Gamelin—together they had attended the War College in 1899 and served in General Joffre's entourage in 1914—Maurin at first declared himself much surprised by Sarraut's speech: "because I could hardly see how we could prevent Strasbourg from being within range of German guns."[43] On two points he contradicted Flandin and Sarraut: He said 1) that no voice was raised in favor of immediate war and in any case not that of Mandel;[44] and 2) on the contrary, someone said, "nobody here wants war" and nobody else protested.

Maurin thus suggests that Paul-Boncour and Flandin used hindsight to endow themselves with the gift of prophecy. Nevertheless he notes that after he had mentioned the inclusion of protection forces in his plan, Sarraut asked, "And what then?" And then he replied, "that depends on what the government wants to do." Paul-Boncour asked about the recall of available troops and Maurin replied, "But what do you want us to do with them?" He was convinced that if they were called up simply as a threat, Hitler would hold to his position.

Maurin also says[45] that he mentioned a limited operation in the Saar region. But what then?

Nothing would be gained unless we forced Germany to repudiate Hitler. . . therefore it would mean war and unless we are to strike out senselessly a general mobilization would have to be planned. This is what led me to discuss a general mobilization in the Council of Ministers, but I never said that it ought to be immediately ordered.

One point remains clear despite these disagreements: In Maurin's words, "at this meeting of the Council of Ministers, in the end we decided nothing."

Two days had already been lost. On Monday March 9 the Germans, uncertain the day before, began to be confident. François-Poncet reports that between nine in the morning and two in the afternoon ruling circles in Berlin were anxious because of "the energetic and definite attitude of the French government."[46] But then they quickly realized that the French government was neither energetic nor definite. On March 11,[47] François-Poncet was able to write, "As of today the great majority of Germans no longer expect a strong reaction from France and her allies."

Nevertheless one last inclination to military action showed itself on March 10 and 11. On March 10 at 9:00 P.M.,[48] a meeting was held in the private rooms of Premier Sarraut, attended by the three ministers of defense and their chiefs of staff. In an atmosphere of free discussion, the possibility of using the left bank of the Saar for bargaining purposes was taken up. In the files of the General Staff there was a plan drawn up by Colonel Vaulgrenant, designed to replace Plan D, Part Four, of October 22, 1932, dealing with the reoccupation of the Saar. This plan, dating from the period when the German army had not been reconstructed, was to reoccupy the entire Saar with three divisions of infantry, one of cavalry and one brigade of Senegalese. On the evening of March 10, 1936, only the left bank of the Saar—between Saarbücken and Merzig—was in question. The force envisaged was ten divisions of infantry, one of cavalry, and the special armaments and services of an Army Corps, that is, one-third of the available defensive forces.[49]

During the discussion, according to the account of Gamelin himself, the military men showed that they did not favor such an operation. They did not ask for the immediate calling-up of three classes of reserves. "If Germany yields, everything will be easy." But if Germany resisted, it would mean war, and a general mobilization was called for. "With Germany mobilizing its superior resources in manpower and industry, France would need allies." Maurin supported Gamelin. Piétri and Déat couldn't imagine such an operation without the support of the League of Nations—this was tantamount to burying it.

Indeed, the note of March 11,[50] formulated by Gamelin and signed by Maurin, which Sarraut received in the late morning, constituted a long list of difficulties to be overcome and conditions to be met before action could be taken. Moreover, it specified that the operation "could not be launched until a week after the decision was taken." It was to be implemented within the framework of the League of Nations, with 1.2 million men to be mobilized and a general mobilization anticipated.

The High Military Commission, meeting at three in the afternoon of this same day, hardly touched upon these questions.[51]

It may be said that on this day, March 11, the die was cast. France had not taken independent action, a right given her by Article 4 of the Locarno Treaty, and there was no chance of obtaining anything more than verbal support from Great Britain and Italy, the powers associated with her in the treaty. The British government—despite Eden's reluctance—had already decided to follow an appeasement policy. They thought it possible to sign further pacts with Hitler along the lines of the Naval Accord of June 1935. The German aim to revise the treaties in order to correct injustices therein seemed to them to have some merit. Of course, they disapproved the methods Hitler used—force and the unilateral repudiation of treaties—but they thought Hitler would become more tractable once his object had been obtained. The idea that they were rewarding aggression did not occur to them any more than it did to Sir Samuel Hoare and Pierre Laval when they cooperated in the partition of Ethiopia in December 1935. Moreover, Great Britain and Italy were much more concerned with the Ethiopian problem than with the Rhineland. To Mussolini, even though he had not yet begun to ally himself with Hitler's Germany, the mere idea of intervention seemed impractical so long as the bulk of his forces were fighting in East Africa.

This does not alter the fact that for three or four days France had a critical responsibility and that she was unwilling to carry it out. To be sure, certain government leaders, especially Flandin, Paul-Boncour, and Mandel, had inclined to reaction by force more than the others, although we must be skeptical of their later statements, based on hindsight and naturally affected by intervening events. At the Quai d'Orsay, it would seem that Alexis Léger and René Massigli saw what was at stake more clearly than others, but what could they do confronted with a government resigned in advance to a do-nothing policy?

The new fact brought out by the *Documents diplomatiques français* is the extent of the responsibility of the military chiefs, especially Maurin and Gamelin. Of course they did what they believed to be their duty. What is noteworthy is that they thought the German army was already stronger than the French army,[52] at least for purposes of a long war. They therefore wanted to avoid action by France alone at all costs and they did not realize that if she *did* act, France's allies would be obliged to follow suit.

Finally, the French military chiefs were victims of the currently dominant military strategy, developed under the influence of the principal leaders of the 1918 victory, especially Marshal Pétain and General Weygand. As early as 1921, Pétain had said, "The defensive is an infinitely superior position to the offensive, because action kills."[53] The French army, trusting in the Maginot Line, was unwilling to venture beyond it. The General Staff condemned the new theory of action based on tanks, advocated by General Étienne in 1922 and General Doumenc in 1928, which had been developed in two books, Guderian's *Achtung Panzer*, published in

1931 and Charles de Gaulle's *Vers l'armée de métier*, published in 1934 and much discussed in the press. We are forced to agree with Charles Serre, that for the High Command, "inaction had become the supreme wisdom."[54]

In addition, at the time, almost all Frenchmen also preferred a course of nonaction.

The Level of Public Opinion

On this subject I can speak only in general terms, but any study of the press strikingly reveals the absolute inertia of the French people in the face of danger. Still worn out by the frightful bloodletting of 1914–1918, eighteen years after the victory Frenchmen were either unaware of the danger that had arisen in the East or they did not wish to face its implications, which demanded a courageous decision they could not make.

There is no better way to describe this state of mind than to repeat the words of the Greek statesman, Nicholas Politis, in a conversation with the French ambassador, Laroche, in Brussels on March 2, 1936. He said, indeed, that the fears of states friendly to France had unfortunately not been allayed. Even if the attitude of the French government reassured them, the other nations were still troubled by a certain state of mind that seemed to prevail in the country. In their contacts with various elements of the population in different regions, their representatives in France were struck by

a kind of pacifist depression shown in many circles, where there seemed to be a preoccupation with peace at any price, a tendency to barricade themselves behind what they called "the Maginot Wall" and beyond it to let events take whatever course they might. They did not seem to realize that a people who followed such a policy [these are the exact words of Politis] should no longer claim to be a great power nor that they could not even be sure of finding in such isolation adequate protection against any moves [that might be made] by foreign nations.[55]

Let us try briefly to analyze this "pacifist depression." Two elements stand out clearly: 1) Frenchmen were not really informed of the threat to the Rhineland before March 7—hence their *surprise*, and 2) surprise was followed by *refusal to act*.

THE SURPRISE. As far as foreign policy was concerned, between January and March 1936 Frenchmen were chiefly preoccupied with two main issues, the Italo-Ethiopian War and the ratification of the Franco-Soviet Pact. These two problems separated the Right from the Left along fairly clear lines. The Right hoped for the victory of Mussolini, disapproved of sanctions against Italy, and regretted that France was not allying herself with Italy against Nazi Germany. On the other hand, the Right did not consider the USSR a trustworthy ally and feared that alliance with the Soviets would increase communist influence in France. The Right was therefore hostile to the ratification of the pact. The Left detested Mussolini and favored the enforcement of sanctions, which they thought would have the further advantage of strengthening collective security. The Left favored ratification of the Franco-Soviet Pact but from a variety of motives: For the Communists it was a question of party discipline and loyalty, for the Radical Socialists it was a realistic policy.[56] As for the Socialists, who were still very much opposed to seeking security through a system of alliances, they claimed to see in the Franco-Soviet Pact a treaty "open to all" and thus a bulwark of collective security rather than a return to the Franco-Russian alliance of prewar days.

The result of these contradictory concerns was that the growing menace to the East was passed over virtually in silence and that the public was scarcely informed of it—especially on the Left. The vast majority of Frenchmen—Left and Right—feared Germany and criticized the Nazis. To some, the means of opposing them seemed to be an alliance with Italy; to others, it seemed to be alliance with the Soviet Union combined with the collective security system. Both sides desired alliance with England, but nobody thought it possible.

Humanité, organ of the French Communist party, scarcely mentioned the possibility of a violation of the Locarno Treaty[57] and then generally only by a mere allusion. The Socialist organ, Le Populaire, said even less about it; I can find in it no mention of such a possibility before March 7. In the January 11 manifesto of the Rassemblement Populaire (which included Socialists, Communists, Radical-Socialists, the Confédération Générale du Travail, the Communist unions and other groups such as the League for the Rights of Man) foreign policy was subsumed under the heading, "Defense of Peace."[58] It stressed the role of the League of Nations, arms control, nationalization of heavy industry and repudiation of secret diplomacy. In this context it alluded to the Franco-Soviet Pact: "an extension, especially to eastern and central Europe, of the system of pacts open to all, following the principles of the Franco-Soviet Pact."

The Radical-Socialist newspaper, L'Œuvre, made the situation much clearer. The columns of Geneviève Tabouis often stressed the possibility of a coup by Hitler in the Rhineland. As early as January 14, she wrote that "news from Berlin is more and more disquieting in regard to the demilitarized zone." Great Britain "has let it be understood that she will not act in such circumstances." From this Madame Tabouis drew the conclusion that the Franco-Soviet Pact was necessary. Nevertheless, beginning in February, Madame Tabouis began to sound more hopeful. "It is generally thought," she wrote on February 15, "that [Germany] will confine itself to a firm, but entirely conventional verbal protest [against the Franco-Soviet Pact]." On February 22 she judged that a concerted Franco-British-Belgian statement "would certainly prevent Germany from taking any action in the demilitarized zone before next summer." Even on March 6 she still believed that the Germans would confine themselves to a "slow infiltration" of their forces into the zone.

Rightist circles were relatively more effectively warned by their newspapers, but in the context of arguments designed to oppose ratification of the Franco-Soviet Pact. "We should not undertake any political and military commitments with Russia," wrote J. B. (Jacques Bainville) in Action Française on January 2. This newspaper referred to the situation particularly in its review of the press and in the articles of its correspondents, especially in Brussels. I think the most prophetic article was that of J. Delebecque, who predicted coming events quite effectively.

Will [Germany] seize the occasion of the ratification of the Franco-Soviet Pact to denounce Locarno and to reoccupy the demilitarized zone? In that case what will France do? Without presuming to predict the future, it seems reasonable to expect that we will protest "forcefully" together with England and Belgium (we can no longer speak of Italy, alas!) and that we will perhaps take some defensive measures on the frontier. And what then? Can one imagine our government assuming the position of an aggressor?

Le Petit-Journal of February 25 asked, "will the government yield or will it go to war?"

The newspaper that warned its readers most effectively was perhaps *Le Jour*,[59] but it constantly expressed doubts about the resolution of the French government. "I ask the Minister [Flandin] and his friends," wrote L. Bailby on February 14, "will they accept the ultimate consequences of a firm policy?"

In general these examples—and one could find many more—should not be taken out of context. I have picked them out, but actually they are drowned in a mass of articles on all sorts of other subjects. Moreover, very often they are only used as elements in polemical argument rather than as serious warnings. For the most part, Frenchmen could not realize the imminence of danger, and almost nobody told them what German reoccupation of the Rhineland would involve: construction by Germany of a line of fortifications that would render useless French alliances with nations in eastern Europe.

THE REFUSAL TO ACT. The French press of March 8, 9, 10, and 11 constitutes the best illustration of the "pacifist depression" mentioned by Politis. The most widespread reaction is one of shameful relief, as soon as it was realized that no forceful action would be attempted. Many strong statements were made by newspapers, political parties and other groups opposing any policy of reprisal. Others merely expressed resignation.

Another equally striking feature is that Hitler's coup, far from uniting the French people—who, after all, generally hated Hitler's Germany—on the contrary, accentuated their differences, aroused passions, and generally exacerbated the existing divisions over the current question, that of the coming elections to the Chamber of Deputies. Hitler's action provided material for domestic political quarrels.

This is especially true of the two political extremes. The reactions of the Nationalist newspaper *Action Française* and those of the Communist *Humanité* are curiously alike. Across the entire front page of the March 8 edition of *Action Française* ran the

headline THE REPUBLIC HAS ASSASSINATED PEACE. *Humanité*'s head-
line the same day was PEACE IN DANGER. The same issue of
Humanité contained a Communist party manifesto against
"Hitler's agents in France," that is, "the Laval clique," and urged,
"we must unite the French nation against those who would lead
us to the slaughter." In other words, the Communists did not
demand a reaction against Hitler but against the French Right.
Turning to the opposite political extreme, the big headline of
Action Française on March 9 was GET RID OF SARRAUT AND FLANDIN.
In other words, the enemy was not Hitler, it was the French gov-
ernment. On March 10, Charles Maurras wrote in *Action Française:*
"First of all, no war, first of all, we do not want war."

The pacifism of the Socialist *Populaire* resembles that of
Humanité, but it goes even further. "The hypothesis we refuse to
entertain in any case," wrote Paul Faure on March 8, "is that the
difficult conflict created by Berlin's theatrical coup could lead to
war." In the March 10 *Populaire*, O. Rosenfeld deplored the lack
of cool thinking in Sarraut's much discussed speech. The *Populaire*
even went so far as to condemn the ordering of some battalions to
the Maginot Line. "We will not march," wrote Marc Pivert on
March 10. Paul Faure himself (March 10) and Marc Bidaux
(March 11) forcefully repudiated the idea of *l'union sacrée*, a
nonpartisan closing of ranks. "National union", wrote Bidaux, "is
the highest form of delusion for the parties of the Left." On
March 11 a group of Socialist leaders published a declaration,
"denouncing measures arising from panic," that was subsequently
approved by Léon Blum, leader of the party, who was convalescing
in the south of France from wounds received in an assassination
attempt by a partisan of *Action Française* on February 13.

A considerable number of Frenchmen—in the Center or Right
—did not share this uncompromising pacifism. In most of their
newspapers the principal feeling expressed was guilt; a certain
relief was expressed but without enthusiasm. In *Les Echos*, Emile
Servan-Schreiber did not hesitate to declare on March 11 that
France had been wrong in not acting and that she would pay the
price for it. In *L'Œuvre*, Geneviève Tabouis had said on March 8,

the moment has arrived to learn whether France will make respect
for international law prevail or whether she will let it crumble. We

can state that the disposition of the government is explicit, France will not mobilize, she will not even call up certain [military] classes. She will put security forces into position and will apply sanctions, economic, financial and even military, by the member nations of the League of Nations.

No doubt Madame Tabouis was overstating the case when she said, "the effect of economic sanctions will be the ruin of the country [Germany] internally, within a few months at least." But at least *L'Œuvre* was urging France to act. Alone among the leading newspapers, *L'Œuvre* put Sarraut's apparently forceful phrase in big headlines on March 9. That same day, Geneviève Tabouis wrote again, "Germany is undertaking a test of strength, and if the Reich is not stopped in its course this will be the last international crisis that will be able to be handled by diplomacy. Austria and Czechoslovakia will come next. And then what?" As early as March 10, however, *L'Œuvre* stated that England was turning its back and after that there was no possibility of talking about action.

Le Jour's attitudes was approximately the same. Its editors wished for action, but wondered if it would be undertaken:

We may of course react with appropriate security measures. What about reprisal? We favor it and we urge it with all our might—let us do everything to bring it about. But we fear that in order to be effective it must be the result of inter-allied action and not merely of French action.[60]

On March 10, Bailby, referring to England, like Geneviève Tabouis, headlined his article "We would be alone—we have been warned." Wladimir d'Ormesson in *Figaro* adopted a similar position.[61]

The declarations of political parties and other groups generally advocated that France not react to the coup. The CGT [*Confédération Générale du Travail*], which had just merged with the Communist CGTU [*Confédération Générale du Travail Unitaire*], confined itself to proclaiming its support of peace.[62] Among the veterans' organizations,[63] the CNAC [*Confédération Nationale des Anciens Combattants*] "is gratified to see the nation once more exhibiting calm and poise", the UFAC [*Union Féderale des Associations d'Anciens Combattants*] expressed itself opposed to "any gesture . . . that might create anxiety in the country" and proclaimed its confidence in the League of Nations. Only the UNC [*Union National des Combattants*], a more Rightist group, demanded the reorganization of the Cabinet, "in order to form a government of French reconciliation and national defense," the postponement of the elections, and the strengthening of security, "including, if necessary, the recall of certain classes of military reserves."[64] Finally, Colonel de la Rocque, leader of the Rightist movement, *Croix de Feu*, issued an incoherent statement. After declaring that his movement was so strong that "nothing could relax its grasp, both flexible and firm," he merely proposed a government of reconciliation.[65] This was the attitude of Rightist groups in general. They had nothing to suggest other than a nonpartisan government of national union. But how was this to come about? There were no means available. These were not joint resolutions but pious wishes, not unaffected by the coming elections. Such was the case of a small group called *Rénovation Française*. We should also mention the declaration of the *Conseil Françiste* that "the threat of war cannot be avoided except by a sincere and direct understanding between France, Italy and Germany."

Nor should we omit—this was a sure sign—the fact that the French stock exchange, having fallen on Monday, March 9, rallied sharply on Tuesday, March 10. Nobody wanted war and everybody was reassured. The few Frenchmen who saw the situation clearly and who understood that this was the last chance to stop Hitler before the catastrophe were vitually without any means of expression. The "pacifist depression" had succeeded in convincing a government which asked nothing more than to be convinced.

Thus did France almost unanimously refuse to act, to the discouragement of her friends and of all those who feared the Nazi menace. I know of no better way to conclude than by reporting the conversation of French Ambassador de Roux with the Pope on March 16, 1936.[66]

"If you [France] had immediately moved 200,000 men into the zone reoccupied by the Germans," the Holy Father said to me, "you would have done an enormous favor for the entire world." I replied that we had not done so because of our attachment to the cause of peace.

"Yes," he responded, "and that is to your credit. No doubt you also reasoned that the British would not support you, the Italians still less. But I still say that if you had, you would have rendered a great service to the whole world." This is an unexpected opinion, don't you agree, in a man regarded by Maurras [the French nationalist] as a sympathizer with the Germans?

France had not dared. But it was not alone in its hesitation. When the underlying economic and psychological forces were better understood we could measure more fully the direct influence of such factors as the carnage of the First World War and the Great Depression, which was scarcely over and still exerting important effects. British and American reactions echoed the weakness of France; the United States was then launching the policy embodied in the neutrality laws. The nations that were not showing weakness—Germany and Italy—had chosen a policy of insanity. The March 1936 crisis was one manifestation of a general crisis that was to end in the most senseless of all wars.

Notes

1. *Nazi Conspiracy and Aggression.* Washington: 1945–1948, vol. 6, pp. 951–952.

2. *Nazi Conspiracy*, pp. 974–977.

3. Second series (1936–1939), vol. 1 (January 1–March 31, 1936), Paris: 1963, vol. 72. Hereafter cited as *DDF*. These documents fill out earlier studies, notably that of W. F. Knapp, "The Rhineland crisis of March 1936." In James Joll (Ed.), *The Decline of the Third Republic*. New York: 1959.

4. *Souvenirs d'une ambassade à Berlin*, Paris, 1946, pp. 245–246.

5. *DDF*, no. 1, pp. 1–2, January 1, 1936.

6. *DDF*, no. 3, pp. 3–9, January 2, 1936.

7. See especially *DDF*, no. 24, pp. 31–34, January 8; no. 25, pp. 34–35, January 9.

8. *DDF*, no. 30, pp. 40–42, January 10, 1936.

9. *DDF*, no. 49, pp. 71–76, January 14, 1936.

10. *DDF*, no. 95, p. 141, January 22, 1936.

11. *DDF*, no. 242, p. 344, February 27, 1936. See also no. 147, p. 213, February 7, 1936; no. 180, pp. 256–261, February 13, 1936; no. 237, pp. 334–335, February 27, 1936.

12. *DDF*, no. 265, pp. 373–375, March 2, 1936.

13. *DDF*, no. 286, pp. 399–400, March 6, 1936.

14. *DDF*, no. 294, p. 405, March 6, 1936.

15. *DDF*, no. 263, p. 371, March 2, 1936.

16. *DDF*, no. 297, p. 409, March 7, 1936.

17. *Politique française, 1919–1940*, Paris: 1947, p. 191.

18. *DDF*, no. 105, p. 151, January 27, 1936.

19. *DDF*, no. 106, pp. 152–154, January 27, 1936.

20. *DDF*, no. 125, pp. 174–176, February 1, 1936.

21. *DDF*, no. 143, p. 205–207, February 6, 1936.

22. *DDF*, no. 155, pp. 218–221, February 8, 1936.

23. *DDF*, no. 83, pp. 121–124, January 18, 1936.

24. Flandin, pp. 195–196.

25. *DDF*, no. 170, pp. 245–247, February 12, 1936.

26. *DDF*, no. 186, pp. 277–278, February 14, 1936.

27. *DDF*, no. 196, pp. 290–293.

28. *DDF*, no. 203, pp. 301–302, February 19, 1936.

29. *DDF*, no. 223, pp. 317–318, February 24, 1936.

30. *DDF*, no. 269, pp. 377–378, March 2, 1936.

31. *DDF*, no. 298, pp. 410–417, March 7 (received at 11:20 A.M.).

32. *DDF*, no. 299, p. 412.

33. Maurice-Gustave Gamelin, *Servir*, Paris, 1947, vol. 2, p. 201.

34. *Les Événements survenus en France de 1933 à 1943*, Paris: n.d. (Imprimerie de l'Assemblée nationale), Report of M. Charles Serre, vol. 1, p. 30.

35. Gamelin, vol. 2, p. 202.

36. *DDF*, no. 321, pp. 430–431, March 8, 6:15 P.M.

37. *DDF*, no. 322, p. 431, Corbin to Flandin, March 8.

38. Flandin, p. 201, confirmed by Massigli's testimony.

39. Flandin, pp. 198–199; see also testimony in *Les événements* . . . , vol. 1.

40. Joseph Paul-Boncour, *Entre deux guerres: Souvenirs sur la IIIᵉ République.* Paris: 1946, vol. 3, pp. 32–36; *Revue de Paris*, March 1946; see also *Les Événements.* . . .

41. Paul-Boncour, vol. 3, p. 33.

42. *Les Événements*, vol. 3, pp. 559–643, esp. p. 561.

43. *Les Événements*, vol. 5, written testimony, pp. 1262–68.

44. *Les Événements*, vol. 4, oral testimony, p. 905.

45. *Les Événements*, vol. 5, p. 1266.

46. *DDF*, no. 337, p. 449, Berlin, March 9, at 2:17 P.M.

47. *DDF*, no. 394, pp. 508–512, March 11, 1936.

48. Not March 9 as Sarraut says in *Événements.* . . . Gamelin kept a diary and he says March 10 (*Servir*, vol. 2, pp. 204 ff.)

49. *Les Événements*, p. 30 ff.

50. *DDF*, no. 392, p. 504, March 11, 1936.

51. *DDF*, no. 393, pp. 506–508, March 11, 1936.

52. They were not the only people to hold this opinion. Franklin-Bouillon referred in the Chamber of Deputies to a statement by the Radical Deputy, Léon Archimbaud, presenting the war budget, that Germany's army "is twice as big as ours and twice as well-equipped." When questioned about it, Archambaud replied, "I said it because it is true." *Journal Officiel-Débats parlementaires* 1936, p. 140.

53. *Les Événements*, pp. 67 ff.

54. *Les Événements*, p. 67.

55. *DDF*, no. 270, p. 379, March 2, 1936.

56. Note that not all Radical-Socialists supported the Franco-Soviet Pact. The newspaper *Quotidien* campaigned against ratification.

57. Articles of Paul Nizan, January 1, 1936, of M. Magnien, January 6, of Gabriel Péri, January 12, of Paul Nizan, February 2.

58. Text in *Le Populaire*, January 11, 1936.

59. Beginning in January. See January 2, "Will England commit herself on the Rhine?"; January 12, "Germany is attacking the Locarno Treaty, but what really concerns her is the demilitarized zone"; January 17, "The German campaign against Locarno"; January 18, (Léon Bailby) "The world may go up in flames, but they don't care".

60. *Léon Bailby*, "Words without action are nothing," *Le Jour*, March 9, 1936.

61. March 9.

62. Text in *Populaire* of March 12.

63. Texts in *Action Française* of March 10.

64. This resulted in a violent protest against UNC in *Humanité* on March 11: "We understand their motives well."

65. *Le Jour*, March 9, 1936.

66. *DDF*, no. 447, p. 574, Rome, March 17, 1936.

⤳ *JOHN McV. HAIGHT, JR.*

John McV. Haight, Jr., born in Highland Falls, New York, in 1917, received an A.B. from Princeton, an M.A. from Yale, and a Ph.D. from Northwestern University in 1953. He is a professor at Lehigh University, where he has taught since 1949. A captain in the United States Army on active duty from 1942 to 1946, he has been preoccupied with research in the history of the Second World War. He has worked in the various public repositories, especially in Paris, London, and Washington, but he has also had access to private papers of some of the key *dramatis personae* of the late 1930s, such as Jean Monnet. His study of Anglo-American and Franco-American policy in this period, has resulted in the publication of a number of articles on military plan-

ning and diplomacy. Needless to say, the desperate
French effort to close the gap opened by the rapidly
expanded Luftwaffe has been a major concern for
Professor Haight, who gives us the essence cf the
problem in the following pages.

Jean Monnet and the American Arsenal After the Beginning of the War

Jean Monnet, the French financier and confidant of governments, achieved one of his most remarkable triumphs in March
1940, when he persuaded France and Britain to join in the purchase
of some 4600 American combat planes. This was the largest order
placed with the American aircraft industry since 1918, and the
expansion it required determined the tempo of aircraft production
in the United States until September 1941. It has been said that
this order speeded the development of this key section of the
American arsenal by a crucial twelve to eighteen months.[1]

As we look back today, we realize the vital implication of the
Anglo-French order in mobilizing the American aircraft industry,
but in the late 1930s this was not so well recognized. Monnet, of
course, was not alone in seeing the importance of American production for the European democracies, but to him goes the prime
credit for finding the procedure by which contemporary obstacles
could be overcome in the first six months of the war and the
United States could be called upon to overcome Germany's aerial
superiority.

On September 3, 1939, as France declared war upon Germany,
Monnet sent a letter to France's Premier, Edouard Daladier, proposing that a new approach be made toward developing the American capacity for producing planes. He began the letter by referring
to the Air Ministry's recent request that he leave immediately for
the United States to head his third mission to purchase planes.
While he did not disapprove of such a mission, he believed the

Air Ministry's current plan to buy 3000 planes and 10,000 engines for delivery by the spring of 1940 "surpassed by a good deal the known potential of American industry," particularly since the actual maximum number of engines available for export amounted to only two or three hundred a month. He further warned that to obtain such a large order, "it is necessary that we have the aid of the American Administration and of the President, as we had the other times . . . [but] without doubt this aid can only be obtained after the [arms embargo of] the Neutrality Act is eliminated."

Monnet's prime reason for declining to head this mission to the States was his desire to remain in Europe in order to implement a three-step program by which a really significant number of planes could be ordered. Drawing upon the knowledge of American industry and politics that he gained during his two missions in 1938, he sketched out these steps in his letter to Daladier. The first step suggested that the Air Ministry's proposed mission should order every available plane so that the productive capacity of the United States would be fully utilized. This action would force the American aircraft industry to expand its facilities before accepting the large orders that Monnet foresaw France and Britain placing once the arms embargo was repealed. The second step, "as it appeared clearly to me [last January] in the talks I had with President Roosevelt," would be for France and Britain to establish a joint purchasing commission in the United States. This could also pave the way for the two Allies to pool their scarce dollar reserves for the purchase of planes. The third and final step, once Congress removed the barrier to orders from the European belligerents, was to send a further mission across the Atlantic to determine the maximum number of planes that could be manufactured, and Monnet set Daladier's sights high by speaking of "doubling and even trebling" American production. Monnet concluded in his letter to the French premier:

Only in this way can solutions be found and maximum deliveries be attained rapidly. It is possible to expand American industry at a rate unknown in Europe—but to achieve this it is necessary to face the problems with resolution and on the basis not of French need but of Allied need.[2]

The premier apparently welcomed Monnet's three-step program, for his remarks several days later to the American Ambassador, William C. Bullitt, reveal he was already convinced of the importance of American aid:

If we are to win this war, we shall have to win it on supplies of every kind from the United States. We can hold for a time without such supplies but England and ourselves cannot possibly build up sufficient production of munitions and planes to make a successful offensive possible.[3]

Despite Daladier's support, however, six months elapsed before Monnet achieved his ultimate goal, the Anglo-French order of March 1940. The delay came not from the leisurely tempo of the negotiations, but rather from the seriousness of the obstacles that Monnet's plans for mobilizing the American aircraft industry had to face.

Jean Monnet had been developing these plans since his first air mission to the United States in the spring of 1938. In a report he made to the Air Ministry at that time he emphasized that "outside of Europe only American industry possesses the necessary technique and adaptability for rapid expansion in case of need.... [Here] France would possess an extensive rapid assembly plant sheltered from enemy bombings." He also spoke of the possibility of obtaining 500 to 1000 fast bombers before July 1939 and, by July 1940, a year later, a total of 4500 combat planes. To obtain such speedy quantity production, he stated, "it is necessary to select only those which are ready for immediate production with no new types required." In addition, he said, it would be vital "to combine aviation techniques with the mass production techniques of the automobile industry." Monnet returned to the United States on a second mission shortly after the Munich Settlement and again reported prospects of sizeable deliveries if models currently in production were selected.

Both of Monnet's early missions met with frustration, primarily because the technicians in the French Air Staff questioned the combat readiness of the available American models. In the spring of 1938 France ordered a paltry 100 Hawk 75s, which were modeled closely upon Curtiss Wright's new fighter, the P-36, which was just coming into production for the American Army

Air Corps. The French Air Ministry viewed this order as no more than a stopgap affair until these new fighters could come into quantity production. Monnet's second mission led not to the 2500 he had reported available, but only to some 440 combat planes, divided between an additional 100 Hawk 75s, 40 dive bombers, and 300 twin-engined Douglas and Martin bombers. Two hundred trainers were also ordered.[4]

As a result of his two purchasing missions, Monnet recognized that there were other obstacles besides obsolescence that had to be overcome before the governments of France and Britain could be persuaded to join in developing the American capacity to produce planes. Another strictly American obstacle was the limited facilities of the aircraft industry for the manufacture of the new aluminum air frames and high-powered aircraft engines. American management raised a further problem by hesitating to invest capital in a war boom that might suddenly be ended by the success of the appeasers. Other American barriers were raised by the Neutrality Act, with its embargo on the delivery of arms and war matériel to belligerents and with its "cash-and-carry" clause.

Monnet had discovered that answers to these obstacles could be found. As to the inadequacy of American types, it was obvious to him that there was nothing so obsolete as too few planes, and that better types were being developed in the United States. As to the cost of building production lines for these new planes, Daladier's government had already been persuaded in the spring of 1938 to purchase the machine tools for Curtiss Wright and then in the winter of 1939 it had contributed $2.5 million to Glenn Martin for a new factory.

As for the Neutrality Act, Monnet remembered his first conversation at the White House in March 1938, when President Roosevelt spoke of his intention to remove the arms embargo before war broke out, or, if this happened, immediately thereafter. The Frenchman also realized that the president was anxious to develop the American arsenal. In the fall of 1938 Monnet had heard Roosevelt outline his vision of the United States' producing 10,000 planes to provide Britain and France with superiority over Germany's Luftwaffe. From first-hand experience, Monnet knew that Roosevelt would act as well as talk. In January 1939 the President had forcefully overridden his Air Corps' opposition to releasing to France its newest light bombers, which Martin and Douglas were preparing to put into production.

While France had previously been willing to find answers to the American obstacles, Monnet foresaw that the greatest problem would be to persuade Britain to join in a large order for American planes. For one thing, the British were further ahead than France, both in the design and the construction of planes, and thus were less sensitive to the need for American planes, especially as the latter appeared inferior to British models: They were costly and production was slow. Granted that the British Air Ministry had placed two prewar orders for 650 planes, but these were for 400 primary trainers and 250 Lockheed transports that had been hastily converted for coastal patrol. The major British obstacle lay in the policy that Prime Minister Neville Chamberlain's government had adopted toward war imports from the United States. In order to conserve dollars for a long war, these imports were to be limited, except in extreme cases, to machine tools.[5]

Monnet had these obstacles very much in mind when he drew up the three-step program that he presented to Daladier early in September 1939. The first step aimed at expanding the limited American capacity to produce up-to-date planes. If immediate orders that would utilize the entire available capacity could be placed, then American management would be forced to expand before it could accept subsequent Allied orders.

As Monnet knew when he wrote his letter to Daladier, the French Air Ministry had just sent its first war mission across the Atlantic. Working secretly while Congress debated the repeal of the arms embargo, this mission discovered that American industry, as Monnet had earlier predicted, could not produce 3000 planes by the spring of 1940, but only about 1000 by the end of that year. Of this number, 500 were Hawk 75s and 400 were Martin and Douglas bombers, all three being of the same type that France had previously ordered. The remaining 100 consisted of the only new fighter that the United States could put into quantity production in 1940, Curtiss Wright's P–40. This mission best fulfilled Monnet's ultimate plan of expanding the American aircraft industry in the production of high speed aircraft engines, which was the current bottleneck. The French order doubled the American annual capacity from 5000 to 10,000 and Daladier's Government considered this so essential that it agreed to provide the capital cost of $10 million, an unprecedented investment in the American aircraft industry of those days.[6]

By the end of 1939, France had ordered just over 2000 planes. With the removal of the United States Arms embargo, the British contracted for an additional 600 trainers and 350 Lockheed Hudsons, thus bringing their total to 1600. The significance of these orders for the American aircraft industry was that the combined Allied orders surpassed by some 400 the current American Air Corps order for 3200. The latter's final delivery date was set for June 1941, while the Allies' final date was December 1940, six months earlier.

The second of Monnet's steps, that of establishing an Anglo-French purchasing commission, was almost completed by November 3, when Congress finally revised the Neutrality Act, and permitted the United States to fill war orders from the European belligerents. What Monnet sought by this second step was the establishment of a joint Allied policy for purchases in the United States. As early as January 1939, he had talked with President Roosevelt about the problems that might result from Allied war purchases, such as competition between French, British, and Americans for planes, the rise of prices, and the interference with United States rearmament plans. In November 1939 the President had again outlined his solution to these problems. Writing to Ambassador Bullitt, he stated: "What we want is that perfectly possible combination of two head men—one French and one British —who will sleep in the same bed and lay all their cards on the table to prevent crossing of wires."[7]

Monnet sought the same end when he included in his letter of September 3 to Daladier the proposal to re-establish with Britain the Inter-Allied supply organization of 1917 upon which Monnet himself had served. To revive this effort to coordinate economic war policies of Britain and France, Monnet drafted a note which Daladier sent to the British prime minister on September 15. It left no doubt that the initial aim was to coordinate the "necessary imports by our two countries."[8] Monnet followed this note to

London and the success of his negotiations led Chamberlain to write to the French premier on October 22, "I should like to take this opportunity of letting you know how much Monnet's appreciation of our problems and his willing co-operation have assisted in the preparation of this important scheme of Anglo-French war effort."[9]

By November 17 the negotiations had progressed adequately for Britain and France to agree at a meeting of their Supreme War Council to establish an Anglo-French Purchasing Commission in New York under Arthur Purvis. The Council also set up in London the Anglo-French Economic Coordinating Committee and appropriately named as its Chairman, Jean Monnet.

With the second of his steps launched, Monnet called upon France's premier to initiate the third. On November 23 Daladier called Ambassador Bullitt into his office and in the presence of Monnet and Guy La Chambre, the Minister for Air, he proposed that France and Britain purchase 10,000 planes from the United States. The premier stated that he sought thereby to gain what he called "the absolute dominance in the air," and thus permit the Allies to go over to the offensive by the spring of 1941. Remembering the success of the present French air mission in the States, he emphasized that "this problem was enormous [as the existing American factories] had more orders than they could fill for the year 1940 . . . [and] it would be necessary to create enlarged facilities for the production of planes." Remarking that Monnet was currently setting up "the organization for the pooling of the resources of France and England," Daladier announced that he would immediately send René Pleven, Monnet's personal assistant, to the United States to survey the possibility of obtaining these 10,000 planes.[10]

This conference with Bullitt is worth further attention because Daladier went on to threaten that unless sufficient planes could be obtained in the United States, he would resign and turn the government over to "Bonnet or Flandin, either of whom would make an early compromise peace with Germany." He was so determined to buy these planes that he was prepared to curtail all other purchases from the United States and to make every French resource available to cover their cost. As Bullitt reported, the premier even offered "Versailles or any other possession of the French Government."

Although President Roosevelt immediately replied, "I am ready to handle the whole matter over here,"[11] the French premier did not despatch Pleven for the United States until December 10. The delay was caused by the old obstacles. This time, the French center of opposition lay with the Minister of Finance, Paul Reynaud, who stated adamantly on November 30 that French resources were not sufficient for "any additional payments whatsoever for additional planes." As Monnet reported to Ambassador Bullitt, however, Daladier was still prepared to cut all foreign purchases "in order to provide a sufficiently large fund for plane purchases in the United States."[12]

More serious was the hesitancy of Chamberlain's Government, but Daladier determined finally to act alone, and on December 11 he sent to the prime minister another letter which Monnet had prepared for him. It began by summarizing the French position:

In the course of our meetings I have spoken of my desire to see our two countries acquire as rapidly as possible aerial supremacy which in my mind will permit us to impose our initiative on the enemy and hasten the end of the war. I estimate it is indispensable to supplement our national production with American imports. From information furnished me, the present American production is almost utilized by earlier orders and the needs of the American Army. Thus to obtain the supplementary supplies the potential of American production ought to be augmented on a large scale.

This letter concluded by requesting British cooperation with Pleven's mission to survey the size of this expansion.[13]

Though Chamberlain agreed to have a representative join Pleven in Washington, the prime minister made no commitment, for, as he said during a meeting of the Supreme War Council on December 21, "American planes are so expensive that the question of finance was a serious one which the British Government would have to study with care." In reply, Daladier reiterated his determination to go ahead, and he and his advisers carried away the impression that, if France created additional facilities for the construction of large quantities of American planes, the British would ultimately be forced to share at least half the burden.[14]

On the same day, December 21, Pleven finally made his first contact with the American Administration. By then President Roosevelt had taken a major step to facilitate the Anglo-French purchase of planes by announcing on December 6 the establishment of a President's Liaison Committee and stating it would serve as "the exclusive liaison with reference to procurement matters between this Government and interested foreign governments."[15] Roosevelt's purpose was to bypass the Army, Navy, and State Departments where previous obstructions to foreign orders had been located. The way was now so well prepared that Pleven could state in his final report of January 15: "We have been aided in a most cordial manner by the Administration, and the President as well as Mr. Morgenthau have proved their desire to assist us in every way possible." The Frenchman went on, however, to add a warning:

To avoid all disappointments it is necessary to remember that in 1940 the United States enters its presidential elections and that, whatever may be the good wishes of the President, Secretary of the Treasury, and their collaborators, they are obliged at this time to be extremely discreet to avoid providing the isolationists with any propaganda.

As to the prospect of obtaining 10,000 planes by the spring of 1941, Pleven had to report that the American aircraft industry needed an extra six months and even then could only produce 8400. Again the bottleneck was engines. Nevertheless, 8400 was a sizeable figure and it could be attained only if Monnet's original proposal of May 1938 was adopted, the ordering of only those planes currently in production.

Thus Pleven recommended that the 8400 should be divided into thirds between Martin, Douglas, and Curtiss Wright, with the former two producing their light bombers and the latter concentrating upon the P–40. Pleven also followed Monnet's earlier suggestion of utilizing the mass production techniques of the automobile industry, and he persuaded General Motors to set up a new line for engines. The cost for the planes and engines would amount to almost $1 billion while the necessary expansion would cost an additional half billion. It was a staggering total for early 1940. In calling for a rapid decision Pleven noted, "The plan has such consequences for the entire industry that the American

Government cannot develop its own program as long as the question hangs in suspense."[16]

Though Premier Daladier was reported to be "most disappointed at the figures and the delays,"[17] he was prepared to give his government's assent to the plan and to override Reynaud's renewed opposition to such an expenditure of dollars. Again technicians in the Air Ministry expressed doubts that ran very much as follows: "We don't know when the fighting will start. Maybe the Germans will not attack before 1941. If we order planes now, they will become obsolete by then. Maybe it is not wise to buy planes at this time." As Ambassador Bullitt had reported, however, "Daladier's position in France is so strong at the moment that he can put through anything he is really determined to put through."[18]

Britain remained the major obstacle to Monnet's plan for tapping American war production. Its Chancellor of the Exchequer, Sir John Simon, had joined Reynaud on January 9 in announcing that their two nations "positively could not find the dollar exchange for large numbers of planes and materials." Moreover the British Air Ministry raised its technical objections and took particular issue with the selection of only three American models which in British eyes held little promise for improved performance.[19]

Monnet quickly came to see that one more step was needed to clinch the decision to place massive orders for American planes. By January 18 he had persuaded Daladier to propose to Chamberlain that a comparison be made of French and British plane production with that of Germany. So for the first time the Intelligence Services of both nations pooled their figures on the enemy's productive strength and placed these in a balance sheet against the Allied figures.[20]

As soon as Britain's Permanent Secretary for Air, Sir Arthur Street, saw this balance sheet, he realized it revealed "the formidable accumulation of German striking power which can be *instantly* deployed against us." He also recognized that over a long period Germany could continue to confront the Allies with a "big effort." Granted the margin of superiority was being reduced, "but it will take time to establish our supremacy." The conclusion Street drew may well have been the deciding one for the British:

"Under conditions of attack our peoples in their depth of agony would draw comfort and courage from the knowledge that the vast resources of America were firmly and surely at their back." The Secretary went on to state: "We must now create new potential in America which will be productive during this year and thereafter stand ready at our disposal to be brought into immediate use."[21]

Monnet had not only won a convert in the Air Ministry with his balance sheet, but he had also convinced Prime Minister Chamberlain to reverse his policy toward the purchase of American planes. As the British Secretary for Air, Kingsley Wood, reported to Monnet, "the only question is to save the face of Sir John Simon."[22] That question had been solved by February 5 when the Supreme War Council met.

There is no question that Jean Monnet's indefatigable efforts smoothed the way for this development. Amongst the memoranda, letters, and reports that remain in his files there is a copy of the note he prepared for Daladier to present to the Supreme War Council, and that became the basis for final agreement. It summarized the arguments justifying the necessary financial expenditures:

We have before us a formidable accumulation of offensive weapons which can be instantly used against our countries. We are dependent upon our own production, which can be destroyed. American production can provide a "necessary insurance." It is the indispensible duty of our two Governments to mobilize American production. The enemy in spite of blockade has the means to continue considerable production for a long time.

As Daladier presented this note, he spoke of "the urgency of having our decision implemented without delay," and he suggested that Roosevelt and Morgenthau be informed by the end of the week.[23]

Eleven days elapsed before Arthur Purvis, as chief of the Anglo-French Purchasing Mission in Washington, was instructed to inform Secretary Morgenthau that, "the Allies are agreed to combine their efforts to establish a growing potential in the United States for the manufacture of planes and motors. They agree that orders will be of sufficient importance to assure . . . General Motors and the frame makers." The conclusion of this cable, however, reflected the dissatisfaction of the Air Ministries over certain aspects of

Pleven's proposal: "Certain technical questions such as types, divisions between types, nature of armaments must be decided after a new survey here and especially in the United States."[24]

A joint Anglo-French air mission finally assembled in Washington March 4, after having been held up by further red tape and a four-day delay in the departure of a Pan American clipper. Three days later the mission officially proposed that the American Government release all its latest planes and it went on to request that the planes currently under construction for the Army Air Corps be diverted to the Allies.

The details of the civilians-versus-military struggle within the United States over these two proposals were out of Monnet's hands and thus do not belong in this study. Suffice it to say that the releases and certain diversions had been made in time for the Supreme War Council meeting of March 29 to agree to order 4600 planes, consisting not only of three models but of all the latest types being produced in the United States. Engines were still the limiting factor. Thus while frame producers required no major expansion, the French and British agreed to invest $29 million to create new capacity for 6500 engines.

Seven months had elapsed between the outbreak of war in September 1939 and the final placing of the Anglo-French order. The pace, however, had not been desultory. Actually, Monnet had hurried it along as rapidly as possible while still being assured of convincing Britain to share in the development of the American arsenal. What he had to accomplish was a complete change in the British point of view, which had been based on careful consideration of the matters at hand, the Neutrality Act, the inadequacy of American combat planes, their slow rate of production, their high cost, the low level of foreign exchange to cover the required cash payments, and the success of domestic and Commonwealth production plans. Through the three-step program—full utilization of the American aircraft industry by French orders, the establishment of machinery for the coordination of the Anglo-French imports, and Pleven's plans to expand American aeronautical production—Monnet had led the British into a position where one last step was necessary to convince them of the necessity of American planes. This last step was also of his own design, the comparison of British, French, and German air power. It provided the final impetus that propelled Chamberlain's government forward.

Through the Anglo-French order for American planes in March 1940, Jean Monnet had directly contributed toward the opening of the American arsenal, and he achieved one of his greatest triumphs. Though the order for 4600 planes did not match Daladier's original demand for 10,000 and expansion of the American aircraft industry was limited only to the companies producing engines, nevertheless it amounted to the largest order that the American industry had received since 1918. Recognition of the importance of this order was immediately expressed by Secretary Henry Morgenthau, in testimony before Congress, and later verified by Henry L. Stimson when, as Secretary of War in February 1941, he testified in support of Lend Lease. Together with President Roosevelt these two American leaders realized the crucial importance of the Anglo-French order in mobilizing American production.

As an aftermath, it is interesting to note that Monnet, through his efforts to bring about this Anglo-French order, in March 1940 won the confidence of the French, British, and American governments. On the basis of his success he went on after the fall of France to become the only foreign member of the British Supply Council in Washington. There, as I am discovering in my current study, he played an even more vital role in the opening of the American arsenal.

Notes

1. Edward R. Stettinius, *Lend Lease, Weapon for Victory*. New York: 1944, p. 24, cites the testimony which the Secretary of War, Henry L. Stimson, gave in February 1941 at the time of the initial Lend Lease hearings.

2. Letter from Monnet to Daladier, September 3, 1939, contained in File 2A (Paris, October–November 1939) of M. Monnet's private papers, which he kindly opened to this writer during the summer of 1961.

3. Letter from Bullitt to Roosevelt, September 8, 1939, as quoted by William L. Langer and Everett S. Gleason, *Challenge to Isolation*. New York: 1952, p. 219. In later testimony Daladier listed as one of the four reasons why the French Army did not launch an offensive in the fall of 1939, "The need to

stimulate American production so the United States could render effective and substantial aid." *Les Événements survenus en France de 1933 à 1945, Témoignages et documents recueillis par le commission d'enquête parlementaire.* Paris: 1947, vol. 1, p. 66.

4. For detailed studies of Monnet's two prewar missions to the United States see this writer's "Les Négociations françaises pour la fourniture d'avions Américains: 1er partie—avant Munich," *Forces Aériennes Françaises*, December 1963, no. 198, pp. 807–839; and "Les Négociations relatives aux achats d'avions Américains par la France pendant la période qui précéde immédiatement la guerre," *Revue d'Histoire de la Deuxieme Guerre Mondiale*, April 1965, no. 58, pp. 1–34.

5. J. Hurstfield, *The Control of Raw Materials, History of the Second World War, United Kingdom, Civil Series*. London: 1953, pp. 253–257.

6. For a detailed account see this writer's "France's First War Mission to the United States," *Airpower Historian*, January 1964, vol. 11, pp. 11–15.

7. Roosevelt to Bullitt, November 23, 1939, Elliott Roosevelt (Ed.), *F.D.R., His Personal Letters*. New York: 1950, vol. 2, pp. 959–960.

8. Monnet's Papers, Draft of letter, from Daladier to Chamberlain, September 15, 1939.

9. Monnet's Papers, letter, from Chamberlain to Daladier, October 22, 1939.

10. Bullitt to Secretary of State, November 23, *Foreign Relations of the United States, 1939*. Washington: 1956, vol. 1, pp. 564–565. Hereafter cited as *FR, 1939*.

11. Roosevelt to Bullitt, November 23, *F.D.R., His Personal Letters*, vol. 2, pp. 959–960.

12. Bullitt to Secretary of State, November 30, *FR, 1939*, vol. 2, pp. 523–524.

13. Monnet Papers, draft letter from Daladier to Chamberlain, December 10. For published excerpt of this letter, which Daladier forwarded the next day, see Duncan H. Hall, *North American Supply, History of the Second World War*. London: *United Kingdom, Civil Series*, 1955, p. 118.

14. For fullest available account on this phase of the Supreme War Council's Meeting see Bullitt to Secretary of State, December 21, *FR, 1939*, vol. 2, pp. 524–526.

15. Roosevelt to Secretary of War, Harry Woodring, December 6, 1939, War Plans Division, File 4244, War Department Records, National Archives, Record Group. See also Under-Secretary of State, Sumner Welles, to Roosevelt, December 4, and to the Treasury Department, December 5, 1939, State Department Records 841.24/135A,136, National Archives, Record Group 19.

16.   Pleven Report, January 15, 1940, is filed as no. 13 of "Commandes Américains" among the private papers which the former Minister for Air, Guy La Chambre, opened to this writer in the summer of 1961.

17.   Bullitt to Secretary of State, January 17, 1940, S.D. 851.248/322.

18.   Bullitt to Secretary of State, January 9, 1940, S.D. 851.248/318 and 319.

19.   The reaction among the French General Staff for Air and the RAF is based upon the author's personal interviews during the summer of 1961 with M. Pleven and General Paul Jacquin, his technical adviser.

20.   Monnet Papers, Daladier to Chamberlain, January 18, 1940. In file 2A, under subheading "Comité co-ordination française-anglaise" there is a copy of "Report on German Air Force War Potential, January 1940."

21.   Monnet Papers, Memo from Sir Arthur Street, undated.

22.   Monnet Papers, Memo of Monnet from London to Daladier and La Chambre, January 31, 1940.

23.   Monnet Papers, Memo from Monnet to Daladier, February 5, 1940, forwarding "note I have prepared for your presentation to the Supreme Council on the program concerning American planes" and note presented by Premier Daladier to Supreme War Council, entitled "American Motors and Planes; Comparison Allied-German Forces; Use of American Production Facilities; Resolution Proposed to Supreme Council" (Note dated February 5). See also La Chambre Papers, "Commandes Américains" no. 15, La Chambre to Daladier, February 7, summarizing the proceedings of the Supreme War Council on February 5.

24.   The original draft of this cable from Monnet to Purvis was approved by Chamberlain and forwarded to Daladier February 10; see La Chambre Papers, "Commandes Américains," no. 17. Hall, *North American Supply*, p. 120, cites excerpts from the cable actually forwarded to Purvis, February 16.

⚮ *JOHN C. CAIRNS*

At the 1964 Franco-American Colloquium in Wilmington there was a commentator for only one of the sessions, that at which Professors Duroselle and Haight spoke. In view of the uniqueness of his role and the contributions of the two papers he was to discuss, the commentator was undeniably faced by a difficult challenge. The challenge, however, was more than met by the former Royal Canadian Air Force pilot, who deftly tied together the points of view offered by the two speakers, while presenting fascinating observations of his own. Professor Cairns was born in Canada in 1924, received his schooling largely in England, obtained his B.A. and M.A. at Toronto immediately after the war, and completed his work for a Ph.D. at Cornell in 1951, with a study of France on the eve of the First World War. Although he has worked in the field of intellectual history and has written historiographical articles, his prime interest is France on the eve of the Second World War, the subject with which many of his publications and much of his current research are concerned.

Commentary on the Papers by Duroselle and Haight

I have no intention of attempting to refute either of the two excellent papers by Professors Duroselle and Haight. I happen to agree with almost all they maintain. But perhaps I may be permitted to underline one or two points, or to query this one or that.

If I may, I shall turn first to Professor Duroselle's discussion of the March 1936 crisis: On the whole I am in accord with his general view that the country was pacifist and "depressed"; that the army did not wish to move; and that the allies of France deserted her. But really I think that the *Documents diplomatiques français* do not shed a great deal of light on these events. Rather, they seem to me to confirm what we have known for a long time, or to substantiate former suspicions.

Professor Duroselle has placed much of the blame or responsibility, if you like, on the Army, and he has explained the Army's attitude by reference to the general "pacifist depression" prevailing in France. Certainly there can be no doubt about the obtuseness of General Gamelin or General Maurin concerning what was "wanted" in the spring of 1936 by the politicians in office. This comes through very clearly in the documents. And anyone undertaking a defense of Gamelin would have his work cut out, since the general spent the rest of his life in his own defense—with the results as we have seen in his memoirs. But, on the other hand, it is worth saying that, with the exception of a few notes by René Massigli in the *Documents diplomatiques français*, there is little to show that either the politicians or the Quai d'Orsay pushed very hard for some tough line vis-à-vis Hitler. Where, one must ask, is Alexis Léger in all this? Although memoirs are promised for some unforeseeable date, we have had nothing from him so far; we have virtually nothing of him in this volume. What was his attitude? Gamelin, it may be recalled, quoted him as being ready for action in March; Vice-Admiral Durand-Viel here suggests Léger *was* prepared to act; Madame Tabouis, for what it is worth, once maintained that Léger had even threatened resignation unless action were taken.[1] But the documents are all but silent. Thus we are left with many questions. Just how "obstinate" *was* Gamelin? *How* hard did Flandin hammer away at the Army to produce some military proposal?

So much is missing. We have, for instance, a paper requesting some scheme from the Army to deal with some hypothetical but likely situation. Days pass. The resulting proposal is duly drawn up and delivered. It is judged unsatisfactory. More time passes, and a reply is sent. But what took place between these draftings and deliveries? Who talked to whom? What was said? What positions were stated or assumed? We do not know. Obviously the missing pieces are many. Are they not also essential? We have only the barest record of a part of the whole transaction. Again, what was said in London at the time of George V's funeral? The *Documents diplomatiques français* editors tell us that on the French side they could find no record of those talks. Yet this is a matter of major importance. Thus far the British records are not available, and we have only the Earl of Avon's later recollections, which assuredly are not especially favorable to Flandin and France. And then, one remembers Paul-Boncour's story, related in his memoirs and repeated to the parliamentary commissioners, of the March 8 Council of Ministers meeting, when Flandin at length leaned toward Sarraut and said, "Je vois, Monsieur le Président du Conseil, qu'il ne faut pas insister."[2] What could this mean? How was it possible to get to March 7 without any plan of action? How *did* they get there? In all this, for instance, what was the rôle, what was the influence of Ambassador François-Poncet? He surely is the *grande vedette* of the new documents, with those lengthy despatches (a mere fragment, presumably, of the total outpouring), perceptive, prophetic, but cautious too, and self-defensive, more fit really for the pages of *Le Figaro* than for the Quai's bureaus. Monsieur Duroselle has suggested that with this avalanche of words from Berlin no one had time to read the warnings of Jean Dobler from Cologne, and one can see that François-Poncet did not expect a coup in the immediate future. Can we yet begin properly to assess responsibilities?

Of course it is blindingly apparent that on March 10 and 11 Gamelin and Maurin made any serious action almost inconceivable. But what can explain that the matter was still being debated from the ground up at that date? What had the politicians, what had Laval earlier, what had Flandin and his colleagues done since January to meet the Army's basic condition, however intended, whatever the *arrière-pensées* with which it was maintained: that France obtain a prior agreement for joint action from the United Kingdom? It is all that one wishes to know. And thus far no one has been able to tell us.

With the view that public opinion did not want war, there can be no disagreement. But I am puzzled by Professor Duroselle's statement that "No one understood that Germany, in reoccupying the Rhineland, would proceed to fortify it, and the French Army, essentially defensive, would find itself henceforth unable to help its Eastern allies, who were thereby condemned." This was not at all the impression I had. Indeed I think there are contemporary statements suggesting on the contrary that the implications of the successful coup were evident to some Frenchmen at least.[3] More seriously, something of the complexity of this whole situation is lost to sight if one proposes such a total myopia at the time. It tends to make later French policy still more of a mystery.

One or two final points concerning the Army. Doubtless it is true that the prevailing military doctrine was an expression of the general lassitude in the country, a reaction to the losses of the First World War—although one should be careful here because there is, after all, something to be said for the defensive (as the Second World War would show at certain stages), and, above all, because no one, neither Gamelin nor any other responsible military leader, seriously proposed that in the end there could be a substitute for the offensive that alone would bring victory. The question was rather, when, how, and by whom? Finally, I think that the elusive subject of Gamelin's hesitations must in part be spelled out in terms (*pace* his own too-transparent denials) of his extreme political sensitivity, the lessons of General Weygand's recent collisions and conflicts with the civil authority, and the shifting political climate of the hour. None of this should be taken to imply the wish on my part to lift all historic responsibility from the shoulders of the old Army. It is a matter merely of trying to consider whether there was not some larger sharing of the guilt—if that is what it is —for the apathetic policy in March 1936.

Professor Duroselle has been forebearing enough not to say too much about the other Locarno powers. Their attitudes were certainly unhelpful, to say no more. As for France's major partner, it would be difficult to be too critical of Great Britain in those unfortunate years. Her point of view was not less blind for being reasonable. Even A. J. P. Taylor's brilliant argument (that March 1936 represented not the last chance, but the necessary prelude to a first chance to deal with Adolf Hitler) is not sufficient to exonerate the British. The preceding paper naturally avoided the completely erroneous interpretation given by many and recently, most notably, by George F. Kennan, that the French wished to move but were dissuaded from this by the British.[4] Yet I think it did imply that British policy was more clear-cut than it may actually have been. Here again, one would wish to know much more about the approaches made by Laval and Flandin to London. For whatever reason, in the *Documents diplomatiques français* we have almost nothing. It is, for instance, remarkable how little there is in this volume from the Embassy in Knightsbridge. Compared with the lavish materials coming out of Berlin, those representing the views of Charles Corbin are extraordinarily small in quantity. What can explain this relative silence? Doubtless some of our

French friends know the answer to such a question; but I do not, and I should like to. It is even now sad, and disturbing, to see these French despatches from London containing the suspicion that Great Britain *knew* the coup was coming. Did she? And in what sense "knew"? And disturbing, if diverting, to read François-Poncet's bitter retaliatory description of all the clergymen, old ladies, pacifists, intellectuals, and Socialists across the Channel, eager to display their germanophilia, anxious to welcome home the black sheep strayed from the fold. Disturbing, too, is Corbin's view that London wanted ratification of the Franco-Soviet Treaty so that when Hitler did move, Great Britain would be covered.

All in all, the *Documents diplomatiques français* raise, in my opinion, far more questions than they answer concerning the role of the United Kingdom in these grave events.

One is left still asking, again and again, how it came about that France permitted herself to be treated so shabbily by her former allies. Why, amidst the wreckage of Lansdowne's and Delcassé's work, should she have been so summarily challenged—taunted, really—by Anthony Eden (as the now Earl of Avon has not shrunk from revealing) to state her position and intentions clearly before Great Britain would even deign to discuss the implications of the German threat hanging over Locarno before March?[5] To this moment, it is not, I think, at all clear why all this was so.

There are other points, but time does not permit us to consider them now. The problem of Italy, the burden of sanctions formally imposed upon her, the Anglo-French rift over this matter—all this should be taken into account. But let me end here by agreeing completely with Professor Duroselle's statement that "the fundamental historical problem" is that of relating "the pacifism of exhaustion" to "the general plan of strategy." Only one last matter I would question, his closing determinative description of France in 1936, ". . . and finally condemned to defeat." That is a very weighty pronouncement indeed, and if I may be permitted to say so, I think it implies too long and too methodologically uncertain a jump for us to make with any degree of comfort.

Turning now to the second paper, we see that it is, I think, closely connected with the first. It concerns an aspect of the last act in this sad series of events for France and for us all. Jean

Monnet's success was, as Professor Haight has so well shown, a "remarkable triumph." Monnet is given credit—"the prime credit" —for persuading the allies to place the large aircraft order of March 1940 in the United States. Professor Haight notes, however, that Monnet was "not alone," and I hope it is not some misplaced chauvinism on my part that makes me propose that more might be said in this connection of Arthur Purvis. A big businessman with a wide experience, Purvis, until his death in the crash at Prestwick in August 1941, expedited matters greatly, not least because of his close and good relations with Henry Morgenthau. I know of course that this paper is not about Purvis, but I ask whether it may not be that to this Scots-Canadian servant of the Allied cause should go some notable proportion of the credit for speeding up the development of the American arsenal "by a crucial twelve to eighteen months"—to quote Professor Haight's estimate, although such estimates are necessarily difficult to be quite precise about.

The obstacles facing Jean Monnet have been clearly outlined to us. There can be no doubt of their reality. But I should like to consider some of them, because I think there may be a little more to be said about this one or that. In the first place, there is the matter of the French air staff's questioning the combat worth of American aircraft. I have the impression that Professor Haight feels that this attitude was unreasonable.[6] But was it entirely so? Here, I hasten to admit, we are plunged at once into an area of technical considerations in which of course I have not the slightest competence. But I believe that there is evidence to show that the French hesitations in this regard were not entirely out of place; that, in short, United States combat aircraft then available to the Allies were not in those days up to the level of the corresponding British and German, or even French, types already on active service. We have been told that to Monnet it was "obvious" that "there was nothing so obsolete as too few planes." But one might say too that there is nothing so obsolete as dead pilots. The supply of pilots was in those days an exceedingly critical issue; they were far from expendable. The British opposition which Monnet encountered was also partly to be explained by this matter of a pilot shortage. I believe it is quite certain that, at least in the area of advanced fighter aircraft, the Royal Air Force types, like the best Luftwaffe types encountered in the great battle that summer, were superior to their American counterparts. Thus, again, it all came back to pilots, for you will recall that, in the British case, the Commonwealth Air Training Scheme was scarcely under way. Rightly or wrongly— and it must now seem, quite wrongly—the British believed that they could produce aircraft almost as they produced the pilots to fly them. We now know that aircraft production in the United Kingdom was in fact bad, indeed in a mess, when Lord Beaverbrook stepped in to take a hand during the dark days. But all this was by no means universally clear the previous winter, and we have Arthur Purvis's comment on the Americans as late as July 1940, "Armamentally, they are passing through the same phase as we did eight years ago." It is all too easy and misleading to remember only the later phases of United States war production. Who now recalls that the most successful American fighter aircraft operating in Europe at the long war's end, the Mustang, was the product of cooperation between British experts and the North American Aviation Company, the original designs having been drawn in the spring of 1940?

The problem of British insistence upon purchasing machine tools is similarly worth a word. Today it may seem absurd that those islanders could have believed in their ability to produce domestically what the war would require, if only they obtained the requisite American machine tools. Absurd that they should have feared the crippling of their own production should United States manufacturers be encouraged to expand production and thus compete for the same equipment. These absurdities were not so obvious then. It is true that Sir Edmund Ironside, Chief of the Imperial General Staff, noted crossly in his diary, December 4, 1939, that the Minister of Supply "can only mumble that he has such and such an output,"[7] and that during a secret session in the House that same month the Minister's references to the First World War brought derisive cries of "Tell us what we did in the Crimean War!"[8] But many in high places truly believed that production would pick up, that there would be time to produce. Above all, one must recollect the atmosphere in the Allied camp that winter, the great hopes placed in the blockade of Germany. Think of Neville Chamberlain's view that he did "not believe that holocausts are required," and his reluctant "beginning to wonder whether we shall do any good with them, unless they first get a real hard punch in the stomach."[9] And not only men in England.

In France, too, this unwillingness to contemplate massive violence prevailed. Flandin—and how far he had then traveled from the March days!—later complained that it had not been possible for him to express his opinion, in the Foreign Affairs Committee, October 4, 1939, that the blockade was *not* working.[10] Think of Jean Giraudoux's cry (he was, after all, High Commissioner for Information), "Oh precious blood! . . . The French élite is more necessary for the world than any other élite at this precise moment of history. . . . Today we are the bearers of the antidote to Europe's poison."[11] Think of François Mauriac's reminding the troops, the homesick, wet and frozen troops lingering on in the wretched, warless winter, that Edouard Daladier had said he was thinking of them *fondly*.[12] My point is just this, then, that all this anguish, this tortured hopefulness, this clinging to the notion of blockade and attrition of the enemy, this was not the mood that propelled governments into a crash program of purchasing aircraft abroad, at apparently ruinous cost, and almost despite the serious technical criticisms leveled at the types then available from America.

Two more obstacles stood in Monnet's path. These were the men who held the Allied purse strings. And here, somewhat curiously, Paul Reynaud has not, through all the many versions of his own defense, tried to explain away his opposition to larger purchases from America. It is certainly not my purpose, then, to try to do what he has not undertaken on his own behalf. All I should like to note is that the background to this reluctance on the part of the Minister of Finance must also be considered: the improbably confused domestic struggle about the real condition of the French air force. If René Fonck was in despair, it seemed almost impossible to know the true situation, as Senator Maroselli and others found out. The secret hearing in the Chamber Air Committee, January 1940, was really quite wild, with Commandant Robbe presenting a lamentable catalogue ("If a German attack is launched, we are lost!"), with Guy La Chambre replying with inflated figures on French strength, and with General Bergeret stepping in to say that if he had to answer the questions being put, he would have to give figures even less optimistic than those advanced by Robbe.[13] The French aircraft position was, in short, a scandal; and the scandal was not much clarified by being dragged through the Chamber's secret session of February 9, 1940,[14] and coming to involve the highest military echelons. All that does not excuse or justify Reynaud's policy; it may help to explain it. The facts of the situation were not known properly, or were hidden by the government and even within the government. One must recall also the continued strong opposition to purchases in the United States from both air-force personnel and from French aircraft manufacturers. The minister of finance's opposition was, in a word, only a part of a larger, if different, movement of hostility to American supply; and, given the efforts—in many ways understandable, of course—to mask the actual state of French air power, less unreasonable than we might now be inclined to judge.

As for the obstacle of Sir John Simon, Chancellor of the Exchequer, a distinction ought to be made, I believe, between his views and those of the government as a whole. Simon was a strong personality. The fact is that, as early as September 16 and 22, 1939, the prime minister tackled him vainly in the hope of getting him to adopt a more liberal policy. "The Chancellor," noted the CIGS, who was present, "watches his money like a hen cackling over her chickens."[15] It appears that Simon and his men were strong enough to impose their policy and that others were not willing or not powerful enough to override them—and here one might say that thus far there is no evidence that even Winston Churchill (then First Lord of the Admiralty) actively opposed the chancellor's careful procedures. It was a curious war in those days, and hence that American limerick, so old you may have forgotten it, so recent as not quite to have passed into history,

> An elderly statesman with gout,
> When asked what the war was about,
> Replied with a sigh,
> My colleagues and I
> Are doing our best to find out.[16]

A view of Chamberlain which, at least in the case of these purchases, was hardly quite fair. For the essential opposition to putting out more money came not from him but from Sir John—and hence, it may be, that French view cabled by Ambassador Bullitt, November 11, 1939, that Simon wished "to have the economic and financial as well as the human resources of France exhausted before Great Britain reaches a stage of considerable difficulty."[17] This was nonsense, of course, the sort of nonsense Bullitt too often indulged in and reported. But it did accurately locate the center of opposition to increased aircraft purchases. What it did not do was point out the early and contrary view that flickered—and, as Professor Haight has so conclusively shown us, drew encouragement from Jean Monnet—at No. 10 Downing Street.

So much for the obstacles in Jean Monnet's path. Doubtless all had their part in the story. I have wished only to question the interpretation of them and to ask what may be impossible in a brief paper, that important contiguous factors not be lost from sight.

In addition, I should like to say a word about Professor Haight's presentation of Daladier. Here we have the intransigent premier, resolute, ready to sell Versailles or the collection in the Louvre, or ready to resign. I wonder, however, whether this is not really Daladier as seen through the eyes of the American Ambassador. Is not the Daladier in *Foreign Relations* . . . , or, as I take it, in the State Department archives, to some considerable extent the creation of William C. Bullitt, the President of the Council, one might say, as Bullitt, for so many reasons, wished him to be? Certainly this Daladier makes the British, by contrast, seem worse than they were—and heaven knows, they were, in retrospect, an unhappy lot, "a collection," as that sharp critic, the CIGS, noted on September 16,

of old men without vigorous leadership. The PM sits and does nothing but offer a few sage remarks about things. He initiates nothing but discussion of the most futile kind. We sit around the table, avid for news which doesn't come and listen to little details of air battles, submarine heroics and a simple story of the extermination of the Poles.[18]

What I should like to suggest is that if this kind of unvarnished (probably somewhat unfair—and, to this moment, unpublished) reporting of a comparable French cabinet meeting were known— and the nearest thing may be Anatole de Monzie's fragmentary jottings—the almost heroic stand Daladier appears to make in Bullitt's bulletins might have to be modified. Indeed, there is, I think, evidence already that Daladier also assumed quite different attitudes. Let me hasten to say that I have not the slightest wish to denigrate Daladier; rather I would ask whether he does not have the right to share very considerably in the credit ascribed to Monnet. But Daladier ought not to be portrayed quite so monochromatically as we have him here. Camille Chautemps often said (especially in his *Cahiers secrets*,[19] which ought perhaps to be called "Cahiers discrets") that there was a psychological problem involving Reynaud. I think the same thing may be true of Edouard Daladier, and consideration of it might modify the account of this important negotiation that Professor Haight has unfolded before us.

To conclude, then: It is quite certain that the case for giving the major credit to Jean Monnet is strong. But the ambiance may be more complicated than we have been told. We have to weigh Arthur Purvis's role; we must consider the part played by such men as Henry Morgenthau; we cannot ignore Daladier, let alone the United States Ambassador. On December 22, 1939 Jay Pierrepont Moffat rightly noted "Bill Bullitt is violently espousing the French thesis, while the British, who control the purchasing mission in New York, are going calmly on their way."[20] All that taken into account, Monnet remains in reality what the first President of the Fifth Republic would one day call him in derision, "the Inspirer." If I may suggest a slight modification of Professor Haight's conclusion, it may be that Monnet's principal success and contribution was not so much the March 1940 aircraft order as the obtaining of an enormous increase in the American capacity to build aircraft engines. At all events, it was the view of Henry Morgenthau that this achievement of the French was "the best thing that has happened to this country. . . ."[21] Time has not really invalidated that judgment, and Jean Monnet's case at the bar of history will one day be impressive if only for his service at this particular moment when the blow was about to fall on both France and the other Western democracies.

Notes

1. Geneviève Tabouis, *They Called Me Cassandra*. New York: 1942, p. 274.

2. Joseph Paul-Boncour, *Entre deux guerres: Souvenirs sur la IIIᵉ République*. Paris: 1945–1946, vol. 3, p. 35; *Les Événements survenus en France de 1933 à 1945. Témoignages et documents recueillis par la Commission d'Enquête parlementaire*. Paris: n.d., vol. 3, p. 799.

3. For instance, *L'Europe Nouvelle*, January 1936, before the event; and René Pinon in *Revue des Deux Mondes*, June 1, 1936, and Raymond Recouly in *Revue de France*, April 1, 1936, quoted in Charles Micaud, *The French Right and Nazi Germany 1933–1939*. New York: 1943, pp. 87 and 94 fn. 15. See also the remarks of Henry Lémery in the Senate, March 12, 1936, *Journal officiel de la République française. Débats parlementaires. Sénat*, 1936, 25A, and the remarks of Jean Montigny in the Chamber, June 23, 1936, quoted in Arnold Wolfers, *Britain and France Between Two Wars: Conflicting Strategies of Peace Since Versailles*. New York: 1940, p. 67.

4. George F. Kennan, *Russia and the West under Lenin and Stalin*. Boston: 1961, p. 286.

5. A more extended discussion of this is in John C. Cairns, "March 7, 1936 Again: The View from Paris," *International Journal*, vol. 20 (Spring 1965), pp. 930–1246.

6. In justice to Professor Haight, the editors point out that in a longer version of this paper, which was prepared before the Colloquium, this matter was handled in a way which would not have brought forth this observation of Professor Cairns.

7. "The position of our armaments is calamitous and the Minister of Supply has no idea of pushing things along to fit the crisis. He can only mumble that he has such and such an output." Unpublished diary of General Sir Edmund (Later, Baron) Ironside.

8. December 15, 1939, Ironside diary.

9. Keith Feiling, *The Life of Neville Chamberlain*. London: 1946, pp. 426, 427.

10. Paul Allard, *Les Journées pathétiques de la guerre*. Paris: 1941, pp. 42–44.

11. Giraudoux at the American Club in Paris, quoted by François Mauriac, *Journal 1932–1939*. Paris, 1947, pp. 424–425.

12. Mauriac, *Journal*, p. 404.

13.　Allard, *Journées*, pp.46–53.

14.　See the remarks of Robbe, Guy La Chambre, Edouard Daladier, *et. al.*, February 9–10, 1940, *Journal officiel* . . . *Chambres des Députés, Comité secret*, published in *Annales de l'Assemblée nationale. Débats. Ier législature*, vol. 22. *Session de 1948*, XI, 1–47.

15.　September 16, 1939, Ironside diary.

16.　Quoted in Sir Robert Bruce Lockhart, *Comes the Reckoning*. London: 1947, p. 78.

17.　*Foreign Relations of the United States, 1939*. Washington, 1956, vol. 1, p. 567.

18.　Ironside diary.

19.　*Cahiers secrets de l'armistice* (*1939–1940*). Paris: 1963.

20.　The Moffat diary, December 22, 1939, Houghton Library, Harvard University.

21.　William L. Langer, *The Challenge to Isolation, 1937–1940*. New York: 1952, p. 291.